Edwin Troxell Freedley

Home Comforts

Things Worth Knowing in every Household

Edwin Troxell Freedley

Home Comforts
Things Worth Knowing in every Household

ISBN/EAN: 9783337306847

Printed in Europe, USA, Canada, Australia, Japan

Cover: Foto ©Lupo / pixelio.de

More available books at **www.hansebooks.com**

HOME COMFORTS;

OR,

THINGS WORTH KNOWING IN EVERY HOUSEHOLD;

BEING A DIGEST OF FACTS ESTABLISHED BY

Science, Observation and Practical Experience,

RESPECTING THE IMPORTANT

ART OF LIVING WELL AND CHEAPLY,

PRESERVING HEALTH AND PROLONGING LIFE.

EDITED BY

EDWIN T. FREEDLEY,

AS A COMPANION VOLUME TO HIS "COMMON SENSE IN BUSINESS."

S. A. GEORGE & CO.,
15 NORTH SEVENTH ST., PHILADELPHIA.

Copyright, 1878, by EDWIN T. FREEDLEY, in the United States and in France; also entered at Stationers' Hall, London, England.

TO

EVERY YOUNG WOMAN

WHO ASPIRES TO BE

A GOOD WIFE AND GOOD HOUSEKEEPER,

AND WHO BELIEVES THAT

TRUE WISDOM CONSISTS IN KNOWING WHAT IS BEST WORTH KNOWING,

THIS BOOK IS INSCRIBED,

IN THE HOPE AND BELIEF THAT IT CONTAINS FOR HER WORDS FITLY SPOKEN, WHICH
SOLOMON COMPARED TO

"Apples of gold in pictures of silver."

PREFACE.

THE title of this book is so comprehensive, that an explanatory preface must be superfluous. It may, however, be stated that, inasmuch as the success or failure of men in business is often so intimately dependent upon the influences that surround them in their homes, the editor's work, entitled "Common Sense in Business," seemed incomplete without a companion volume on the Art of Living comfortably, yet economically. Moreover, so many books have been written on Domestic Economy and Hygiene—most of them containing very few grains of wheat to the bushel of chaff—that there is apparently an urgent need for a Digest of what may be called well-established facts in Housekeeping. This volume contains hundreds of such facts, each one of which, if worth anything at all to the reader, will be worth much more than the cost of the book.

The greatest part of every work of this kind, as Dr. Johnson observed even in his day, is made by transcription, and any attempt at originality, except in arrangement, is a fault. The editor has accomplished all that he proposed, if he has succeeded in selecting from "the crude and undigested mass of suggestions" those which are true and reliable, distinguishing between assertions and facts; and if he has done this, those on the threshold of life, who use this book aright, will have at their command an amount of practical knowledge, every day useful, which most persons in a lifetime of experience do not acquire.

Among the works partially digested, or extracted from, in this volume, are Beecher and Stowe's "Domestic Science;" Bellows' "Philosophy of Eating;" Beeton's "Englishwoman's Cookery Book;" Prof. Blot's "Lectures on Cookery;" Chase's "Recipes;" Dr. Chavasse's "Advice to Wives and Mothers;" Dr. Delamere's "Wholesome Fare;" Devoe's "Market Assistant;" Dwyer's "Economic Cottage Builder;" Eastlake's "Hints on Household Taste;" Freedley's "Opportunities for Industry;" "The Gas Consumer's Guide;" Harland's "Common Sense in the Household;" Dr. Hall's "Health by Good Living;" Dr. Hufeland's "Art of Prolonging Life;" Lyman's "Philosophy of Housekeeping;" Ruskin's "Lectures on Art;" Savarin's "Physiology of Taste;" Dr. Strange's "Restoration of Health;" "Scientific American;" Soyer's "Culinary Campaign;" Mrs. Warren's "Home Management;" and numerous works on Cookery and Hygiene.

CONTENTS

CHAPTER I.

ELEMENTS OF COMFORT.

The most interesting of studies—Where comfort is worshipped as a deity—Meaning of house-thrift—The rich as well as the very poor often have no homes—Why few have comfortable homes—An English manufacturer's remark—Soyer's remarkable calculation—Ignorance of good cookery—Men as cooks—The health of cooks carefully guarded—Dr. Johnson's plan of making a cook-book—The French as cooks—McCullough's observation—A good wife a fountain of comfort—How to promote health of women—Walking in the open air recommended—Care in ventilating chambers—Importance of thorough ablution—Meagre breakfasts condemned—Importance of sleep—A surprising statement as to the drinking habits of young ladies—Value of cook-books to house-keepers—American women excel in fancy cooking—How to cultivate cheerfulness—How a Quaker mastered his temper—Causes for jealousy to be guarded against—A good wife something of a physician—A lad in the wilderness and the two fairies.......... 33

CHAPTER II.

ON PLANNING, PAINTING, AND PAPERING HOUSES.

Elements of good taste—A well-planned house essential to domestic comfort—*Points to be observed in erecting or selecting a house*—Best site for a country house—Aspect of a house—Time should be taken in planning a house—Where the kitchen should be located—The stairs—The cellar—The windows—Sills of windows should be low—Defects in English palaces—Chimneys should be curved—

Ceilings only moderately high—Where the sleeping apartments should be located—The best woods for finishing—A good protection against fire—Rubber-lined tubing for water-pipes—Defects in water-closets—An abundance of room-closets recommended—Importance of trapping drain-pipes—Dwyer's plan for heating and cooling rooms—Suggestions on *painting* and *papering rooms*—An artist's idea for decorating mansions—Selection of paper governed by the light and size of rooms—Suggestion on *buying wall-paper*—How to make a small room look large—How to clean paper-hangings—A recipe for a permanent whitewash................ 44

CHAPTER III.

THE ART OF HOUSE-FURNISHING.

Modern furniture condemned by art critics—The fashionable woods a century ago—Uses of different woods—*What to avoid in buying furniture*—A salesman's opinion of beauty not to be regarded—Tendency in upholstery to run into curves—Chairs and sofas so curved as to be uncomfortable—Tables and sofas should be strong and comely rather than light and elegant—Usefulness the first qualification—Size should be adapted to the dimensions of the apartment—Comfortable and elegant *parlor chairs* difficult to find—Selecting *dining-room chairs*—Cane seats unsuitable for bedroom chairs—Drawers in bureaus should not be too deep—Bedsteads—Novel articles in combination furniture—*Pictures and picture-frames*—Oil pictures should not be hung with water colors and engravings—Picture cords should correspond with the wall-paper—Framed pictures should not be suspended from one nail—How to select *marble-top furniture*—How to extract stains from marble—Recipe for marble cement—How to take *bruises out of furniture*—How to clean mirrors—How to clean and tighten cane-seat chairs—How to take oil or grease from cloth—To remove stains from tables—How to cement broken china—CARPETS—First point to be regarded in buying a carpet—The cheapest floor-covering that can be made—The most desirable quality in a carpet—What colors to avoid—Large patterns to be avoided—The best carpet for an ordinary drawing-room—For bedrooms—Most economical way to lay down carpets—What to do when a carpet begins to wear—*How to sweep carpets*—How to preserve brooms—How to destroy moths in carpets—*How to clean and brighten Brussels carpets*—Selecting oil-cloths—How to clean oil-cloths—*Moths in furniture*—Only effectual preventive known... 55

CHAPTER IV.

HOUSEHOLD CONVENIENCES NOT IN GENERAL USE.

Housekeeping art—Novel mode of shelling beans—Importance of kitchen conveniences—Why there should be an abundance of kitchen cloths—Conveniences in a cook's galley—Articles to be found in a well-kept kitchen—What kind of *tinware* should be bought—Novel articles—The *stock-pot* a standard fixture in French kitchens—Whitewood boards preferable to tables—The Dutch oven highly commended—The French *bain-marie* a very useful utensil for stewing—Faults of modern frying-pan—Scales and weights should be in every kitchen—Pasty-pans useful articles—*Revolving gridiron*—A novel *egg-boiler*—A bronze egg-steamer—Different kinds of egg-beaters—Best kind of coffee-pot—French *turn-spit* preferable for roasting meat—Warren's cooker commended—*Apple and peach parers* save labor—Ingenious invention for slicing potatoes—A new machine for shelling peas—A tendon separator a boon for bad carvers—How to choose *refrigerators*—Table gas-stoves useful—Rotary knife-cleaners save time—A *griddle-greaser* of recent invention—The best clothes-line protector—How to *remove rust from knives*, forks, etc.—How to prevent rust on iron or steel articles—Novel mode of sharpening edged tools—How to prevent lamps from smoking... 69

CHAPTER V.

THE ART OF MARKETING—HOUSEKEEPING HINTS.

Dr. Kitchiner's rule for marketing—How to choose beef—What parts furnish the choicest beef—Sirloins—Why so called—*Porterhouse steaks*—Where the tenderloin is taken from—How the rump is divided—Beef-à-la-mode—What the chuck contains—What the brisket-piece is used for—Which are the best beef's tongues—How to distinguish good beef's liver—How to cook a beef's heart—Points in *good veal*—How the hind-quarter is divided—Veal cutlets—*Most economical piece of veal to buy*—Calves' *sweet-bread* a delicacy—How to tell when a *calf's head* is fresh—How to buy *calves' feet*—How to select *mutton* and *lamb*—Appearance of poor mutton—What the two loins are called—Points of good lamb—Usual weight of a quarter of lamb—How to distinguish good pork—Measly pork—How to select good hams and bacon—What are the best sau-

sages—How lard is adulterated—How to keep meat from spoiling
—*How to tell when chickens are fresh*—How to tell a *young turkey*—
Ducks and *geese*—How old pheasants may be known—Old partridges, wild fowl, hares and rabbits—How to choose *venison*—What
vegetables are appropriate to different meats—How to select
potatoes, turnips, tomatoes, cauliflowers, celery, egg-plant—
How to distinguish bad from good mushrooms—Where potatoes
should be kept—How cabbages and celery are best preserved—How
to keep apples—How to keep oranges, lemons and cranberries all
winter—How to test seeds—How to distinguish *fresh fish*—How to
judge whether *oysters* and *clams* are fresh—A hint to oyster-eaters
—How to buy lobsters, crabs and terrapin—How the Chinese catch
fish—Best mode of buying *flour*—*Indian meal* to be bought in small
quantities—Rye and buckwheat should be kept in covered kegs—
Sugars should not be bought by the barrel—Coffee and tea may be
bought in considerable quantities—Difficult to get good *indigo*—
Saleratus should be kept in glass bottles—*Salt* should be kept in
the dry—Where to keep *oils* and *molasses*—How to keep spices—
How to test *nutmegs*—Which is the best *cheese*—How to preserve
eggs—How to test *coal-oil*.................................... 80

CHAPTER VI.

ON FUELS AND FIRES, SAVING GAS, ETC.

Great waste of fuel—Principal substances used as fuel—What is
charcoal, coke, peat—Different kinds of *woods*—Which is the best
—Advantages of black birch, white oak, maple—How pine and
chestnut may be made useful—Best trees make best fuel—*What
kind of wood most profitable to buy*—When wood is cheapest—COAL
as a fuel—How to judge *hard coal*—How coal-dealers judge coal—
How to kindle a coal fire—How to remove clinkers from stove
grates—How to use coal economically—Experience of an old
housekeeper—Good coal thrown out as cinders—How to measure
coal—GAS as a fuel—Improvements in *gas-stoves*—How to regulate
and save gas—Different kinds of burners—Importance of good
burners—A good regulator economizes gas—Novel method of
enriching gas—The best way to regulate flow of gas—How to
extinguish fires and prevent conflagrations—Fire-proof buildings
a failure—Every building should be provided with fire apparatus
—A reorganization of the fire department recommended—*How to
preserve life when clothing is on fire*—What persons should do at night

when they discover smoke in the room—*How to use kerosene oil safely*—Tricks of sellers of patent oils—How to save a person on fire—Best remedy for burns 105

CHAPTER VII.

ABOUT EATING AND ARTICLES OF FOOD.

Animals directed by instinct to the right food—Food of the Esquimaux—Classes into which food may be divided—What kinds of food produce heat, muscle, brains—Mistakes made in eating—Infinite variety of articles adapted for food—*Wheat* contains all the elements of the human system—*Rye* valuable to persons predisposed to constipation—Qualities of *Indian corn* as food—*Oatmeal* promotes muscular and mental activity—What *rice* should be eaten with—*What vegetables are the most nutritious*—Peas more easily digested than beans—Value of potatoes, carrots, turnips, etc.—Meats as food—*Pork* suited for cold weather and *veal* for warm—Value of *beefsteak*—*Fish* said to contain food for the brain—*Chickens* and *poultry* as food—What parts are the best—Best meat in *birds*—What *oysters* are good for—*Food makes the man*—One of the most important discoveries ever made—What kind of breakfast for students to eat—For laborers—What every one can test for himself—What to eat before going out in the cold—What to eat in summer—All kinds of food wholesome under certain circumstances—Dr. Bellows' remarkable statement that rattlesnakes may be eaten—What kinds of foods are the most digestible—*How and when to eat*—What suppers are the best—Dangers of nightmare—How Cornarro prolonged his life 121

CHAPTER VIII.

CHEAP LIVING AND ECONOMICAL FOOD.

To teach art of living the greatest charity to the poor—Why American cookery is extravagant—How thousands of Frenchmen live—What may be done with *ten cents a day* in New York—Thoreau's experiment—Cost of keeping prisoners—What is actually needed to sustain life—Soyer's cheap soups—Value of grits or *crushed wheat*—Where the nutriment in wheat is—Food thrown to pigs exactly suited for children—Nutritious qualities of *beans* and *peas*—Cheapest of all food—How to cook *pork and beans* —Baked beans—*Indian corn* nutritious and cheap—Mistakes in grinding and boiling it—How to make *corn bread*—How to make *Indian pudding*—How to cook *hominy*—How they cook rice in Italy—How to make *rice pudding without eggs*—Utility of *lentils*—Recipe for *farmer's rice*—Oatmeal said to contain the most material for hard work of any known grain—Recipe for *oatmeal porridge*—What are the most economical *meats*—What is the best corned-beef—A cheap and excellent *beefstew*—A good and economical breakfast dish—How to fry *rashers of bacon* and poach eggs—Roasted *ox-heart* stuffed, a savory and economical dish—A genuine *pepper-pot*—English celebrated for cold-meat cookery—What can be done with *cold roast beef*—Cold *mutton*—Cold *veal*—Cold poultry—Mixed coffees the best—Wheat and coffee afford an agreeable mixture—*Peas* used largely to adulterate coffee—Excellence of sturgeon, veal-cutlets, and *vegetable beefsteaks*.................. 131

CHAPTER IX.

VALUABLE SECRETS KNOWN TO GOOD COOKS.

Bad cooking is waste—The regret of Mrs. Warren's friend—Value of family kitchen maxims—What comprise the essential operations in cookery—How to bake meats—Should meat to be boiled be put in cold or hot water—How to *boil cabbages*—What is the most important thing in *broiling*—Should a beefsteak be turned once only or often—Soyer's opinion—What the French understand by frying—How to test the heat of fat in frying—What careful cooks do with their frying-fat—How to *roast meat*—Slow roasting the best—How veal, fowls and rabbits should be roasted—Use of covering with bacon fat—What fire is best for *stewing*—The proper rule for seasoning—Wash greens in warm water—What a cook should be—Cleanliness in kitchen utensils a cardinal requisite—A good cook regards appearances—How punctuality in meals can be assured—How to avoid waste—Cooking-aprons with bibs desirable—How to treat frying-pans—Few cooks can make good biscuits—How to neutralize acid in fruit pies—How to make good family bread—Marion Harland's directions—Miss Leslie's recommendation—How to make *stale bread or cake fresh*—Convenient uses of bread dough—Soyer's recipe for good buttered toast—*How to fry ham and eggs*—Blot's beef-broth and soup—How to *boil eggs*—How to *boil potatoes*—The Irish method—What may be done with cold potatoes—How to boil sweet potatoes—How to *boil turnips*—To make cabbage digestible—To cook *onions without smell*—To make maccaroni cheese—Lyman's method of cooking mackerel—What good cooks do with cold veal—To boil bacon—Novel mode of making coffee—Cabbage made digestible to all—Should coffee be ground or beaten—Professor Blot's method of making tea—Soyer's plan—Hints about *chocolate*—How to prepare *salads*—Bill of fare for the sick—Food for young children—Food suited to delicate persons—Standard breakfast dishes—Sunday dinners that save cooking—Dr. Lambert's *bill of fare of brain-making food*.......... 150

CHAPTER X.

DAINTY DISHES FOR DAINTY PALATES.

1. DOMESTIC COOKERY.

In what the art of cookery consists—High-class cookery—How to roast beef English style—Proper fire for roasting beef—Length of time required—How to roast *canvas-back ducks*—How to extract their fishy flavor—Lady St. Clair on roasting game, ducks, partridges, woodcock, etc.—How to *barbecue rabbits and squirrels*—To broil pigeons or squabs—*Roasted guinea-fowls* richer than chickens—Harland's recipe for baking *salmon-trout*—How to cook *brook-trout*—Broiled *reed birds* a dainty dish—Charles Lamb on roast pig and apple-sauce—How to make *mutton eat like venison*—Best mode of broiling oysters on the shell—*Finest way of cooking oysters* for company—How to dress chicken as terrapin—Soyer's French *pot au feu*—Eggs and cheese a favorite dish—Professor Blot's recipe for French *omelets*—Good cheap omelet—How to make a *Swiss rarebit*—A genuine *Welsh rarebit*—Good sauce for every kind of fish—The Harlem river boatmen's recipe for *clam chowder*—Tom Riley's clam bakes—Soyer's wholesome summer salad—French method of *dressing salad*—Parkinson's recipe for *strawberries with orange juice*—A delicious custard—Very fine cold *cup custard*—The queen of puddings—A pleasant fruit dessert—A delicious *apple sauce*—A nice breakfast dish—Dainty dish for farmers—Green-corn fritters and pudding—Buckwheat short-cakes—The nicest pie ever eaten—A rare strawberry short-cake—National French cake—An exquisite marmalade—Saratoga *fried potatoes*—Philadelphia fried potatoes—An *exquisite mince pie*—How to make superior ice cream............................. 179

CHAPTER XI.

DAINTY DISHES FOR DAINTY PALATES.

HIGH-CLASS COOKERY—Large salaries paid to head-cooks—Expense of banquets in fashionable restaurants—Cost of flowers—Admirable arrangement of kitchens—Dinners that are marvels of culinary skill—Costly bills of fare—A Nevada senator's bill of fare engraved on silver—Recipes of dainty dishes invented in Delmonico's restaurant and furnished by the chief cook—A menu for twelve persons—How to make *Crème d'asperge*—How to cook brook-trout—Duchesse potatoes—Fillet de bœuf, salvandy—Fillets of chickens à l'aquitaine—Force meat—Salpicon—English snipe—Ananas à la Bayration—How to make Sorbet au kirch—Parfait au café and numerous French and other dishes belonging to high-class cookery.. 206

CHAPTER XII.

PRACTICAL SUGGESTIONS ON CLOTHING.

Chesterfield's opinion on dress—Shakspeare's ideas on proper apparel—BUYING CLOTH—What should be kept in view—Advantages of a frock coat—What may be made from old clothes—HOW TO CLOTHE CHILDREN—What should be worn next the skin in childhood—Clothing should be free and loose—An expensive custom in MEN'S CLOTHING—Advantages of laying woollen garments away a while—What suits a gentleman should have—Best goods for business suits—What should be avoided in striped trousers—How to cleanse broadcloths—How to treat a wet hat, or coat, or boots—How to render cloth water-proof—How to obtain easy boots or shoes—How to preserve boots and shoes—A cure for squeaking shoes—WOMEN'S CLOTHING—The first rule in buying dress goods—Advantages of chintzes and calicoes—How to choose calicoes—How to select silks—The best way to test their quality—Utility of black alpaca—What style of women look well in plaids—In stripes—In flounces—In shawls—BONNETS—Selecting colors that harmonize with the complexion—What colors become blondes—Brunettes—*Hints to wearers of kid gloves*—How to *wash chintzes* and summer dresses, including buff-linen, pique, cambric—HOW TO JUDGE LINEN—Healthfulness of flannels—When to take off and put on flannels—Proper method of washing flannels—Washing clothes made easy—Advantages of refined borax—How to preserve the lustre of silks—How to protect woollens, furs, etc., from moths—The test of good furs............   216

CHAPTER XIII.

THE SECRETS OF THE TOILET.

Cleanliness a test of civilization—The two great enemies of beauty of form—*How to reduce corpulence*—Excessive corpulence is a disease—Stock-raisers know how to fatten or reduce flesh in animals—Banting's experiments in reducing corpulency—What he was allowed to eat and what was forbidden—The effect in a year—How ladies may reduce excessive development of the breast—Sir James Clark's advice for increasing its development—*How to cure leanness*—What to eat and drink—*Beauty of complexion*—Importance of keeping the pores of the skin open—Cosmetics that are not injurious—What to do to prevent sunburn—How to cure *freckles*—Recipe for removing *tan* and *sunburn*—How to remove *birth marks* and *moles*—To prevent wrinkles—Recipe for curing *tetter*—A novel cure for *ringworm*—The HAIR—Favorite colors—Rules for securing a beautiful head of hair—How baldness may be cured—A wash for dandruff—How to darken the hair—How to secure beautiful *eye-lashes*—HANDS AND NAILS—Wearing kid gloves improves the appearance of the hands—What water should be used for washing and why—How to treat the nails—Cures for chapped hands—Best ointment for the hands—How to remove *warts*—CARE OF THE EYES—When to use spectacles—Best remedies for inflamed eyes—How to remove cinders from the eye—Squinting may be cured—White veils injurious—*How to preserve the* TEETH—What to do to avoid having decayed teeth—A safe tooth-powder—Infallible cures for toothache and faceache—*Bad breath*—Causes of offensive breaths—Best remedy for bad breath—How the taint of onions may be removed—*Care of the feet*—How to keep feet in good condition—Remedy for tender feet—Treatment of chilblains—Astley Cooper's remedy—To relieve feet itching from frost bites—How to prevent frosted feet—A remedy for cold feet—Cures for ingrowing nails—Proper ways of cutting nails—Causes of FETID FEET—Cures for odorous feet—*Corns and bunions*—Origin of, and how they may be speedily cured—Corns cured in ten minutes—A capital ointment for bunions—*How to remove body vermin*—Peculiarities of these insects—Simple remedies for their speedy destruction—How to drive away *roaches*—How to banish *flies* from a room and from horses, etc.—*Bedbug* exterminators—How to destroy *rats*—Humphrey Davy's infallible rat poison—How to drive them away alive—What *ants* do not like—How to banish *flea* from houses and from animals—How to get relief from *musquitoes*—What a smart editor does—Remedies for bites of insects.................. 240

CHAPTER XIV.

THE FAMILY MEDICINE CHEST.

Sickness one of the great burdens of society—The best room for a sick-room—Advantage of sun-light—Well-aired bedding essential—Best night-light—How to purify the air in a sick-room—Dr. Smythe's recipe for preventing infection—COLDS AND COUGHS—Treatment recommended by the regulars—What Dio Lewis recommends—How to avoid taking cold—Sir Astley Cooper's preventive—The best and cheapest cough-syrup ever made—Dr. Chevasse's advice not to stop a cough in children—ASTHMA—A cheap palliative—Dr. Finley's prescription—What has cured asthma and what is considered a specific—AGUE—Dr. Chase's prescription—A novel cure for ague—*How to prevent fever and ague*—Experience of the French Creole planters—How to prevent *bleeding from the nose*—How to arrest bleeding from the lungs—A *cheap blood-purifier*—A remedy for *bruises and black eyes*—Remedy for pinched fingers—Cure for *chilblains and frosted feet*—Proper treatment for *diarrhœa*—Hints for travellers—Dr. Locock's remedy for *dysentery*—Warm bath recommended—Raw minced beef found effective—DYSPEPSIA OR INDIGESTION—What is the first essential element in the cure—Secret of the New York doctor who charged five hundred dollars for each case—Voltaire's remedy—How Mrs. Swisshelm cured her dyspepsia—A remedy for the indigestion resulting from overeating—EARACHE AND DEAFNESS—Best treatment for removing concreted wax—Several remedies for *erysipelas*—What to do when a person faints—How to cure a felon in six hours—Recipe for felon ointment that has been sold for ten dollars—Remedies for *headache*—How to cure *heartburn* or *waterbrash*—Remedies for *hysterical fits* and *nervousness*—Preliminary treatment of *pleurisy*—Relief for *liver complaint*—The most successful treatment for *piles*—Dr. Hariman's sure cure for blind or bleeding piles—Remedies for *sore throat*—The best gargle—Smoking mullen leaves recommended — SMALL-POX OR VARIOLA — A Californian's remarkable statement — Dr. Getchell's opinion that small-pox may be utterly exterminated — *How to prevent pitting in small-pox* — What a person should do who has been bitten by an animal supposed to have been rabid — A cure for scrofula — Sprains — A French *remedy for sea-sickness* — Simple remedy for *curing ringworm and barber's itch* — How to prevent *curvature of the spine* — Uses of cold water in disease — Value of alcohol as a medicine — Opinions of Surgeon-General Hammond and Mrs. Swisshelm — Why *ammonia* should be kept in the house — What may be done with chlorate of potash... 266

CHAPTER XV.

CHILDREN AND THEIR DISEASES.

Macaulay's remark — Healthy children a monument of their parents' thrift — Proper food for infants — Dr. Combe's observation — Dr. Clarke on animal food — When should an infant be spoon-fed — Advice to suckling mothers — The proper period for *weaning a child* — Good pap for infants — A good breakfast dish for infants of twelve months old — Good *porridge* — *What to do when a baby cries* — Character of the cry indicative of the nature of the trouble — Cry of earache — Bowel-ache — Bronchitis — Croupy cry — When tears are a favorable indication in illness — Proper treatment of infants — Treatment during *teething* — Importance of fenders around a stove in nursery — Cause of *weak ankles* and *curved legs* — Proper clothing for infants — INFANTILE DISEASES — Remedy for red gum — For vomiting — How thread-worms may be removed — *The best vermifuges* — Value of *onions* — Diseases of the mouth — Treatment of convulsions or *fits* — What to do in *remittent fever* — CROUP — Promptness in treatment essential — An English doctor's recommendation — What to do for child-crowing or *spurious croup* — MEASLES — Little medicine required — The nurse more important than the doctor — *Mumps* — Treatment for — How they may be removed in four or five days — Palliatives for WHOOPING-COUGH — Dr. Dailey's prescription — A remedy for soreness in the chest — Dr. Delamere's *quick cure for whooping-cough* — When a change of air is beneficial — What to do in cholera-morbus or *summer complaint* — How to treat diarrhœa in children — A *specific for all bowel complaints* — Dr. Newell's treatment of DIPHTHERIA — How two hundred and ninety-three cases were treated without losing a single patient — Instant relief for

EARACHE—How to treat BURNS, SCALDS, etc.—Recipe to cure itching feet from frost-bites—Cheap cure for the *itch*—Dr. Chase's ointment for the seven years' itch—Dr. Bird's prescription—Cure for *tetter*—A remedy for *hiccough*—SCARLET FEVER—How to distinguish scarlatina from other eruptive diseases—Dr. Chevasse's treatment of scarlet fever—Best external application for the throat—What he regards as a specific for scarlet fever—Food to be eaten in scarlet fever—Gartland's scarlet fever disinfectant.. 305

CHAPTER XVI.

SLEEP AND ITS APPLIANCES.

Napoleon's remark on sleep and death—Shakspeare's beautiful tribute to sleep—What is the proper length of time to sleep—For children—For adults—For women and students—What kind of BED is best—Dr. Strange's opinion—What is the best MATTRESS, and which the cheapest and most economical—Domestic mattresses—Best springs to put under mattresses—Best covering for beds—BLANKETS—Treatment of—How to wash blankets—Cotton sheets preferable to linen—Best pillow-slips—How to sweeten sheets—Hair pillows better than feathers—How to ventilate sleeping apartments—A doctor's objection to the present method—How long should bed-room windows remain open—Fires in bed-rooms—*What can be done to produce sleep*—Which side is best to sleep on—Sleeping on the back—Should food be taken just before going to bed—What Dr. Strange recommends—Digestion goes on during sleep—A nap after dinner recommended—Coffee and tea for supper considered—What narcotics are unobjectionable—Onions soporific—FRANKLIN'S ART OF PROCURING SLEEP—Two beds are recommended for invalids—When all rules for procuring sleep will fail.. 333

CHAPTER XVII.

THE ART OF PROLONGING LIFE.

Chronology of early ages was not the same as at present—A remarkable statement—Methuselah's age reduced to two hundred—Erasmus Wilson's remark—What things tend to shorten life—What errors students commit—How cold bathing may shorten life—What things tend to prolong life—What remedies to employ in case of suffocation—Cut the rope—The tepid bath useful—Conveying air into the lungs—Rubbing with a cloth or flesh-brush—How to restore persons struck by lightning—The earth bath recommended—How to restore persons frozen—The two great antidotes for poisoning—Best antidotes for arsenic or corrosive sublimate—How the old may prolong their lives—Heat essential—What old people should eat—Regularity in all natural operations—Danger of indulging in violent passions—Old folks should associate with children and renew their life.. 344

HOME COMFORTS.

CHAPTER I.

INTRODUCTORY.—ELEMENTS OF COMFORT.

"There is no more intensely interesting subject, among the many questions of the day, than the great problem of Domestic Economy. How to live well and comfortably, and yet cheaply, without descending to niggardliness, is, and has been, the study of wise men and philosophers in all ages."—ANON.

COMFORT has been called the principal household god of the English people. Home and Comfort are certainly the two most significant words in the English language. In countries where the air is genial throughout the year, and to bask in the sunshine imparts health and pleasure, the dwelling and its management may be matters of secondary consideration; but in England and the United States a comfortable home is the first essential element in the art of living happily.

Home comfort is the result of knowing how to manage the details of a household in the best manner, so that its machinery will work smoothly, without jar or friction, and applying that knowledge daily, which is sometimes called House-thrift. Wealth, though it can purchase luxury, cannot buy comfort. The rich, as well as the very poor, are often without homes, or have homes that are not homes. When the spirit of domestic disorder or unthrift enters the door, whether it be of a mansion or of a cottage, all the good angels fly out of the windows. So when the genius of Good Management comes within a household, Comfort follows soon after, erects her shrine and distributes daily blessings to every member of the family.

It is remarkable that though the ambition to live comfortably is so general as to be almost universal, yet very few attain the object of their wishes. Those who have made their fortunes are wheedled into the meshes of fashionable society, bound with silver chains, and delivered over into the hands of the most remorseless of taskmasters. The middle classes sacrifice comfort in their attempts to imitate the rich in their style of living, and involve themselves in debt and its attendant vexations. Even among the working classes, their daily meals are often miniature banquets. Living to eat, rather than eating to live, they consume the nest-egg of independence and wonder there is no increase. An English manufacturer remarked that he could not really afford to buy spring lamb, and green peas, and salmon, and new potatoes, and strawberries, for some weeks after his hands had been feeding on these delicacies.

Some one has naively remarked there is nothing so expensive as living, except, perhaps, it be dying and employing a fashionable undertaker. Alexis Soyer, one of the noted authorities in gastronomy, in order partly to magnify the importance of his calling, has attempted to compute the quantities of food which an English epicure probably consumes, if his life be prolonged to threescore years and ten; and taking for the basis of his calculation the average or medium consumption at daily meals, he estimates that a moderately good liver consumes 300 oxen, 500 calves, lambs, pigs, etc., 1200 fowls, 1000 ducks, turkeys, etc.,

3600 birds of various kinds, 500 hares and rabbits, 40 deer, 120 Guinea hens, 360 wild fowl, 5000 smelts, 4000 other kinds of fish, not counting whitebait, 30,000 oysters, 1500 lobsters or crabs, 300,000 prawns, shrimps, sardines, etc., 500 lbs. of grapes, 360 lbs. of pine apple, 240 melons, some hundred thousand apples, pears, plums, etc., and some millions of cherries, strawberries, currants, and other small fruit, as walnuts, chestnuts, and figs; 5475 lbs. of vegetables of all kinds, $2434\frac{3}{4}$ lbs. of butter, 684 lbs. of cheese, 21,000 eggs, $4\frac{1}{2}$ tons of bread, half a ton of salt and pepper, and near $2\frac{1}{2}$ tons of sugar; and that he will drink 2736 gallons of water, 2394 gallons of coffee and tea, 1368 gallons of beer, and 4200 gallons of other liquids. This calculation, if only approximately accurate, demonstrates most forcibly how great is the cost of our daily subsistence, and how important is that knowledge which enables us to select and prepare these vast quantities of food without loss or waste, and in accordance with the laws of health. It is undoubtedly true that the greater part of human labor is directly employed in producing materials for human food.

Another serious drawback to the attainment of Domestic Comfort is ignorance of the elements of comfort, especially of good cookery. In the princely establishments of Europe and the mansions of the wealthy, where a dinner is not merely a necessity, but a luxury, all the great chiefs of the kitchen are men. The Francatellis, the Soyers, the Blots, and the Gouffés, whose names are familiar in both continents, are simply by profession male cooks, but they are also men of genius, and deservedly take rank with artists, for it requires as much talent to prepare a modern banquet as to paint a modern picture. In the homes of luxurious living the health of the chief cook is a most important matter, and is guarded with assiduous care, because when there is any ailment in the body the palate cannot be relied upon. Some enthusiastic gourmand recommends an employer to feel the pulse of his cook every morning, and examine his tongue, for he says if his system be out of order, and "the cook's palate is dull, his master will find the ragouts and sauces too highly seasoned."

It is the conceit of some philosophers that men are not only the best cooks, but the only fit persons to write books of cookery. The oldest and one of the best books in this class of literature, known as "Mrs. Glasse's Cookery," was written, it is said, by Dr. Hill. "Women," said Dr. Johnson, "can spin very well; but they cannot make a good book of cookery." The learned doctor himself thought of writing a book upon the philosophy of cooking, and said that as "a prescription, which is now compounded of five ingredients, had formerly fifty in it, so in cookery, if the nature of the ingredients be well known, much fewer will do. Then, as you cannot make bad meat good, I would tell what is the best butcher's meat, the best beef, the best pieces; how to choose young fowls; the proper seasons of different vegetables; and then how to roast, boil, and compound."

In France, all classes, the men as well as the women, study the economy of cookery and practise it; and there, as many travellers affirm, the people live at one-third the expense of Englishmen or Americans. There they know how to make savory messes out of remnants that others would throw away. There they cook no more for each day than is required for that day. With them the art ranks with the fine arts, and a great cook is as much honored and respected as a sculptor or a painter. The consequence is, as ex-Secretary McCullough thinks, a French village of a thousand inhabitants could be supported luxuriously on the waste of one of our large American hotels, and he believes that the entire population of France could be supported on the food which is literally wasted in the United States. Professor Blot, who resided for some years in the United States, remarks, pathetically, that here, " where the markets rival the best markets of Europe, it is really a pity to live as many do live. There are thousands of families in moderately good circumstances who have never eaten a loaf of really good bread, nor tasted a well-cooked steak, nor sat down to a properly prepared meal."

But in American households it is not the fashion for men to concern themselves with the details of the kitchen. The wife is the prime minister in the administration of the household, and within the limits of her jurisdiction her power over the fortune and well-being of her subjects is more absolute than that of the most despotic sovereign. If she be ignorant of the arts of frugal management, or willfully extravagant, or carelessly indifferent, not only the exchequer but the health of the family will suffer. The wife is the central figure in the household, and the secret or philosophy of Home Comfort consists principally in getting a good wife, who knows the things worth knowing in household management, or is teachable and willing to learn.

The Qualifications of a Good Wife.

A good wife, it may be remarked, is not a natural growth, springing from the soil without care or cultivation. Something undoubtedly is due to parentage and example, but in the main a girl is trained to be what she becomes. Writers on physiology and hygiene, as well as those on morals, have had a good deal to say on the education of women, but probably no one has written so much that is practical and useful as Dr. Chavasse, in his little books entitled "Advice to Wives" and "Advice to Mothers."

First of all in the list of qualifications that fit a woman for marriage, and above all others, he, in common with most other sensible writers, places GOOD HEALTH. Life without health is a burden; life with health is a joy and gladness. It is a fearful responsibility both to men and women to marry if they be not healthy, and the result must, as a matter of course, be misery. How needful it therefore is that all necessary instruction should be imparted to every young wife, and the proper means shown by which she may preserve her health.

How to Preserve a Wife's Health.

In order to maintain health, a young married woman ought to take regular and systematic *out-door exercise*, so far as it can be done without interfering with her household duties. Walking expands the chest, strengthens the muscles, promotes digestion, and exhilarates like a glass of champagne, but unlike champagne, it never leaves a headache behind. "If ladies would walk more than they do, there would be fewer lackadaisical, useless, complaining wives than there at present are; and instead of having a race of puny children we should have a race of giants."

In order to preserve health a young married woman must attend to the *ventilation* of her house. Ninety-nine out of every hundred bed-rooms, doctors assert, are badly ventilated; and in the morning after they have been slept in they are full of impure and poisoned air. "I say advisedly impure and poisoned air, for the air becomes foul and deadly if not perpetually changed—if not constantly mixed, both by day and by night, with fresh, pure, external air. Many persons, by breathing the same air over and over again, are literally poisoned by their own breaths. This is not an exaggerated statement—alas, it is too true!" For ventilation open the windows both at top and bottom, that the fresh air may rush in one way, while the foul air makes its exit through the other. This is letting in your friend and expelling an enemy.

In order to preserve health a young wife should *wash her body thoroughly* every morning. "There is nothing," says Dr. Chavasse, "more tonic, and invigorating, and refreshing than a cold ablution. Moreover, it makes one feel clean and sweet and wholesome; and you may depend upon it that it not only improves our physical constitution but likewise our moral character. A dirty man has generally a dirty mind."

In order to preserve health a young wife should have a nourishing diet, and especially a substantial breakfast. She must frequently vary the kind of food, of meat especially, as also the manner of cooking it. Where a lady is very thin, good fresh milk, if it agree, should form an important item of her diet. The meagre breakfasts of many young wives, eating scarcely anything, is one cause, the doctor thinks, of so much sickness among them, and of so many puny children in the world. A woman who has no appetite for her breakfast is not in perfect health, and should consult her medical adviser.

In order to preserve health a wife should have seven or eight hours of *sound, refreshing sleep.* "Sleep is of more consequence to the human economy than food. Nothing should therefore be allowed to interfere with sleep. And as the attendance on large assemblies, balls, and concerts interferes sadly, in every way, with sleep, they ought one and all to be sedulously avoided." Early rising, not later than six in summer and seven in winter, is also recommended, as it imparts health to the frame as well as gives animation to the household. "The early risers make the healthy, bright, long-lived wives and mothers."

In order to preserve health it is necessary to avoid the use of *alcoholic stimulants*, except as a medicine. "It is surprising," says Dr. Chavasse, "the quantity of wine some young ladies, at parties, can imbibe without being intoxicated; but whether if such ladies marry they will make fruitful vines is quite another matter; but of this I am quite sure that such girls will, as a rule, make delicate, hysterical, and unhealthy wives. The young are peculiarly sensitive to the evil effects of over-stimulation. Excessive wine-drinking with them is a canker, eating into their very lives. Time it is that these facts were proclaimed through the length and breadth of our land before mischief be done past remedy."

Other Qualifications of a Good Wife.

A good wife is not only a healthy woman, but one who thoroughly *understands household duties*. In Sweden, it is said, the young ladies of wealthy families esteem it a privilege to be permitted to cook the family dinner; and in France every woman can cook, hence good cookery is with them the rule, while with us it is the exception. It is true, as Dr. Johnson remarked, that a man is in general better pleased when he has a good dinner upon his table than when his wife speaks Greek. But it is also true that a good house-wife is of necessity an educated woman, learned not in the dead languages, but in the physical sciences.

She is a chemist, technologist, and a physician. On the walls of her laboratory are hung texts of practical wisdom for the instruction of her domestics, and in an appropriate corner, within convenient reach, is a small but select library of books on Household Science, Domestic Economy, and Common Sense Cookery. "The practical value of cookery books," says Delamere, "consists not so much in the instruction they afford to persons totally ignorant of the art, as in their suggestiveness to heads of households who do know something about it. A lady is puzzled how to vary agreeably and economically her day's bill of fare. She consults her books, and there are many good ones; and without slavishly following their indications, adapts them to her own tastes and circumstances. A clever housekeeper, with only half a hint, will improvise pleasing culinary novelties—novelties, that is, to the habitual diners at her own family table, whereas without the hint she might have gone plodding on in a wearisome routine of roast, boiled, and cold.

A good wife not only knows the details of household duties, but the secret of *economical management*. There are many women who have the disposition to do, and succeed tolerably well, provided they have plenty of means; but their management is inordinately extravagant. They throw away as remnants what would suffice a good cook for a meal. They cook more than is required and allow the surplus to spoil. They spend the time in making iced cakes which should be devoted to making good bread. It has been said of American women that there are more who can furnish you with a good ice-cream than a well-cooked mutton-chop; a fair charlotte-russe is easier to gain than a perfect cup of coffee; and you shall find a sparkling jelly to your dessert when you sighed in vain for a well-cooked potato. They forget that to do common things perfectly is far better worth our endeavor than to do uncommon things respectably.

A good wife also cultivates *cheerfulness,* and placidity of temper and disposition. Nothing disturbs digestion and consequently injures health so much as a fretful, easily ruffled temper. "Our passions," says Dr. Grosvenor, "may be compared to the winds in the air, which, when gentle and moderate, fill the sail and carry the ship on smoothly to the desired port; but when violent, unmanageable and boisterous, they grow to a storm and threaten the ruin and destruction of all." Fortunately temper is susceptible of cultivation, and may be controlled. A Quaker, who was remarkable for the mastery he had acquired over his temper, was asked by one, who had roundly abused him, the secret, and he replied that in his youth he was also hot and irritable, but having observed that those who got into a passion elevated their voices he resolved never to allow his voice to rise above a certain pitch, and that was his secret.

A good wife, moreover, avoids giving *cause for jealousy.* There are some women who delight to test their husbands' affection by flirting with others and mean no harm, but jealousy is too dangerous a passion to trifle with. When aroused it is rarely ever allayed; it grows by feeding on apprehension, and magnifies mole-hills into mountains. Trifles light as air

> "Are, to the jealous, confirmations strong
> As proofs of Holy Writ."

Lastly, a good wife is something of a physician, and in the minor ills, and especially infantile complaints, the best of physicians. She knows the proper remedies for cuts and bruises, mumps and measles, as well as the best cosmetics for the complexion, and pomades for the hair; and is an expert in destroying bugs and banishing fleas. All the information contained in the subsequent pages of this volume is in substance familiar to a properly educated woman, though we may wonder

"That one small head could carry all (she) knew."

It is related that a lad who had been brought up in a wilderness by a hermit, and had been kept from the sight of women, saw by chance two girls walking, and inquiring what they were, was told they were fairies. Long afterward, when he was asked what was the pleasantest thing he had ever seen in all his wanderings, he replied, "The two fairies in the wilderness." So a man who has known a good wife or mother treasures her memory as the pleasantest recollection of his life.

CHAPTER II.

ON HOUSE-PLANNING AND SELECTING WALL-PAPER.

"Taste—which has been described as the finest ornament and purest luxury of a land—is a thing of culture, and to its full enjoyment we may not hope to attain till the eye has been trained as well as the mind. Everything that is strained, forced or unnatural, is repulsive. An excess of color, an elaboration of carved ornaments, or extravagance of any kind, in matters of taste, should meet a well-merited censure."—MASON.

ONE of the fundamental principles or elements of domestic comfort is, for most persons, a convenient and well-planned dwelling. Much has been written on the subject of house-building, but a digest of it would probably be of very limited practical value. Those who intend to build for themselves will be likely to study the works specially devoted to architecture; those who have already built do not need to be told what mistakes they have made, and those who have not the means to build for themselves must take such houses as they can get. There are a few points, however, that have such an important influence upon economy in housekeeping, that they they should be borne in mind when erecting or selecting a house.

Points to be Observed in House-Planning.

In building a house in the country the first consideration is a selection of a site or location, and this should always be, if possible, on dry, gravelly soil, moderately elevated and slightly declining on every side to afford good drainage. Trees upon a site always improve it, but they should not be too numerous or too near the house, or they will make the rooms gloomy and injure the walls and roof by their continual shade and dampness.

With regard to the aspect of a house, all architectural writers concur that the principal front should be towards the *southeast*. . Mr. Repton remarks, " I consider the *aspect* of infinitely more consequence to the enjoyment and comfort of the inhabitant than any *prospect* whatever; and every common observer must be convinced that in this climate a southern aspect is most desirable; but few are aware of the total difference in the effect of turning the front of the house a few points to the east or to the west of south, because, although the southeast is the best, the southwest is the worst of all possible aspects, for this reason, that all blustering winds and driving rains come from the southwest, and consequently the windows are so covered with wet as to render the landscape hardly visible."

With regard to the plan of a proposed house, it is desirable to spend a good deal of time during the winter in discussing and considering it, and it is well to take counsel from an intelligent woman. Women generally have a much better idea of what constitutes real comfort in a house than men; and on all points connected with the relative arrangement of apartments, so as to save labor on the part of servants, we would far sooner take the opinion of an intelligent woman than that of the cleverest architect who ever handled drawing square and pencil. The following points deserve careful consideration in any plan that may be adopted:

1. Let the kitchen if possible be on a level with the principal floor, and for strong light and free ventilation it

should have windows on opposite or nearly opposite sides.

2. The pantry, or dish closet, should be between the kitchen and dining-room and easily accessible from either.

3. There should be a set of easy inside stairs from the kitchen to the cellar, and also an outer set into the cellar for admitting barrels, hogsheads, etc.

4. Every entrance, except the one to the kitchen, should be from an entry or hall, not only to prevent the abrupt ingress of cold air and for proper seclusion, but to prevent the too common evil of passing through one room to enter another.

5. Let the partitions of the upper floors stand over those of the lower, as nearly as may be, to secure firmness and solidity.

6. If possible arrange that the windows be placed diagonally to the four cardinal points, so that at no lookout will a living or sleeping room be all day deprived of the sun's rays, nor all day be exposed to them.

7. Let the sills of the windows be low, so that while sitting you can easily, without effort, see out; say not much exceeding two feet.

8. Avoid having too many doors opening into an apartment of moderate size.*

---

* Mr. Huggins, in the "London Building News," remarks: "I have noted plans of recently erected noblemen's and other mansions, showing four or five doors opening into one room of but moderate dimensions, sometimes two of them in the same wall with the fire-place, which must render freedom from draughts impossible, and give all ideas of domestic enjoyment to the winds that ride rampant through them. At one of Her Majesty's residences, if it be not belied by the engraved plan of it, scarce one of the rooms contains a snug corner, so numerous are the doors opening into them from every direction, one-half of which might be built up with great advantage to the place."

9. The chimneys should be curved gently in the form of an S, instead of having them perpendicular. By this means the draft will be good, the heat having a longer passage through the wall, and the wind outside cannot puff the smoke down further than the bend. The inside surface should be perfectly smooth, which will prevent the accumulation of soot.

10. The ceilings should be only moderately high, as it is difficult to heat rooms with high ceilings, except with an enormous expenditure of fuel.

11. The bedrooms should be roomy, not less than twelve by twelve feet if possible, with ceilings at least eight feet high, and well ventilated. Sleeping apartments should never be placed on the ground-floor when it is possible to avoid it. The unwholesome exhalations which affect the atmosphere are more concentrated near the surface of the earth. Dr. Rush observed, during the prevalence of yellow fever in Philadelphia, that those who occupied apartments in the third story were far less liable to attacks than those who resided lower.

12. The best woods for the different apartments are: oak, ash and yellow pine for the kitchen; oak for the dining-room; butternut for the sitting-room, parlor and library; oak and black walnut for the main hall; curly maple for the bath-room; chestnut for the principal sleeping room, and ash, maple and birch for the other chambers. A very handsome wainscoting may be made from alternate strips of light and dark curly maple.

13. As a protection against fire lay a flooring of thin sheet iron over the joists and the wood upon that, and sheathe the stairs with the same material. This is the advice of the eminent sculptor, Hiram Powers, who says that during the thirty-four years of his residence in Florence,

Italy, he never knew of a single house being consumed by fire, because there all the floors, above and below, are covered by thin brick tiles, which prevent ventilation, and a fire cannot rise and burst into flames. A Boston chemist recommends that in all wooden buildings, the wood should be covered with coarse mortar. He says the fire fiend craves light wood-work, loosely arranged, and full of draft channels. Let him find everything plugged solid with mortar.

14. Have your water pipes made of rubber-lined tubing, which, though patented, is furnished at a very reasonable price at the Paschal Iron Works, in Philadelphia. "Deceive ourselves as we may," says Dr. Bellows, "*there is no water incapable of acting on lead, or zinc, or copper under some circumstances*, and these metals should never be used for or connected with service pipe; and the sooner the people fully understand this fact the better. But how shall we protect ourselves in the meantime? It takes a long time for the most palpable truths to get control of corporations, proverbially conservative. Meantime we should never use water to drink or for cooking that has stood for any length of time in the pipes, and never use at all for these purposes water that has come from a leaden or zinc-lined cistern."

15. Inside water-closets should be connected, by means of a pipe, with the flue of a chimney, which will carry off their gases and prevent noxious exhalations. If this be not practicable, they should be placed against the outside wall, where there is a window which opens into a yard or unobstructed space. This window should be left partly open at night, for it is then, even more than during the day, that the close, unhealthy air from a water-closet per-

vades a house, unless some aperture for escape is provided.*

16. Have a closet wherever a recess in the masonry may afford space for one. A dwelling can hardly have too many closets, and women especially appreciate the comfort and advantage of having plenty of these convenient receptacles for old clothes and dirt.

Lastly: It is an important precaution to have all the drains properly trapped, not forgetting rain-water pipes where they enter into underground drains. These are a frequent source of bad smells and malaria, and from a neglect of this precaution, and the want of cleanliness in

---

* Man's ingenuity seems to be equal to the achievement of most difficult things, except the proper construction and arrangement of necessary houses and water-closets.

In the country these conveniences are generally located so far from the dwelling that they are decidedly inconvenient, and women are compelled to trudge to them through storm and exposure, to the injury of their health and the loss of their modesty. Many for this reason do not attend to the demands of nature with that regularity the maintenance of health requires, and thus the stupidity of country designers is often the cause of much suffering and probably the loss of many lives.

In the cities, water-closets inside of dwellings become, from faulty construction, decided nuisances. They are continually out of repair, and often emit a noisome odor that is far from being wholesome. Within a few years it has been discovered that dry earth possesses the remarkable property of not only deodorizing the refuse of the human body, but converting it into an inoffensive material that can be handled as earth. Advantage has been taken of this discovery for the construction of EARTH-CLOSETS, which dispense with the machinery of water-closets and the vaults of privies. The apparatus resembles a commode, with a vibrating hopper, on which the pulverized earth is placed, and a movable hod to receive the deposits. They are made either fixed or movable, and circulars giving directions for their use are easily obtainable in the principal cities. Those who have used them commend them highly, and they seem a valuable addition to the resources for promoting comfort in the household.

cellars, many a princely mansion has proved to be a pest-house to its owner.

Novel Method of Heating and Cooling Rooms.

Among the most important and desirable objects to be observed in the erection of a dwelling-house is a constant supply of pure and wholesome air. Mr. Dwyer,* an American architect, recommends a *Reciprocating Furnace and Refrigerator*, by means of which rooms may be warmed in winter and cooled in summer. He says, "The principle I would apply is the well-known philosophical law of temperature, viz., that warm air ascends and cold air descends. For this purpose I would construct a furnace in every cellar, surrounded with an air chamber with a current of water circulating through it to prevent its becoming too dry. The air thus purified and warmed, I would convey to every room in the house it was desirable to warm, by tubes leading to a refrigerator in the attic. These tubes I would close in the middle opposite each room, with an opening both above and below it. Supposing it is winter; I would unfasten the lower opening and admit the warm air from the chamber in the cellar, until the room was of an agreeable warmth. In summer I would close the lower opening and open the upper one. In the refrigerator in the garret, I would place a quantity of ice daily, the cool air from which descending the tubes, would enter the rooms and keep them at any requisite temperature. Thus, in the warmest days in summer, a refreshing coolness can

---

* Mr. Dwyer has made a specialty of economic cottage building, and has published two books to aid Western pioneers in the construction of houses suited to their circumstances. He furnishes designs for log houses that could be erected at an expense not much exceeding fifty dollars.

be maintained at the daily expense of a little ice—the furnace in the cellar and the refrigerator in the attic reciprocating with each other."

Suggestions on Wall-Paper and Interior Decoration.

The ornamenting of apartments with hangings and coloring involves so many points of nice consideration and artistic effect, that very few painters or paper-hangers understand them. Where expense is not an object, a genuine artist should be called in that the owner may have the benefit of a trained and cultivated taste. If a master in his profession, he will have a preference for God's favorite colors, green and blue; and for the dining-room of a fine mansion he will probably recommend that the carpet be of ultramarine blue, with a broad border of green oak leaves, and that the walls be covered with dark green velvet in panels; and the carved oak chairs covered to match. Each of the principal rooms, he will probably suggest, should be decorated and furnished according to some dominant color, that it may be known by a distinctive title, as the green room, the crimson room, blue room, etc.

But as we are not gathering information for the benefit of the wealthy and luxurious, but for those who are satisfied with comfortable homes, we would remark that the first consideration before purchasing wall-paper for any description of house, large or small, is to note the supply of light in the rooms and their dimensions. If the view be north, northeast or northwest, or due east, the general tone of coloring should be positively warm. Blues, greens, and all shaded colors which involve any predominant use of blues, must be avoided. In such aspects the choice should tend towards reds, and all their various combinations with yellow. As the aspect approaches east and west, so the color should verge towards yellow rather than red tints. In an eastern aspect tints of light yellow, lemon colors, etc., are always effective and cheerful.*

Another point to be looked to, and which has an important bearing on the selection of wall-paper, is whether it is to form a decoration in itself, or whether it is to become a mere background for pictures. In the latter case the paper can hardly be too subdued in tone. Very light drab, silver gray, and dark maroon (with a pattern of the same color glazed running through it), and two shades of the *same* color are all sufficient for one paper. Where water colors are hung, embossed white or cream color, with a very small diaper or spot of gold, will not be amiss. As a rule, the simplest patterns are the best for every situation,

---

* A writer in the London "Athenæum" remarks: "The supply of light, the size of the room, and its purpose, appear to be the chief circumstances which ought to regulate the strength or depth of the colors to be used. Where the light is strong, unobscured and plentiful, the tone of the coloring may be full; on the other hand, where the supply of light is small, the tone of the coloring should be light. Under a strong and abundant light, full-toned colors preserve their brightness and distinctive character, but when the light is feeble and the supply of it limited, they become dull and gloomy. Full-toned colors *lessen* the apparent size of the room; light coloring enlarges it. If you wish to *make your room appear as large as possible,* then exclude dark coloring not only on the large surfaces, but even in the patterns of the paper-hangings, and in the mouldings and ornamental parts. The nature of the use to which the room is applied should also influence the decision as to the tone of the coloring. If the room is used mostly by artificial light, which, being less pure than daylight, materially modifies the appearance of most colors—much or little, according to their strength—then keep the coloring light. If on the other hand it is a room for occupation during daylight, then the tone of coloring must be deep. Red and green with black appear dark and grave; with white they appear gay."

but where the eye has to rest upon the surface of the wall alone, a greater play of line in the patterns may become advisable.

Paper-hangings, according to Eastlake, should in no case be allowed to cover the whole space of a wall from skirting to ceiling. He says, "a 'dado,' or plinth space of plain color, either in paper or distemper, should be left to a height of two or three feet from the floor. This may be separated from the diapered paper above by a light wood moulding, stained or gilded. A second space or frieze left just below the ceiling, and filled with arabesque ornament, painted on a distemper ground, is always effective, but of course involves some additional expense. The most dreary method of decorating the wall of a sitting-room is to cover it all over with an unrelieved pattern of monotonous design."

Nothing is more difficult than to estimate the effect and intensity of colors, when spread over a large surface, from the simple inspection of a pattern-book. The purchaser will frequently find that a paper which he has ordered will look either darker or lighter when hung than it appeared in the piece. For this reason it is advisable to suspend several lengths of the paper side by side in the room for which it is intended, and it is only by this means that a correct idea of the ultimate effect can be arrived at.

How to Clean Paper-Hangings.

To clean paper-hangings, take small pieces of stale bread, about two days old, commence at the top of the room, and with the crust wipe lightly downward about half a yard at each stroke, till the upper part of the hangings is completely cleaned all around, and so continue until the whole is gone over. This operation, if carefully performed, will frequently make old paper look almost equal to new. Great caution must be used not to rub the paper hard, nor to attempt cleaning it the cross or horizontal way. The dirty part of the bread must each time be cut away, and the pieces renewed as often as at all necessary.

How to Make a Permanent Whitewash.

Make the whitewash in the ordinary manner, then place it over a fire and bring it to a boil. Then stir in to each gallon a tablespoonful of powdered alum, a half pint of good flour paste, and a half pound of glue dissolved in water, while it is boiling.

This wash, it is said, nearly equals paint, and the expense is trifling.

CHAPTER III.

THE ART OF HOUSE-FURNISHING.

"Whatever has nothing to do is a positive incumbrance; and following out this rule, the greater part of the ornaments introduced only add to the defects of a design that has nothing of elegance, strength or utility to recommend it to our attention. Had it any of these qualities it would not require such an oppressive weight of meaningless scrolls and figures to secure a favorable notice; and any resort to this method of hiding defects is as unbecoming as it would be for a lady to wear a brooch that fastened no portion of her dress, or a chain of gold without a watch or some other article of value attached to it."—MASON.

IT is the fashion of certain art critics to condemn all modern furniture and upholstery as inferior not only in design but in substantial excellence to that made by hand in the Mediæval age. This, with men like Ruskin and Eastlake, is carried to the extreme of cynicism, but it is, nevertheless, true that since the introduction of steam-mills, and the abolition of long apprenticeships among cabinetmakers, the markets are overstocked with vast quantities of inferior furniture which it is not good economy for any one to purchase.

A century ago the fashionable woods for furniture were ebony and rosewood; at a later date, and until recently, mahogany was the favorite; now walnut is more in demand than all the others combined. Poplar is used largely by cabinetmakers as an underwood for veneering, and maple for chamber furniture; while bass, or white wood, is employed principally in making cheap, painted bedroom suits, and is said to be as durable as finer woods. Oak is used to some extent for dining-room and library furniture, but the American oak is a very different article from that of Europe, being not only more difficult to work but more liable to warp.

What to Avoid in Buying Furniture.

In selecting furniture the cynical critics to whom we have referred caution buyers not to attach the least importance to any recommendation a salesman may make on matters of taste. "If he says one form of chair is stronger than another form; or that the covering of one sofa will wear better than that which is used for another, you may believe him, because on that point he can judge, and it is to his interest that you should be correctly informed so far. But on the subject of taste his opinion is not likely to be worth more, but rather less, than that of his customers, for the plain reason that the nature of his occupation can have left him little time to form a taste at all. He neither made the furniture in his shop nor superintended its design. His business is simply to sell it, and it will be found that his notions of beauty are generally kept subservient to this object. In other words, he will praise each article in turn, exactly as he considers your attention is attracted to it with a view to purchase. If he has any guiding principles of selection, they are chiefly based on two considerations, viz., the relative price of his goods and the social position or wealth of those customers in whose eyes they find favor."

Secondly: They advise the selection of furniture which is simple in its general form and free from extravagant contour or unnecessary curves. The tendency of the present age in upholstery is to run into curves. Chairs are frequently curved in such a manner as to insure the greatest amount of ugliness with the least possible comfort. The backs of sofas are curved so as to be manifestly inconvenient; either too high in one place or too low in another to accommodate the shoulders of a sitter. Drawing-room tables are curved in every direction, perpendicularly and horizontally, and are therefore inconvenient to sit at and always rickety. This system of ornamentation is called shaping. It always involves additional expense in manufacture, and therefore by avoiding "shaped" articles of furniture the public will not only gain in an artistic point of view but save their money.

Thirdly: There is a notion very prevalent among people who have given themselves but little trouble to think at all on the matter, that to insure grace in furniture, it must be made in a flimsy, fragile manner. Thus we constantly hear the expression "light and elegant" applied to a set of drawing-room chairs which look as if they must sink beneath the weight of the first middle-aged gentleman who used them. "Now lightness and elegance," says a critic, "are agreeable qualities in their way, and under certain conditions of design art should be aimed at. For instance, the treatment of mere surface ornament, such as painted arabesques, etc., or of details purely decorative and useless, as the filagree gold of a lady's earring, may well be of this character; but objects intended for real and daily service, such as a table which has to bear the weight of heavy books or dishes, or a sofa on which we may recline at full length, ought not to look light and elegant, but strong and comely; for comeliness, whether in nature or art, is by no means incompatible with strength."

What to Choose in Buying Furniture.

In the choice of furniture the first and principal qualification is its *usefulness or fitness*, or, in other words, the combination of convenience, ease and propriety. Furniture is made to be used, and a couch upon which you cannot lie, or a table from which you cannot eat, or a chair upon which you cannot sit, is neither useful nor ornamental. In selecting furniture also the style of the house, the room and domestic surroundings must be constantly borne in mind, and especially that the size of the furniture will be adapted to the proportions of the apartment for which it is destined. To illustrate, a buffet, or any other article of furniture of large size, which might adorn a rich man's mansion, would look ridiculous and out of place in a poor man's dwelling.

Passing from general principles to details, we would remark that in selecting chairs it will be extremely difficult to find those that are comfortable and strong yet elegant. This is especially true of drawing-room chairs. Either the backs will be found too straight, or too high, or full of painful projections, or the springs too weak, and, except those with arms, it will be a task to find in all the cabinet-shops a comfortable yet handsome chair or sofa. With regard to coverings the most elegant and the most costly are satin brocade and silk damask. The latter differs from the brocade, which is all silk, in being woven even on the surface instead of having the figures raised. The most serviceable and most durable furniture-covering is *plush*, and it is always fashionable.

Dining-room chairs should be high enough to bring the diners well above their plates. The high chair occupied by a carver gives him an advantage. The dining-room table should be large enough to accommodate the dishes without crowding.

Bedroom chairs should be substantial, with low seats and high backs. The cane-seat chairs that come with chamber sets of cottage furniture are not well suited for use in bedrooms. With respect to *washstands*, those should be selected which have high splash-boards to protect the wall, and which are oiled or painted, not varnished.

In selecting *bureaus,* or chests of drawers, it is important to select those which have drawers not exceeding five or six inches in depth; for every one knows the inconvenience of being obliged to delve down below innumerable strata of clothes to find some article of clothing which is wanted in a hurry, and by the additional height gained in saving depth, another drawer may be added to the set. *Bedsteads* can now be obtained of all kinds and sizes, in wood or metal, and those with a canopy and head-curtain, made of cretonne, chintz or damask, add much to the picturesqueness of a modern bedroom.

Combination Furniture.

During the last quarter of a century the ingenuity of cabinetmakers has been directed to the production of articles that serve a twofold purpose, or what may be called combination furniture. A round table has been made which at a touch can be converted into a comfortable arm-chair and writing-desk. High chairs for children have been made which in a minute can be converted into a low chair and play-table. Ottomans are so constructed that they can be changed into two small settees and two arm-chairs. An arm-chair is made that can readily be converted into an invalid couch and a library chair, the back of which turns over to form a pair of steps. At the New York Crystal

Palace in 1853 a cabinetmaker exhibited a palace secretary which combined a bedstead, writing-desk, bookcase, washstand, gentleman's wardrobe, medicine-drawers, secret silver closet, dressing-bureau, ladies' wardrobe and secret jewelry case, the whole surmounted by a musical and alarm clock. This combination furniture, if well made, is often very useful, especially for rooms of narrow dimensions.

Pictures and Picture Frames.

A room, however elegantly furnished, looks naked and cold without pictures on the walls. They must not, however, be too numerous, and a few good ones are better than a hundred poor pictures. The proper height for hanging a picture is given at five feet six inches from the floor to its centre, or so that the eye can fall upon the lower part. Art critics recommend not only that oil pictures should be hung by themselves, but to separate water-colors, drawings, photographs, and engravings. Each may be beautiful in itself, but to place them together is to destroy the effect of all. The print will look cold and harsh by the side of the water-color sketch, the sketch will seem unreal and gaudy by the side of the photograph. Keep them all apart—if not in separate rooms, at least on separate walls. Never hang glazed drawings, where it can be avoided, opposite a window. The sheen of the glass reflects the daylight, and annihilates the effect of the picture behind it. Take care that your picture-cord either matches or harmonizes with the color of the wall-paper behind it. Some use wire instead of cord, because the former is almost invisible at a little distance, but this seems a disadvantage.

Never suspend a framed picture, however small, from one nail. This may seem a trifle, but, independently of the consideration of safety, the effect produced by two points of support is infinitely better. The triangular space enclosed by a picture-cord stretched between three points must always be inharmonious with the horizontal and vertical lines of a room.

Marble Tops on Furniture.

The use of marble by the cabinet-makers is increasing, notwithstanding some critics contend that marble is fit only for tombstones and should be rejected from the interior and exterior of dwellings, and very few fine tables are now made without marble tops, either carved or plain. The Italian is the favorite variety, and of this the purest white is preferred by most persons, though the dark veined is usually harder and more durable. Purchasers in choosing should take care to observe that the marble has a good *metallic* ring when struck, which shows that it is capable of resisting the action of acids and grease. When stains have come upon a marble top, the following is the best recipe for extracting them:

Saturate the soiled places frequently with *pure spirits of benzine*, which will penetrate the marble and carry the grease from the surface. This is about the only remedy known, and will answer for every kind of marble. If soiled with wine or acids, and the surface is decomposed, scrub with a strong solution of soda, and afterwards rub briskly with whiting-paste on a woollen rag. If the edges are chipped, file off the roughest part, and then rub with cuttle-fish until smooth; afterwards polish with whiting as above.

The following is said to be a very valuable receipt for MARBLE CEMENT:

"Take plaster of Paris and soak it in a saturated solution of alum, then bake the two in an oven, the same as gypsum is baked, to make it plaster of Paris, after which they are ground to powder. It is then used as wanted; being mixed with water, like plaster, and applied. It sets into a very hard composition, capable of taking a very high polish. It may be mixed with various coloring minerals, to produce a cement of any color capable of imitating marble. This is a very rare receipt, worth twenty dollars to many readers, who can prepare it for themselves."

To Take Bruises out of Furniture.

Wet the part with warm water; double a piece of brown paper five or six times, soak it and lay it on the place; apply on that a hot flat-iron till the moisture is evaporated. If the bruise be not gone, repeat the process. After two or three applications the dent or bruise will be raised level with the surface.

To Clean Mirrors, Looking-Glasses, etc.

Take a soft sponge, wash it well in clean water, and squeeze it as dry as possible; dip it into some spirits of wine and rub over the glass; then have some powder-blue tied up in a rag, dust it over your glass, and rub it lightly and quickly with a soft cloth; afterward finish with a silk handkerchief.

To Clean and Tighten Cane-seat Chairs.

Turn up the chair-bottom, and with hot water and a sponge wash the cane-work, so that it may be thoroughly soaked. Should it be dirty, use a little soap. Let it dry in the air, and it will be as tight and firm as when new, provided the cane be not broken.

To Take out Oil or Grease from Cloth.

Drop on the spot some oil of tartar, or salt of wormwood, which has been left in a damp place until it is fluid; then immediately wash the place with lukewarm soft water, and then with cold water, and the spot will disappear.

This will be found very useful, says Stokes, in his *Cabinet-Maker*, and by proceeding as above, every spot of grease in cloth will be completely taken out.

To Remove Stains in Tables.

Wash the surface with stale beer or vinegar; the stains will then be removed by rubbing them with a rag dipped in spirits of salts. To repolish, proceed as you would do with new work.

If the work be not stained, wash the surface with clean spirits of turpentine, and repolish it with furniture-oil.

How to Cement Broken China, etc.

Stokes says: Beat the whites of eggs well to a froth; let them settle; add soft, grated or sliced cheese and quicklime; beat them well together, and apply a little to the broken edges. This cement will endure both fire and water.

Another good receipt, and which is nearly colorless, is the following:

Dissolve half an ounce of *gum acacia* in a wineglass of boiling water; add *plaster of Paris* sufficient to form a thick paste, and apply it with a brush to the parts required to be cemented together.

Buying Carpets.

In buying a carpet, the first point to be regarded is its capacity to wear well without becoming shabby. It is a waste of money to buy a carpet of loose texture. If a cheap floor-covering be desired, sew two strips of the cheapest cotton cloth of the size of the room, and tack the edges to the floor. Then paper the cloth with any sort of room paper, and after being well dried, give it two coats of varnish, and your floor-covering is complete. This can be washed like a carpet without injury, and on chambers or sleeping-rooms, where it will not meet with rough usage, it will last two years as good as new. Another mode of providing a cheap carpeting is to have a handsome border around the room and floor-drugget in the centre, so arranged as to seem to cover and protect a handsome carpet, when in reality it covers nothing but paper on the floor. Next to texture, the most desirable quality in a carpet is cheerfulness in figure and color. The most tasteful carpets are those made of various shades of the same color, or of all shades of two colors, such as salmon and yellow, or blue and buff, or salmon and green, or all shades of green or of brown. All very dark shades should be brown or green, but not black. Avoid, in selecting colors, those which have black threads, as they are always rotten.

But while aiming at cheerfulness, care should be taken to avoid those designs which are remarkable for over-brilliancy of color. They are apt to be inharmonious with the rest of the furniture, and rich, oriental dyes frequently have a deleterious effect on the material which they stain. The crimson used in Scinde rugs, for instance, is especially destructive, and the portions dyed with this color wear out long before the rest. The dull, Indian red is far more enduring, and is also more likely to blend well with the surrounding tints.

Another precaution to be taken in buying carpets is to *avoid large patterns,* unless the room be of extraordinary dimensions; for large figures, both in wall-paper and carpets, have a tendency to make rooms look smaller than they really are. About the best carpet that can be selected for ordinary drawing-rooms is a good Brussels, provided that the pattern is one that bears some resemblance to something in the world, and that in both figure and color it is cheerful. For a sitting-room a substantial three-ply carpet, of some medium dark pattern, but cheerful, is desirable. For bedrooms the ingrains are suitable, but the pattern should be of soft colors, a prominent one of which should be green, and the figures flowers and foliage.

In *laying down carpets* the most economical way is not to fit them into the recesses of the room, the portions uncovered by the carpet being painted in oil or covered with oil-cloth, baize, or drugget. A square carpet, it is said, may be changed eight times, and an oblong one four times, when not fitted into recesses, whereas one fitted to the room cannot be altered in position, except the apartment be symmetrical. Some authorities insist that bed-room carpets should never be tacked down, so that they may be taken up easily and frequently. They also direct that carpets "should be sewn on the wrong side, with double waxed thread, and with the ball-stitch. Take a stitch on the breadth next you, pointing the needle towards you, and then take a stitch on the other breadth, pointing the needle from you. Draw the thread tightly, but not so as to pucker. Bind *the whole* of the carpet with carpet-binding, and nail it with tacks, having bits of leather under the heads."

When a carpet begins to wear, its position should be changed so as to wear equally, and when mended, a needle should be used, and proper colored worsteds, as in embroidery. Before *sweeping carpets* with a broom it is best to sprinkle them over with damp tea-leaves or Indian meal, and when ready, the *Scientific American* gives the following directions for

Sweeping Carpets.

Place the broom upon the carpet in an inclined position, with the handle inclining forwards; drawing it quickly over the surface in this position, and scarcely raising it from the floor, will prevent the raising of very much dust. In order to do the work effectually, however, the motion should not be given by long strokes, but by a quick succession of short ones. It would be worth fifty dollars to any housekeeper, who does not understand the business, to see these two modes (one holding the broom upright and the other aslant) distinctly performed. By the former, or thrusting mode, the coarser dirt, or that which does not rise in the air, is shot ahead several feet, and spread over a large surface; by the latter, or drawing mode, it is kept more compactly together, something like the winnow of hay in the meadow. The broom, instead of being bent around like a hook, as above stated, is kept straight and smooth, and lasts much longer.

The sweeping should commence from the upper end of the room and proceed toward the fire-place, or the lower end of the room, according to the pile of the carpet. The sweeping must go with and not against the pile. When the sweeping is done, the chimney and other ornaments are to be removed, and their places dusted. Clean soap and water should occasionally be used with a flannel cloth to the marble chimney pieces and slabs. The various articles of ornament should be carefully wiped or cleaned, and then replaced. The ledges, panels of doors, window-frames, mirrors, chairs, and tables, etc., should be dusted and restored to their places. Picture-frames must be dusted with a feather broom, and not with a linen duster.

If a broom be inserted every week in *boiling suds*, it will be toughened and last much longer, will not cut the carpet, and will sweep as elastic as a new broom.

Moths in carpets may be destroyed, both worms and eggs, by spreading a wet sheet on the carpet, and passing a hot flat-iron over it quickly. The steam, it is said, destroys them.

To Clean and Brighten Brussels Carpets.

Take a fresh beef-gall, break it into a clean pan; pour one-half into a very clean bucket, and nearly fill it with lukewarm water: take a clean, coarse cloth, and having brushed the carpet well, rub it hard with the cloth thoroughly wet with the gall water; do a small piece at a time, have ready a dry coarse cloth, and rub the carpet dry; so proceed until the whole carpet is cleaned.

A few drops of carbonate of ammonia, in a small quantity of warm rain-water, will change, if carefully applied, discolored spots upon carpets, and indeed all spots, whether produced by acids or alkalies. If one has the misfortune to have a carpet injured by whitewash, this will immediately restore it.

Oil Cloths.

In buying an oil cloth for a floor, endeavor to obtain one that has been manufactured for several years; as the longer it has been made, previous to use, the better it will wear, from the paint becoming hard and durable. An oil cloth that has been made within the year is scarcely worth buying, as the paint will be defaced in a very little time. An oil cloth should never be scrubbed with a brush; but after being first swept it should be cleaned by washing with a large soft cloth and lukewarm or cold water. On no account use soap, or take water that is hot, as either of them will bring off the paint. When it has dried you may sponge it over with milk, which will brighten and preserve the colors; then wipe it with a soft, dry cloth.

Moths in Furniture.

Within a few years it has been discovered that there is a peculiar kind of moth, which infests furniture, destroying alike in summer and winter. It penetrates sofas or chairs between the backs or seats, or under the seats, where an opening in the springs permits a path of exit. The only effectual preventive known is to remove the furniture from the walls frequently, and whisk it well under the seats to prevent the lodgment of the fly. The usual remedies of Cayenne pepper, Scotch snuff, camphor, turpentine, etc., avail little against the furniture moth. They may be removed by taking off the muslin from under the seats, and from the outside ends and backs, and exposing it to the air. A whisk, or the open hand, will beat all off, and may cause their absence, as they do not like to be disturbed. Whisk well twice a week, and in furniture as yet free from moths, which is to be left without attention during the summer, protection may be afforded by camphor in small bags, or *patchouli* highly concentrated.

CHAPTER IV.

HOUSEHOLD CONVENIENCES NOT IN GENERAL USE.

"It is sometimes said that there are less improvements in the art of housekeeping than in any other. It is quite clear that there are not enough of them, and those which are made are not generally adopted. Let us refer now to what we regard as an improvement in the little art of shelling beans. The old method was making use of the thumb and fingers; then the use of a needle to prepare the pod to open readily. Now the method is to pour upon the pods a quantity of scalding water, and the beans slip very easily from the pod. By pouring scalding water on apples, the skin may be easily slipped off, and much labor saved."— ROBINSON.

SOME one has remarked that it would be better for a lady to give up some expensive article in the parlor, and apply the money thus saved for kitchen conveniences, than to have a stinted supply where the most labor is to be performed. If our countrywomen would devote more to comfort and convenience and less to show, it would be a great improvement. A full supply of all conveniences in the kitchen and the cellar, and a place appointed for each, very much facilitates domestic labor, and for want of this, much vexation and loss of time are occasioned while seeking vessels in use or in cleaning those employed for various purposes.

An experienced housekeeper has also remarked that you must have plenty of *kitchen towels*, or the chances are ten to one that the first hired girl you have will take a damask tablecloth to wipe the dishes and a fine wiping towel for a pot-cloth. The best material for kitchen cloths is the ordinary American tow linen, and it is worth far more than the imported crash, which almost everybody uses.

It is a great economy of time and labor to have the articles in constant use in cooking and housework arranged in compact form and close together. In the cook's galley of a large steamship, every article used in cooking for two hundred persons is often contained in a space not over nine feet square, and so arranged that with one or two steps the cook can reach all that he uses. Around the sink is probably the best place to arrange the shelving and compartments for holding the articles in constant use, such as boxes for holding Indian meal, rye and wheat flour, shelf-boxes for scouring materials, dish-cloths, and can-pails for sugars. Wooden can-pails are said to be the best articles in which to keep sugars, both white and brown, and a tin can with a tight movable cover and a cork in the spout is the best for molasses.

A well-equipped kitchen will contain, among its iron ware, pots of different sizes, a long iron fork with a handle, a large and small gridiron with grooved bars, a bake-pan, two skillets of different sizes, and a flat skillet for frying, a griddle and a waffle iron, tin and iron bread-pans, two ladles of different sizes, a skimmer, a toasting iron and two teakettles of different sizes, of which the handles do not lie flat on the sides of the kettle, for they are very inconvenient, and burn the hands when heated, as we know by experience. Portable furnaces of iron or clay are very useful in summer for washing, ironing and stewing. A spice box and a mill for grinding coffee, strong knives and forks, a sharp carving-knife, an iron cleaver and board, a fine saw, steelyards, chopping tray and knife, knife sharpener, iron spoons, flat irons, ruffle iron and crimping iron, are all desirable. A kitchen should be also supplied with tinware and tubs, pails and other wooden ware, and baskets of various sizes for clothes, marketing, eggs and fruits.

In buying tinware and kitchen utensils generally, it is economy to purchase the best at first. The very best double plate tinware will last a lifetime, while the poor cheap kind will not last a year. We would also caution housekeepers against the low-priced earthenware, " particularly that which looks like the substance of a common brick when broken. The solid, strong stoneware costs perhaps a quarter more, but it is worth ten times as much as the other."

Assuming, however, that our readers are familiar with the articles that are regarded as indispensable by all housekeepers for kitchen service we proceed to call their attention to some

Labor-Saving Contrivances not in General Use.

The *Stock-pot* is a standard fixture in French kitchens, but it is little known in America, though its introduction would be a great and economical convenience. It is always kept simmering to receive trimmings of meat, bones, remnants of fowl or game—in short, to be a save-all for the conversion of worthless scraps into wholesome nutriment. Whether flavored with vegetables or not, the contents of the stock-pot will prove invaluable, both to furnish occasional basins of soup, and to assist in compounding all sorts of made dishes, where something better than mere water is required to moisten them. If the odds and ends of the kitchen do not supply enough materials, a few coarse fresh bits of meat from the butcher will easily make up for the deficiency. "Broth," says Ude, "is the foundation of cookery."

Larding-*pins* or larding-*needles*, for introducing strips of bacon into veal, the breasts of fowl, calf's liver, etc., and *iron skewers*, for trussing meat and poultry previous to cooking, are very common utensils in French kitchens, but so little is known of them in America that it is probable our cooks would leave the skewers in the fowl or joint when placed on the table, to puzzle and confound the carver.

Two or three *whitewood boards*, about twenty inches or two feet square, on which to chip vegetables, cooked or uncooked, meat, suet, sweet herbs, etc., are not too many to have. They are both neater and more convenient than the surface of a deal table, which is generally used for that purpose.

The *American oven*, or *kitchen*, for cooking small things before the fire, is very highly commended by English writers on cookery.

The French *Bain-marie*, or *hot water bath*, is a very useful utensil for stewing gently without the possibility of burning, for warming up cold dishes, and keeping things hot for travellers, sportsmen and professional people. It is a stew-pan with a double bottom, containing water between the fire and the inner bottom. Turtle, ox-tail, and such like soups, when once made, should always be heated up again in a bain-marie, which not only saves the meat, etc., from sticking to the bottom, but preserves the delicacy of the flavor.

The *frying-pans* commonly sold are much too shallow to fry meats or fish by *plunging* them into hot fat, which is the French idea of frying. Every kitchen should possess a frying-pan not less than six inches deep, oval, not round, and long enough to accommodate a respectable-sized fish.

Scales and *weights* to proportion the quantities of ingredients used, and to verify the weight of goods received into the house, are not as common in American kitchens as they ought to be.

Pasty pans are a useful article for making a savory and delicious preparation of meat and potatoes. They consist of a circular pan with a perforated lid, having a valve pipe screwed on to it. The meat is placed at the bottom of the pan, with seasoning, butter, and a little water, and the perforated plate is laid over it. Some mashed potatoes mixed with milk are next arranged on this plate; filling up the whole space to the top of the tube, and finishing the surface in an ornamental manner. If carefully baked the potatoes will be covered with a delicate brown coat, and retain all the savory steam arising from the meat.

Revolving gridirons are made, having fluted bars lined with enamel. The gravy that flows from the meat runs into the fluted bars, and thence into a small receptacle in the middle of the handle, so preserving a nice quantity of the gravy. As the part on which the meat rests turns round, the necessity of frequently moving the meat is obviated.

A novel *egg boiler* has been invented, to which the name of the "Whistler" has been given. It consists of a cylinder in which the eggs are placed. Attached to the cylinder is a whistle which, acted on by the steam, gives notice that the cooking of the eggs is completed, and renders it unnecessary to watch the process.

A bronze *egg steamer* has recently been invented. A little water is poured in, the eggs placed in a frame inside, and the spirit lamp being lighted, the steam cooks the eggs. It is egg-shaped, in bronze, and very neat.

Several different kinds of *egg beaters* are to be had, but purchasers should remember that eggs should be beaten with a circular motion from right to left.

Of *coffee pots* the number is so great, each possessing some point of excellence, that a selection is bewildering. One of the most useful styles, however, is the "Old Dominion Coffee Pot," made in Philadelphia. In this the ground coffee is placed in a strainer, forming the lower portion, and boiling water poured on it; a condenser containing cold water is then placed over, forming the upper part; the aroma-bearing vapor rises, is condensed, and returned into the coffee, the aroma being thus perfectly retained.

Another plan forces the boiling water to filter through the coffee, carrying away the aroma, and leaving the bitter principle in the worthless grounds.

An elegant but rather pretentious utensil is "The French Balance Coffee Machine," composed of two parts connected by a tube. The coffee being heated in one receiver, passes through the tube and strainer into the other perfectly clear and containing all the aroma.

A very useful and at the same time neat coffee pot is "The Vienna Coffee Machine," especially for summer use. The water is poured in, and the coffee then placed in a strainer over it; a spirit lamp is lighted under, and as the water boils it rises through the coffee and overflows into the main holder. This coffee pot swings on a stand, and a slight motion pours the coffee into the cup. Some shapes are very elegant.

For roasting meat and game or poultry, which is always preferable to baking, a *French turnspit* is useful. In this the spit runs through an improved form of Dutch oven, and is kept revolving by machinery, which, when wound up, runs for about two hours, a gong calling the cook's attention when it stops.

But the most useful meat-cooker for a family of any size is *Warren's Cooker*, the invention of a captain in the English navy. The principle is cooking by the heat of water and steam; the meat being placed in a pot without water, which fits into a boiler and just touches the water, the steam from which encompasses the sides and rises by a passage into another chamber, in which puddings are cooked, and heating a third, in which are vegetables, escapes through the lid. When cooked enough the meat is placed for about ten minutes in the oven to brown.

The advantages are, that no meat juices evaporate in the cooking; no trouble is needed in watching the meat after the water boils; it cooks easily over a small gas jet, and the most inexperienced help can use it after once being shown. Fish and game it cooks in perfection.

An economical way of using cold meat is to mince it, and a *mincing knife* with two or more blades, for a small family, is useful. For large families and hotels mincing machines are now made.

Apple and peach parers are great labor savers, and are now made to core in addition to paring. *Raisin seeders* of different kinds have been invented, and also *cherry stoners*.

A little machine for slicing potatoes is an ingenious invention, and can be used for slicing beets and other similar vegetables. A graduated spring pushes the potato forward after each cut.

In families where sausages are much appreciated, a

sausage machine, which can be purchased for a small sum, is desirable. It can also be used for chopping vegetables so that they will dissolve perfectly in soups and stews and afford many savory dishes.

A *pea sheller* has been invented that will shell a peck of peas in ten minutes. The pea pods are thrown into a hopper, and after a handle has been moved backward and forward a few times, the pods fall out in front, while the peas pass into a drawer underneath.

A *tendon separator* is pronounced by some to be the greatest boon ever conferred on unskilled carvers. Soyer says of it, "If it were more generally used there would be no more birds flying across the table in the face of guests; no more turkeys deposited in a lady's or gentleman's lap; no more splashing of gravy to spoil satin dresses; but all would be divided with the greatest facility and in the most elegant manner, and the poultry would look much better at table."

Refrigerators are valuable articles of household convenience not so much in general use as they ought to be. They serve for keeping meat wholesome, vegetables crisp, drinks of different kinds cool, milk from souring, butter solid, etc., etc.; but it should be remembered that an often renewed jug or open dish of lime-water adds much to their efficiency, absorbing the impure gases which meat, fish, etc., give off at even a very low temperature; and in purchasing a refrigerator be particular to choose one in which the ventilation is perfect.

Portable refrigerators are now made, easily carried from room to room, and placed on the table at meals.

Ice-cream freezers, too, are useful in many families, adding greatly to comfort at a small expenditure. Various styles are made, each claiming a peculiar excellence; but the most simple are the most efficient.

For the summer, *gas cooking stoves* are very desirable. Several kinds are now made, giving great heat with small consumption of gas; one—The Table Gas Stove—being especially useful. This connects with the ordinary gas burner by a flexible tube, will stand on the breakfast table, and boil sufficient coffee for an average family. It cannot be overturned, and the flame burns so well as not to soil the brightest tinware.

A griddle *greaser and scraper* is a recent invention for saving lard, and for cleanliness.

A no-drip molasses jug saves much discomfort.

Knife-cleaning is a duty which often becomes irksome in small families, and is always laborious. The *Rotary Knife Cleaner* saves a great deal of time and labor, and cleans very effectually, but unless care is exercised it is apt to wear the knives quickly.

A *cinder sifter* is useful and economical. One we have seen will stand in a corner and occupy little space. The ashes, as taken from the grate, are poured in at the top, and falling on a cone and sieve, the cinders fall into a hopper at the front and the ashes into a hopper at the back, and are easily removed.

Among the patented articles there is also a *funnel strainer*, or a funnel and strainer in temporary combination, united very simply by a catch and spring handle, so arranged that when the funnel and strainer are used jointly, they are held firmly together; and when either one is to be used alone, they can be easily separated.

There are also a number of contrivances patented for filtering water, many of them worthless; but a good and cheap *domestic filter* can be made as follows: Take a flower pot, and insert a sponge in the hole in the bottom, fill the pot with alternate layers of sand, charcoal, and small pebbles. The flower pot thus filled up may then be placed on a jar or other convenient vessel, into which the water can be received as it filters through.

A *clothes line protector* is not a new invention, but it cannot be said to be in general use. It consists simply of a little box fastened to a post and enclosing a wheel and a crank, with which a hundred feet of line can be wound up in one minute. When the line is wanted it can be run out with equal facility, and by a turn of the wheel can be tightened, then a catch holds it in its place.

How to Sharpen Edged Tools.

It has long been known that the simplest method of sharpening a razor is to put it for half an hour in water, to which has been added one-twentieth of its weight of muriatic or sulphuric acid, then lightly wipe it off, and after a few hours set it on a hone. The acid here supplies the place of a whetstone, by corroding the whole surface uniformly, so that nothing further but a smooth polish is necessary. The process never injures good blades, while the badly hardened ones are frequently improved by it, although the cause of such improvement remains unexplained. Of late this process has been applied to many other cutting implements. The workman, at the beginning of his noon-spell, or when he leaves off in the evening, moistens the blades of his tools with water acidulated as above, the cost of which is almost nothing. This saves the consumption of time and labor in whetting, which, moreover, speedily wears out the blades. The mode of sharpening here indicated would be found especially advantageous for sickles and scythes.

In this connection we may remark that, *to remove rust from steel articles*, as knives, forks, razors, etc., cover with sweet oil, well rubbed on, and let it remain for forty-eight hours, then rub with unslacked lime, powdered very fine, until the rust disappears.

"To *prevent rust* on iron or steel," says Dr. Brewer, in his "Guide to Science," "take one pint of fat oil varnish, mixed with five pints of highly rectified spirits of turpentine, and rub with a sponge. This varnish may be applied to bright stoves, and even to mathematical instruments, without hurting their delicate polish, and they will never contract any spots of rust."

We have already advised our readers not to buy a teakettle of which the handle rests against the bulge, as it may burn your fingers; and for the same reason do not buy a soup ladle except it has a non-metallic handle: that is, one either of wood, bone, or ivory.

To prevent a lamp from smoking, soak the wick in vinegar, and dry it well before you use it.

CHAPTER V.

ON THE ART OF MARKETING.

"Tell me what kind of food you eat, and I will tell you what kind of man you are."—SAVARIN.

DR. KITCHNER, in his well-known "Cook's Oracle," says the best rule for marketing is to pay ready money for everything, and to deal with the most respectable tradesmen in your neighborhood. He thinks if you leave it "to their integrity to supply you with a good article at a fair price, you will be supplied with better provisions, and at as reasonable a rate as those bargain hunters, who trot 'around, around, around about' a market, until they are trapped to buy some *unchewable* old poultry, *stringy* cow-beef, or *stale* fish, at very little less than the price of prime and proper food." But on the other hand, it is reported that two Frenchmen, in order to test the question, agreed to buy precisely the same articles on the same day in the Paris markets, the one to take everything at the dealer's prices, and the other to bargain, jew, and beat down, and on comparison of cost it was found that the latter bought his marketing for twenty-five per cent. less than the one who did not bargain. Those who are really good judges of provisions can, with cash in hand and plenty of assurance, no doubt derive an advantage from buying in the open market, but others will do better by adopting Kitchiner's advice, and deal with "respectable tradesmen;" and especially those whose conceit is greater than their knowledge, or who pretend to know more than the dealers, when they really know nothing, should not trust themselves among the Philistines of the markets.

How to Choose Beef.

Of beef, that from the steer or ox is generally considered the best, though heifer beef is but little inferior to that of the ox. Good beef will exhibit a grain of deep coral red with white rather than yellow fat, and will yield easily to the pressure of a finger or knife, rising up quickly after pressure. Yellowish fat is an evidence that the meat is of an inferior quality. In old beef the texture of the meat will appear closer, the flesh coarser to the sight, as well as harder to the touch.

Mr. De Voe, superintendent of one of the New York markets, and author of books relating to markets, makes the following remarks on

Beef and its Different Kinds.

The hindquarters, as is well known, furnish the choicest cuts, and supply the celebrated "baron of beef," so much esteemed in England as the crowning dish for a Christmas dinner. The thick part, in which is the hip-bone, gives the largest pieces, while the small end cuts to pieces each from eight to twelve pounds. The best of these is usually called "the middle-cut sirloin." The other part near the ribs is the *thin-end sirloin*, resembling the middle-cut sirloin, but with less tenderloin, and is sometimes taken in preference by those who have small families, or who like it on account of its closeness to the prime ribs. It is cut up also into small loin or porter-house steaks. The thick part of the sirloin contains the largest part of the tenderloin (*fillet-de-bœuf*), making a large and choice piece of from twelve to twenty-five pounds for roasting, sometimes called the *thick-end sirloin*. When not used for roasting it is cut into three kinds of the finest dinner steaks, of which the first and best contains the largest quantity of tenderloin, and is known as the "hip sirloin steak." The next in order is the "flat bone sirloin steak," of which there is about the same number as the "hip sirloin steak." Next comes the same number of the "round bone sirloin steak," which is cut up to the socket bone, and makes excellent beefsteak pie, beef tea, minced collops, etc., as it is leaner than either of the foregoing. The *small-end sirloin*, when not used for roasting, is commonly known as "porterhouse steaks." The *tenderloin*, the most tender portion of the beef, is taken from the kidney side of the whole sirloin, and is considered by many the choicest portion of the animal. This choice piece owes its tenderness to its situation in the living animal, this muscle being seldom used or called into action.

The whole rump piece is usually divided into two or more pieces. The one that joins on the sirloin is the "socket piece," the other is called the "rump of beef." When this last is divided through the centre streak of fat, cutting about half way across the dark bone on the left side of the fat, the smallest piece on the left side is called the *edge bone*, and the other side the "rump piece." From the rump of beef are also cut pieces for bouilli, stewing, potted beef, fricandeau, etc.

The buttock forms three pieces for smoking—the *inside piece, outside piece*, and *veiny piece*—of which the first is generally preferred, but the last is the most tender. If the buttock be cut into two rounds of beef—the first and second cuts—the first will be larger and better than the latter; they are used for *à la mode, à la doube,* bouilli, stewing and corning.

There are thirteen ribs in the forequarter, nine of which are cut off from the *chuck*. The first seven are called prime ribs, and are cut into the choicest roasting pieces, by subdivision into three or more pieces. The *chuck* contains the last four ribs running under the shoulder-blade, and the neck piece. The second-cut chuck rib is a very sweet, juicy-eating piece of beef, as well flavored but not quite so tender as the first-cut chuck rib. This joint costs much less per pound. The next cut being the twelfth and thirteenth, or both ribs together, is commonly known as a chuck piece. They are not so good, but with the blade out and a piece of nice fat or suet placed within, makes an excellent piece to "roast in the pot," *à la mode* or for potted beef, bouilli, mince pies, soups, etc. The *brisket piece* is much used by the French for bouilli, soup, and a very good piece corned or salted.

Of beef, the back part of the rump is a convenient and economical piece, especially for a small family. It is a long and rather narrow piece, weighing about ten pounds, and contains less fat and bone than any other, equally good, in the ox. The thickest end affords nice steaks, and next to them is a good roasting piece, and the thinnest end, which contains the bone, is very good corned or for a soup. The whole is an excellent piece for roasting in case so large a one is needed.

Dr. Kitchiner advises that you should never think of ordering beef for roasting, except for Sunday, and when you order meat, poultry or fish, tell the dealer when you intend "to dress it, he will then have it in his power to serve you with provisions that will do him credit, which the finest meat, etc., in the world will never do, unless it has been kept a proper time to be ripe and tender."

A beef's *tongue* has always been regarded as a delicacy. The best tongues are those which are thick, firm and fat on the lower side. When fresh, they are used for stews, mince pies, etc.; when pickled or smoked, for boiling, and when cold are choice eating.

A beef's *liver*, which is of a clear, dark color, is good, but the best is of a clear, bright, yellowish-red color. A certain sign that it is tender is when it is easily mashed when pressing on it with the finger. Those that have streaks, dark and "sedgy," sandy spots and abscesses, are unfit for food.

A beef's *heart* is best when it has a large portion of nice clear fat around the top part. The purposes for which it is commonly used are for stuffing, roasting or stewing, and it is a good, wholesome and nutritious food as well as one of the cheapest which the animal affords.

Points in Good Veal.

Veal, to be good, must not be too young and must not be tainted. When too young the bones are very tender, resembling nerves more than bones, and the meat is gluish, with little or no flavor. Many diseases, especially in children, arise from eating such meat. The best veal is made out of calves not less than four nor more than ten weeks old, and in appearance is juicy, finely grained, with pinkish white fat. If the meat be very white, that shows the animal was bled before it was killed, which injures the flavor. If the meat be yellowish, or contain yellowish spots, it is not fresh.

The choice part in veal, as in beef, is the hindquarter, which is usually subdivided into *leg* and *loin*. The loin is the best portion for roasting; it also makes fine chops for broiling, frying or stewing, and when too large is divided into two small joints, of which the thin is called the "kidney end," and the other the "thick end." The leg is used whole for roasting, and from it is cut the "fillet of veal," or veal cutlets. The part of the leg after the fillet is taken out is the "knuckle of veal," which makes a good, light stew or boil.

The forequarter includes the shoulder, neck and breast. A small family can make two dishes from the shoulder by having the blade taken from the thin end for roasting and stewing. The "knuckle," left with the flesh on, with the blade-bone, will make an excellent and economical soup or stew.

A leg of veal is also an economical piece to buy, for you can take off cutlets from the large end, make broth of the shank and roast the centre.

Calves' sweetbreads are considered by some as the greatest delicacy of the meat kind. The calf has two, known as the "throat sweetbread," from the neck and throat, and that from or near the heart, called the heart sweetbread, which is the more delicate. The color should be clear and a little darker than the fat.

In calves' heads, when fresh, the eyes have a bright, full look, and the skin seems firmly fastened to the head. The young horn should appear, to indicate the animal was old enough to kill, for a small head and the absence of the horn show the animal was too young to make wholesome food. Never buy calves' heads or feet with a yellowish look, or which are slippery or slimy to the touch. When the head is split open, the sense of smell will detect any unsound condition of the brain.

In buying *calves' feet* for use in soup always get those

that are singed, not skinned. Much of the glutinous or jelly property is located in the skin.

When you roast or broil a piece of veal, baste often. Veal is better when a little overdone; it is not good and operates as physic if underdone.

How to Select Mutton and Lamb.

Mutton depends for its quality partly on the breeds of sheep and the age of the animal. The best mutton comes from sheep from three to five years old, and even older. The best is of a fine grain, the lean firm, succulent and of a color rather darkish red, the fat white, clear and hard, and the leg bones clear and nearly or quite white. Poor mutton is seldom fat, but, if so, the fat will look yellowish, and if the animal has been driven far, or is in a diseased state, the flesh will be flabby, the kidney fat small, stringy in appearance, while a bluish shade will appear in the lean, seen through the skin on the back. Ram mutton may be known by the redness of the flesh and the sponginess of the fat, which has a darker and sometimes a more yellowish shade than is seen in the best mutton.

The two loins together are called the "saddle of mutton," which is the finest and choicest part for roasting.

To choose lamb, examine the fat on the back, and then that on the kidneys, both of which should be white, or light in appearance, and hard. When lambs have been roughly handled, exposed to cold and stormy weather, or kept without food and far driven, a feverish state results, and the flesh becomes of a dark red color, the fat rather yellow, and the meat is tasteless, tough and dry.

Not less than a quarter of lamb is sold when it is first brought to market, and then its weight seldom exceeds five or six pounds. Age and the milk of a grass-fed ewe, and the genial heat of the sun, speedily increase the weight of the quarters from eight to twelve pounds each, and with age and forced feed these later in the season reach as much as twenty-five pounds.

Pork, Ham, and Lard.

A pig until six months old is called a shoat; after that age it is entitled to be called a hog. When the rind is tender and thin, or semi-transparent, the pork is young; when thick and hard it is old. In prime pork the fat on the back should be half an inch thick, firm and white, while the lean should be of a pale, reddish color, and sappy. The best pork is dairy-fed.

Measly pork may be known by the yellowish lumps or kernels seen through the fat, and the lean and the heavy and dull appearance of the flesh—reject it.

Every part of the hog, even the bristles, is available for some useful purpose. For roasting, the *chine* of pork is considered the best, and for various other purposes many prefer this to the small quarters, or that on which the skin is usually permitted to remain, as the flesh is leaner and thicker.

Pork, like veal, when properly cooked, should be well done.

In selecting *hams*, run a knife along the bone, and if it comes out clean the ham is good, but if it comes out smeared it is spoilt.

Soyer says the best plan to test the freshness of pork, or any meat, is to take with you to market in hot weather two wooden skewers, and insert them in the flesh near the bone and remove them, and the nose will detect any taint immediately; this is much better than touching and feeling the meat. These skewers should be scraped after having been used.

Good *bacon* has a thin rind, clear, red flesh, and the lean adheres closely to the bone. If the bacon has yellow streaks, it is rusty, and not fit to use. When purchasing either hams or shoulders in a cured state, you may conclude, if their appearance is white or dried, they will be very salt, and much of their sweetness extracted in consequence of having been long preserved in a strong, harsh pickle; or they have been badly cured. To be good, they must be bright, clean and firm.

Of *sausages*, the best are made altogether from pork, chopped small, seasoned and run into "casings." The city sausages are small, being meat run into lamb "casings," while those usually made in the country are large and run into beeves' or hogs' "casings." Some of these are well and cleanly made, and others are as bad and quite as dangerous food as city sausages. Deceit is practised by mixing a large percentage of water with the meat; some will put in one-eighth more before it is pressed into the skin. This gives them a very moist, soft and flabby appearance, while a good article is firm and nearly dry on the outside. There is danger too in the kind and quality of the flesh that some use, and it is hard to tell from what animal it came, or whether it was in a diseased condition. The only way by which the buyer can be protected is to make his purchases from a well-known dealer, who is found reliable, or to prepare the meat himself.

Sausage meat is prepared in the same manner as sausages, and not being put in "casings," is more easy of inspection. This meat and sausages are both excellent food, when one is confident they have been cleanly and properly made, and if not, the less one has to do with them the better. The same remark is applicable to all kinds of prepared meats.

Lard is frequently adulterated. It is a common practice among the dealers in lard to mix from two to five per cent. of milk of lime with the melted lard. A saponaceous compound is formed, which is not only pearly white, but will allow of the stirring in, during cooling, of twenty-five per cent. of water.

When there is water in lard, it flies all over the fire; in that case, boil it a few minutes with a cover on the pan, and then use.

How to Keep Meat from Spoiling.

The following is a recipe for this purpose, for which hundreds of persons have paid ten, and even twenty dollars, amounting in the aggregate to thousands of dollars:

Take a quart of the best vinegar, two ounces of lump sugar, two ounces of salt. Boil these together for a few minutes, and when cold, anoint with a brush the meat to be preserved. For fish the mixture is to be applied inside; for poultry, both in and outside.

Meat, either before or after it is cooked, may be preserved for a considerable time, even in warm weather, by being placed in the centre of a clean earthenware vessel and closely surrounded with common *charcoal*. To prevent the flies from "blowing" the meat, the vessel ought to be covered with a wire gauze.

Another mode of preserving meat sweet and good for several days in the warmest weather, is to cover it lightly with bran and hang it in some passage where there is a current of air.

How to Judge Poultry.

In chickens that are *fresh* the eyes will be full and bright, and the feet moist, soft and limber. If stale, the eyes will be dry and sunken, and if any part of the body is dark-colored or green it is spoiled. If the rump is hard and stiff, says Professor Blot, it is fresh enough; but if soft, it is necessary to examine the bird carefully, for it may be tainted.

Buy a chicken with white flesh and pale yellow fat. If young, the cock will have small spurs, and the hen will have the lower part of the legs and feet soft and smooth; in old chickens these parts are rough, as if they had seen hard service in many travels. In young poultry the lower end of the breast-bone will yield readily to the pressure of the finger, but some dealers arrange this in old fowls in order to deceive.

Soyer recommends that, where chickens are to be killed in the morning and eaten for dinner, to give each, "shortly before killing it, a *teaspoonful of vinegar*, which will cause them to eat tender. This can be done with all kinds of poultry."

A young turkey has a smooth leg and a soft bill, and, if fresh, the eyes will be bright and the feet moist. For a small family a young hen turkey will be most suitable, as it is likely to be smaller, fatter, and plump.

Young ducks feel tender under the wing, and the web of the foot is transparent. The best are thick and hard on the breast.

Young geese have yellow bills, and the feet are yellow and supple; the skin may be easily broken by the head of a pin; the breast is plump and the fat white.

If the skin be thick and tough, and the bill and legs are of a dark, reddish yellow, let the dealer keep the goose.

An old goose is unfit for the human stomach.

Buying Game.

There is no article of food so deceptive in appearance and so difficult to judge whether it is young, tender and good or not, as GAME.

In general, we may say that young birds may be distinguished by the softness of their quills, and that females are more tender and juicy than males. Old *pheasants* may be known by the length and sharpness of their spurs; in young ones these are short and blunt. Old *partridges* have light blue legs, instead of yellow brown. *Wild fowl* may be known to be old from their bills and the stiffness of the sinews of the legs; those that have the finest plumage are the poorest eating. *Hares* and *rabbits* are tested by tearing the ear, and breaking the jaw-bone between the finger and thumb; if they do not tear or break easily, they are fit only for soup or "jugging." When game is not to be cooked immediately, it is prudent to pepper the place where they were shot.

In buying *venison*, choose the dark-colored meat, not the black, but the rich reddish-brown flesh, with fine grain, and well coated with fat. Keep it hung up in a cool, dark cellar, covered with a cloth, and use as soon as you can conveniently.

Vegetables Appropriate to Different Meats.

Potatoes are good with all meats. With poultry they are nicest mashed. Sweet potatoes are most appropriate with roast meat, as also are onions, winter squash, and asparagus.

Carrots, parsnips, turnips, greens, and cabbage are eaten with boiled meat, and corn, beets, peas, and beans are appropriate to either boiled or roasted meat. Mashed turnip is good with roasted pork and with boiled meats.

Tomatoes are good with every kind of meat, but specially so with roasts; apple sauce with roast pork, and cranberry sauce with beef, fowls, veal, and ham.

Currant jelly is most appropriate with roast mutton and venison.

Pickles are good with all roast meats, and capers or nasturtiums with boiled lamb or mutton.

Horseradish and lemons are excellent with veal.

How to Select the Best Vegetables.

Of all vegetables the *Potato* takes rank as the most useful and wholesome and least expensive. In buying potatoes, those should be preferred which are of good size, free from blemishes, and having a small eye. In order to test their soundness, cut off a piece of the larger end, and if spotted, they are not sound, and therefore very inferior. Those are best which are fresh from the mould, and have never been wetted until they are cleaned to be cooked.

Turnips are among the least nutritious of all food, being nearly ninety per cent. of water, but for those who are disposed to eat too much, they are useful by stimulating intestinal action and removing constipation. Turnips of middle size are the best for the table, as the large ones are apt to be spongy.

Tomatoes are among the most healthful of vegetables, and good whether eaten hot or cold, cooked or raw, fried in sugar and butter, or stewed with salt and pepper. The medium sizes are the best.

Cauliflowers are considered best when they are large, solid, and creamy. They are stale when the leaves are much wilted, and soft dark spots are seen through the head.

In purchasing *celery*, choose the solid, close, clean, and white stalks, with a large close heart, as they are likely to be the most crisp and sweet, though all celery is rather bitter early in the season. The season begins about the middle of August, and celery is sweeter and better after frost.

Of *egg-plant*, the large, purple, oval-shaped kind is the best, and they taste, when fried in thin slices, something like an oyster. They should be firm, not ripe.

Mushrooms are a dangerous article for an inexperienced person to buy, as it is difficult to distinguish the genuine from the poisonous. As a general rule, it may be stated that in eatable mushrooms the stalk and top are dirty white, and the lower part has a lining of salmon fringe, which changes to russet or brown soon after they are gathered. The poisonous manifest all colors, and those which are dead white above and below should be let alone.

A good test is said to be to sprinkle salt on the spongy part, and if they turn yellow they are poisonous, but if they become black they are good. Let the salt remain on a little while before you decide on the color. Mushrooms are in season during September and October, but may be cultivated artificially throughout the year.

Peas should be always bought in the pods, which should feel cool and dry. Close packing gives them a mashed or wet appearance, and a warm feeling, which injures their natural flavor; and when the pods begin to look rusty the pea has a black spot, and is too old to be good. They should be cooked as soon as possible after having been picked.

As a general rule, it may be said of all kinds of vegetables, that if they snap crisply they are fresh, but if, on the contrary, they bend rather than snap, and have a flabby appearance, they have been gathered for some time, and should be bought for stale vegetables.

How to Preserve Fruits and Vegetables.

Potatoes should be put into the cellar or a cool, dark place, as soon as they are dug. They are injured by being exposed to the sun or air or frost. Some housekeepers keep them in barrels, and have sods laid over them. Others lay them in heaps in the cellar, and cover them with mats, or bury them in sand or earth. Others, again, dip them for a minute or two in boiling water, and after they are dried, put them in sacks. This is to destroy the germs, and is a valuable discovery. To prevent them from sprouting in the spring turn them out on the cellar floor. To thaw frozen potatoes put them in *hot* water.

Cabbages may be kept by burying them in sand, with the roots upward. But the best way to keep them through a severe winter is to leave about ten inches of the stem attached to them, and scoop out the pith to the extent of an inch. Suspend the cabbages by means of a cord tied around the stem, so that the portion from which the pith was taken remains uppermost, which regularly fill every morning with fresh water.

Celery should be buried in sand, and *turnips* and *beets* should be put in a dry part of a cellar.

Apples should remain out of doors, in barrels, until the weather becomes cold. They should not be headed up immediately after having been gathered, as a moisture accumulates upon them, which causes decay. When brought in, set them in a back room until the weather requires that they shall be put into the cellar. A linen cloth laid over them will suffice until very cold weather. Many good housekeepers prefer not to have apples headed up at all. There is an advantage in being able to pick them over several times during the winter, as one decayed apple may injure all its neighbors. If they are moist, wipe them. If frosted, put them in *cold* water.

Onions keep best spread out over the floor.

Parsnips should be buried in a pit in the garden, and in very cold climates not opened until March or April.

Squashes should be kept in a dry place, and as cold as may be without freezing.

Herbs should be gathered on a dry day, and when they are just beginning to bloom, as they are then in their perfection.

Medicinal herbs should be dried, put up in paper bags, and labelled. The leaves of those used in cooking should be pounded, sifted, and put in labelled boxes or stoppered bottles.

Herbs retain their virtue best if dried by artificial heat. The warmth of an oven, a few hours after the bread has been taken out of it, is sufficient.

Cranberries will keep all winter in a firkin of water.

Oranges and *lemons* keep best wrapped in soft paper and laid in a drawer.

In purchasing *seeds* there are two excellent methods of testing their quality. One is to throw them into water:

the seeds which float on the surface are worthless, and the other is to place the seeds in a saucer between two pieces of cloth saturated with water. Having lain the time required for seed in the earth to sprout, they will declare their quality, either good or bad. Note that fruit coming from old seed that has retained its germinating power is better than that grown from new seed.

How to Manage Wines and Beer.

All wines, particularly the light-bodied and sparkling, require to be kept on their side, and at a uniform temperature of about 55°.

Claret, Burgundies, and also white wines, except sparkling, should be decanted very carefully in removing them from the bin, when about to be used, otherwise the deposit is liable to become mixed with the liquid, and the flavor destroyed.

Wines, old in bottle, should be drunk immediately on being decanted.

All aërated waters should have their corks kept damp, and placed downwards.

Bottled stout and ale should be placed cork upwards. When required for use, they should be handled carefully, and the whole poured out without putting down the bottle, otherwise the sediment will be shaken into the liquor. Pale ale is sometimes spoiled by standing in a draught.

To *cool* wine, beer or water, wrap around the bottle a piece of linen dipped in water, and place it in a draught.

Fish, Oysters, Lobster, etc

Most kinds of fish lose their flavor within a few hours after being taken from the water. The cod, and one or two others, are an exception to this general rule. Fish are fresh when the eyes are clear, the fins stiff, the gills red, hard to open, and without bad odor. Fresh shad have gills of quite a crimson red, bright scales, and a firm body; and shad are unfit to eat when the gills are a whitish blue and the eyes are sunken. In a good salmon, when cut, the flesh should appear quite red, solid, and flakey. The Dutch and French bleed the cod, which accounts for the better quality and whiteness of their codfish. All large fish, in fact, should be bled as soon as caught.

Almost every kind of fish is either boiled, broiled or fried. Some are better boiled than broiled, others best fried. Any small fish, of the size of a smelt or smaller, is better fried than prepared in any other way. Fish, like salmon trout, are best when baked, and some fine sauce poured over them. A cup of diluted cream, in which is stirred two tablespoonfuls of melted butter and a little chopped parsley, makes an excellent sauce for baked salmon trout.

Bass, weighing about a half pound to a pound, are best fried; those weighing from one to three pounds are best broiled, and larger sizes are best when boiled. Very large bass are dry eating.

Oysters and Clams.

To judge whether oysters and clams are fresh, insert a knife, and if the shell instantly closes firmly on the knife the oysters are fresh. If it shuts slowly and faintly, or not at all, they are dying or dead. When the shells of raw oysters are found gaping open, they are fit for nothing but to be thrown away.

Salt oysters are not good for frying. Bread crumbs are much better than cracker crumbs for fried oysters. A late discovery is, that oysters fried in sweet oil are best.

When too many oysters have been incautiously eaten, and are felt lying cold and heavy on the stomach, there is an infallible remedy, in hot milk, of which half a pint may be drunk, and it will quickly dissolve the oysters into a bland, cream jelly. Weak and dyspeptic persons should always take hot milk after meals of oysters.

Lobsters, prawns, and *crabs,* newly-caught and fresh, will be lively and brisk in their motions. Never buy a dead lobster. If you buy a lobster ready boiled, see that his tail is stiff and elastic, so that when you bend it under it springs back immediately, otherwise it is not fresh. In buying *terrapins,* select only those that are large, fat, and thick-bodied. Small, poor terrapins are not worth the cost of the seasoning. Female terrapins are the best.

How the Chinese Catch Fish.

The Chinese have a method of catching fish that is known to but few in this country. They sprinkle on the water a mixture of dough and pulverized *Cocculus Indicus,* which intoxicates the fish, and they turn belly upwards on the top of the water by dozens or hundreds or thousands. All that the fisherman has to do is to take a boat, gather them up, and throw them into a tub of clean water, and presently they will be as lively as ever. It is said this manner of catching fish does not injure them in the least, but care must be taken to get them into fresh water at once.

Oil of Rhodium put on the bait, when fishing with a hook, will give a fisherman luck, if there are fish in the stream.

Hints on Buying Groceries.

It is a wise economy to purchase the *best flour*, even at an extra cost. By tasting, any sourness in flour may be detected. Good flour, when pressed tightly in the hand, has a yellowish tinge, and the traces of the skin are left upon it. Poor flour will not stick in this way, may be blown off the hand, and sometimes looks as if mingled with ashes. When you have found good flour, purchase a year's supply, if possible, or at least notice the brand, and buy the same kind. Flour and meal of all kinds should be kept in a cool, dry place.

To keep flour sweet in hot weather insert a triangular tube of boards or tin, bored full of small holes, into the centre of the meal barrel, which allows the air to reach the middle of the meal, and it never gets musty. A barrel of good flour, dry as it appears to be, contains from 12 to 16 pounds of water.

Unbolted flour should be kept on hand by the barrel the same as fine flour.

In cooking, new flour is not as good as old; it does not thicken as well and as fast.

Buy your *Indian meal* in small quantities, say 15 or 20 pounds at a time, unless your family is very large. It is apt to heat, mould, and grow musty if kept long in bulk or in a warm place. If not sweet and dry, it is useless to expect good bread or cakes. As an article of diet, especially in the early warm days of spring, it is healthful and agreeable, often acting as a gentle corrective to bile and other disorders. In winter also it is always acceptable upon the breakfast or supper table, being warming and nutritious. In summer the free use of it is less judicious, on account of its laxative properties. In the South, where corn meal is a staple article of diet, the yellow meal, which is used largely in the Northern States, is regarded as only fit for chicken and cattle food.

Rye flour should be bought in small quantities, say forty or fifty pounds at a time, and be kept in a keg or half barrel, with a cover.

Buckwheat meal, *rice*, and *hominy*, should also be purchased in small quantities, and kept in covered kegs or tubs. Several of these articles are infested with black insects, and an examination should be occasionally made for them.

Arrowroot, tapioca, sago, pearl-barley, American isinglass, maccaroni, vermicelli, and *oatmeal,* are all articles which help to make an agreeable variety, and it is just as cheap to keep a small quantity of each as it is to buy a larger quantity of two or three articles. Eight or ten pounds each of these articles of food can be kept in covered jars or covered wooden boxes, and then they are always at hand when wanted. All of them are very healthful food, and help to form many delightful dishes for desserts. Some of the most wholesome puddings are those made of rice, tapioca, and sago, while isinglass, or American gelatine, forms elegant articles for desserts, and is also excellent for the sick.

Sugars should not be bought by the barrel, especially the brown, which is apt to turn to molasses, and run out on to the floor. It is best to keep four qualities of sugar on hand. Refined loaf for tea, crushed sugar for the nicest preserves and to use with fruit, nice brown sugar for coffee, and common brown for cooking some things.

The loaf can be stored in the papers on a shelf. The others should be kept in close-covered kegs, or covered wooden boxes made for the purpose.

Coffee and *tea* can be bought with advantage in considerable quantities, as they do not deteriorate by keeping. Coffee, in fact, improves by age if kept in a dry place, as it loses its rank smell and taste. Several cents a pound may be saved by buying a bag of coffee or half chest of tea. Tea loses its flavor if put up in paper, and should be kept in glass or tin, shut tight. Coffee should be kept by itself, as its odor affects other articles.

Starch may also be bought in large quantities at a considerable discount from the retail price, which, in a large family, makes a difference in the yearly expenses. The best starch is the most economical.

Indigo is not always good. When a good sample is found, it is advisable to buy enough for a year or two, and keep it in a tight tin box.

Saleratus should be bought in small quantities, then powdered, sifted, and kept corked in a large-mouthed glass bottle. It grows damp if exposed to the air, and then cannot be used properly.

Salt must be kept in the *dryest* place that can be found. The best salt for table use is put up in boxes, but if a quantity be purchased, it should be stored in a glass jar, and closely covered. When, as is common, it becomes damp in the saltstands, it should be set by the fire to dry, and afterwards reduced to fine powder again. Coarse or damp salt on a table cannot be reckoned among Home Comforts.

Vinegar which is made of wine or cider is the best. Buy a keg, or half barrel of it, and set it in the cellar, and then keep a supply for the castors in a junk bottle in the kitchen. If too strong, vinegar will "*eat*" pickles.

Pickles should never be kept in glazed ware, as the vinegar forms a poisonous compound with the glazing. In buying pickles, avoid those which have been raised artificially to a *bright green*.

Molasses, if bought by the barrel or half barrel, should be kept in the cellar. New Orleans syrup is best for the table, and Porto Rico for cooking. If bought in small quantities, it should be kept in a demijohn. No vessel should be corked or tightly bunged, if filled with molasses, as it may swell and burst the vessel, or run over.

Hard soap should be bought in large quantity, and laid to harden in bars piled on each other, having the air all round to dry it. It is much more economical to buy hard than soft soap, as those who use soft soap are very apt to waste it, which they cannot do with hard soap.

Spices and *pepper* should be ground fine, and put in large-mouthed glass bottles, or kept in tin cans, in a dry place. Avoid bright *red peppers*, *spices*, and *sauces*. To test *nutmegs*, prick them with a pin. If they are good, the oil will instantly spread around the puncture.

Raisins should not be bought in large quantities, as they are injured by time. Small boxes are the best.

Of *Sago*, the small and white, called "pearl," is the most desirable.

Cheese, soft between the fingers, is richest and best, and should be kept in a box in a cool, dry place. Wipe off the mould with a dry cloth.

Candles improve by being kept for two or three months, and therefore should be bought by the box.

Lastly, weigh and measure all purchases when they are brought home, in order not only to ascertain whether you have got the just quantity, but to cultivate a faculty of distinguishing between genuine and spurious articles.

How to Preserve Eggs.

There are many ways by which eggs may be preserved fresh for months, and families can thus take advantage of the market, and buy large quantities when they are cheap, for use in those months when they are scarce and dear.

One way to preserve eggs is to place them on a sieve, and pour hot water over them slowly. This stiffens or cooks the white to the depth of the sixteenth of an inch. Then smear the outside with a little copal varnish, or a solution of gum arabic, and pack in bran or oatmeal, with the little end down.

Another plan is to dissolve some gum shellac in a sufficient quantity of alcohol to make a thin varnish. Give each egg a coat, and, after they become thoroughly dry, pack them in bran or sawdust, with their points downward, in such manner that they cannot shift about.

Some put them in a brine made of one pint of fresh slacked lime and half pint of salt to three gallons of water, and if fresh eggs are put in, fresh eggs will come out, even for two or four years; but in the opinion of others, lime and salt have a tendency to impair the flavor.

Dr. Delamere says the method he found to succeed best was to dip each egg into melted pork lard, rubbing it into the shell with the finger, and then to pack them in an old fig drum or butter firkin, setting every egg upright, with the small end downwards. "Eggs thus prepared in August, directly after harvest, have been boiled and eaten with relish by myself and family in the following January."

It is said that, for a small family, eggs are a cheaper breakfast dish than meat, even if they cost fifty cents a dozen.

How to Test Coal Oil.

Good kerosene oil should be purified from all that portion which boils or evaporates at a low temperature, for it is the production of the vapor, and its mixture with atmospheric air, that gives rise to those terrible explosions which sometimes occur when a light is brought near a can of inferior oil. To test the oil in this respect, pour a little into an iron spoon, and heat it over a lamp until it is moderately warm to the touch. If the oil produces vapor which can be set on fire by means of a flame held a short distance above the surface of the liquid, it is bad. Good oil, poured into a teacup, or on the floor, does not easily take fire when a light is brought into contact with it. Poor oil will ignite under the same circumstances, and hence the breaking of a lamp filled with poor oil is always attended by great danger. Good kerosene should be free from all matters which can gum up the wick, and thus interfere with free circulation and combustion, and should be also perfectly safe. It ought to be kept in a cool, dark place, and carefully excluded from the air.

CHAPTER VI.

ON FUEL AND FIRES—SAVING GAS—PREVENTING CONFLAGRATIONS.

"The fuel wasted by rich and poor in England is prodigious. The Frenchman would almost cook an ox with the fuel which an English housewife consumes in the roasting of a leg of mutton."—PALL MALL GAZETTE.

NEXT to a smoky chimney or a scolding wife a fire that "won't burn" is one of the greatest vexations in housekeeping. In all culinary operations a fire is the one thing essential, and the best method of making fires, and how to save fuel, are important considerations in Household Economy.

The substances principally used as fuel in America and in Great Britain are—wood, coal, charcoal, coke, and to a very limited extent, peat. The last three may be dismissed with a brief notice.

Charcoal is simply wood which has been exposed to a red heat until it has been deprived of all its gases and volatile parts. Being very pure carbon, charcoal makes a hotter fire than wood, but, as it requires frequent renewal, it is inferior to wood or coal for household use as a fuel. It is valuable in the arts, and being an absorbent of putrescent effluvia, it will remove taint from meat.

Coke is the charcoal of coal, and bears to it the same relation that charcoal does to wood. It, however, has more carbon than charcoal in a small compass, and therefore affords a longer continued heat. It serves a useful purpose when mixed with coal, the two combined making a strong fire, which is often wanted in cooking, as well as in very cold weather.

Peat is the "turf" of Ireland, and is useful where a mild fire, long continued, is desired. There are different qualities of peat, but the "brownish black," found lower down in the beds than the ordinary brown, is the most valuable as a fuel. It is consumed faster than coal, but does not need to be replenished so often as wood. But so long as coal and wood are reasonably cheap, peat is not likely to be used to any great extent as fuel for household purposes, because of its pungent smell, and the fact that its smoke is very trying to the eyes.

Wood, and its Kinds.

Wood is undoubtedly more generally used as a fuel in this country than any other substance, and most persons are familiar with the characteristics of the different species and their relative value.

Hickory is without doubt the best of all woods for household use. Lyman, in his "Philosophy of Housekeeping," says of it, even when but a few weeks cut, it will light with but little reluctance, and give a steady, equable heat, uniform and entirely reliable for cooking purposes. *Black birch* is very much like it, and, on account of its agreeable fragrance, is the pleasantest of all fuels. Both these woods are worth a dollar or two more by the cord than any others, but the satisfaction they give is more than an equivalent for the difference in price. *White oak*, *ash* and *maple* are next to hickory and black birch in value for fuel. There is little or no preference between these varieties when seasoned, but the peculiarity of ash is, that it burns almost as well when green as when dry. In situations where dry wood cannot be obtained, it is well to remember that ash and hickory, though green, if split fine and baked in the stove oven, will make a hot and lasting fire.

When green, *pine* and *chestnut* are almost worthless for fuel; when dry, they burn for a little while with a lively flame, but never radiate heat like the harder varieties. Dry chestnut, mixed with oak, makes a very good winter fuel, but consumes more rapidly than hard wood alone. Persons who purchase woods for fuel, or who use different varieties, will find it greatly to their advantage to make themselves acquainted with the various kinds and their qualities. Possessing such knowledge, a cord of *mixed wood* can be used in such a manner as always to afford the degree and kind of heat needed, the hickory and birch, or choice cuts of white oak and ash, being reserved for baking and other operations demanding a strong and lasting fire, while the inferior grades of oak, chestnut, bass, and hemlock will be used when only a moderate heat is required.

Of all kinds, the best wood for fuel is made from trees that have attained full maturity, without falling into decay. An elm a century old furnishes much better fuel than one of thirty years.

Wood that is straight and solid is the most profitable to buy. A cord of small, crooked sticks does not contain half the wood there is in a cord of straight and solid logs.

Wood is bought by measurement. A cord of wood is 8 feet long, 4 feet wide, and 4 feet high, and contains 128 cubic feet. To ascertain the amount of wood in a load, multiply the length by the breadth, and this product by the height, and you will have the number of cubic feet.

Wood is usually cheapest in August and September, and if cut into short pieces, will furnish the most fuel.

But in the principal cities on the Atlantic coast *anthracite coal* is the principal fuel, and nothing will compare with it for yielding the largest amount of heat from a given weight of fuel. Ordinarily, it is considered that there is no great difference between a cord of seasoned wood and a ton of anthracite coal, but if used with care and skill, a ton of hard coal can be made to go much farther than a cord of any kind of wood.

How to Judge Hard Coal.

Good hard coal is in square lumps, and breaks with a smooth, shining fracture. Bad coal has flat pieces of a dull color, as thick as the palm of the hand, and of greater or less size, which, when burnt, remain hard, heavy, and become whitish, hence called "bone." If a common scuttleful of coal, about twenty-five pounds, yields, after the cinders are washed next morning, half a pound of white pieces, the coal cannot be commended. This explains the reason why, of two carts of coal standing side by side, though an ordinary purchaser would have no choice, a practised coal-dealer would gladly take a cargo of one, while he would not be hired to take the other into his yard, if compelled to send it to his customers. He knows that one kind will burn almost entirely up, leaving only a little ashes, while in a single day's burning the other will leave the grate full of "slag." So, one ton of coal at four dollars a ton may be dearer than another at ten dollars, and yet not one man in fifty could tell the difference from external inspection.

A shiny, square fracture, we repeat, is what an honest coal-dealer loves to see. He considers the article good in proportion as it breaks at right angles firmly. If it shatter in breaking, or break unsquarely, he will not look at it. If the coal have among it flat pieces, with a dull, coal-dust look, it is "bony." Such a piece gives no more heat than a bone; it is a black rock, nothing more; it is hard to kindle, and goes out directly.

How to Kindle a Coal Fire.

Hard coal will not ignite until it is thoroughly heated through and through, and as small coal will not require as much wood to heat it up as large, it is important, where the supply of kindling wood is limited, that the pieces of coal which touch the wood should be small. As wood in cities is more expensive than coal, economy suggests the use of as little as practicable. The coal, then, for kindling, should not only be as small as a pigeon's egg, called "chestnut coal" by the dealers, but to economize the wood, the pieces should not be over four inches long, so that they can be laid compactly, then the heat will be more concentrated on a given point of coal, and thus the sooner heat it through and through to the degree requisite for actual ignition. If the wood is thus placed, and is covered with one layer of chestnut coal, it will redden with great rapidity and certainty. As soon as this is the case, cover over the reddened coal with another layer or two, and in a minute or two put on the larger size. By putting a handful of shavings or paper in a grate compactly, then some splinters of dry wood, not larger than the little finger, and outside of that a layer of pieces an inch or more thick and three or four long, then apply a match to the paper, and while it is catching, put on the small coal as above, there will not be a failure during the winter, nor a growl in the household, for the want of a good and timely fire. To lessen a coal fire, press it from the top, so as to make the mass more compact, giving less room for air. To revive it, lay on small pieces tenderly, put on the blower, and when red, add larger pieces, and riddle out from below. Heaping on more coal, or letting out the ashes below, will certainly put out a low coal fire.

Clinkers can be removed from stove grates and range backs by throwing half a dozen broken oyster shells into the fire when the coal is all aglow, and covering them with fresh coal. When all are red-hot the clinkers become doughy, and are easily removed.

Some one recommends as a cheap *fire-kindler*, cheaper than wood, to melt three pounds of rosin in a quart of tar, and stir in as much sawdust and pulverized charcoal as you can, and then spread the mass upon a board till cool, and then break it into lumps as big as your thumb. You can light it with a match, and it will light a fire, for it burns with a strong blaze. It is economical of time and money.

How to Use Coal Economically.

In the matter of burning coal, says the "Scientific American," there is also a great want of intelligence, and it is not to be expected that common servants will know or care much about saving it. The grate of the range is stuffed so full that the oven top is loaded with it, so that the fire will not die out nor require looking after; then the draft is opened, and the money, or what is the same, the heat, goes flying up the chimney. With a little forethought all this could be prevented, and a ton of coal made to last three months instead of one. A good bright fire can be steadily maintained with coal, with less trouble than with any other kind of fuel, but not by raking, poking, and piling in green fuel continually.

After breakfast, the fire should be cleared of ashes, if there are any, and fresh fuel put on to fill the grate moderately. Let the oven damper be turned up so as to heat it, and leave the small top door open, more or less, according to the intensity of heat required. In this way air enters over the top of the fire, and maintains a far better combustion, and consequently greater heat than when the draft-dampers are thrown down. A washing can be done, or "ironing" accomplished, with one-third less coal than is generally thought necessary to use.

There is also great waste in throwing away half-burned coal under the supposition that it is cinders. One who has experimented with coal for twenty years, both in the house and under the boiler, writes:

In cleaning the grate in the morning, you will find there is a quantity of unburned coal, which has been externally subjected to combustion. It is covered with ashes, and looks to the inexperienced eye like cinder. It is often relentlessly dumped into the ash-box. The fact, in many cases, is, that the lump is only roasted on the outside, not even coked, and is in a better condition for igniting than the fresh coal. We have stated that coal is a *condensed* form of carbon. The superficially burned lumps, found in our grates or among our ashes, sufficiently prove this. But take a lump of anthracite coal from the fire, red-hot and all alive. Throw it into the water until the ashes are washed from it, and it is black externally and cool. Take it out, and break it open with a hammer, and you will find it red-hot and glowing inside. This shows that time, and a plentiful supply of air, are necessary to burn coal, and that large amounts of what we call ashes and cinders are really excellent fuel.

To prove this fact, let any one carefully sift his ashes, throwing out the inevitable slate, which can be readily detected, and start his coal fire on wood or charcoal, kindling his coal fire with the savings. He will find that he can get a good bed of incandescent coal sooner than with green coal on the kindlings.

Solon Robinson says forcibly:

Never, whether rich or poor, suffer your cinders or unburned bits of coal to be wasted in the ash-barrel.

Measure for measure, they are worth more than coal. Save them, soak them, try them. Water renovates the coke, and wet cinders upon a hot coal fire will make it hotter, and keep it so longer than fresh coal.

Saving cinders is not meanness, it is economy.

How to Measure Coal.

Ten times the price of this book may be saved to any family which uses coal largely, by remembering that the quantity of coal is determined as accurately by measurement as by one of Fairbanks' best scales. A bin or box, of thirty-four and a half feet cubical, holds exactly one ton of two thousand pounds of white ash coal, such as is used in ranges, stoves, and furnaces, but it takes thirty-six cubical feet for one ton, or two thousand pounds, of red ash coal, such as is generally used in grates. A lawful ton of coal in Pennsylvania and, we believe, in New York, is twenty-two hundred and forty pounds, or twenty-eight bushels of eighty pounds each. A bin that will hold an honest ton of red ash coal should measure forty feet cubical—that is, the internal length, breadth and height of the bin multiplied together. For instance, thus, four feet broad, five feet long and two feet deep.

Gas as a Fuel.

Within a few years very great improvements have been made in the construction of apparatus for utilizing gas as a fuel. All the culinary operations of roasting, baking, boiling, and stewing are now done to a limited extent by gas, and for some of these purposes it is superior to coal. Meats can be roasted by gas without parting with their juices, and consequently there is less waste, and their flavor is preserved. Boiling and frying can be done with greater perfection than over the open fire, on account of the readiness with which the heat can be increased or decreased at pleasure. Gas-stoves are peculiarly adapted for the French style of cooking, and the production of soups and stews.

For heating apartments of moderate size, gas has been found very effective and economical, when the burners and regulators are properly constructed. Some of these stoves are now so arranged that the flame of the gas acts on an incombustible, fibrous material, called *asbestos*, which speedily becomes incandescent, and this produces a lively and cheerful appearance.

How to Regulate and Save Gas.

In all the principal cities of the United States and Europe, gas is now the most popular agent for producing artificial light, though hardly known at the beginning of the present century. But notwithstanding its general use, consumers have very vague ideas on the proper management of gas, and large sums of money are unnecessarily expended for want of attention to a few simple details.

For the purpose of economizing in the consumption of gas, there is no part connected therewith of more importance than the *burners*. If these are improperly constructed, or their flames unsuitably adjusted, the light derived from gas is reduced in a most extraordinary manner. Under such circumstances the account of the consumer is much increased, and it is no exaggeration to state that a large proportion of consumers, through their own mismanagement, pay twice as much as there is any occasion for, or, in other words, by proper burners and control, they could have their usual light for one-half the money now expended.

Of burners there are three principal kinds in use—the *argand*, which are best for stores and warehouses; the *bat-wing*, which is best for outside light; and the *fish-tail*, which is generally adopted in hotels and dwellings. In all of these the most important considerations for gas consumers to attend to are, to see that the orifices for the egress of gas are perfectly regular in size, smooth, and not rusted, and sufficiently large to permit it to issue with very feeble pressure or force. "Whenever the orifices for the emission of gas," says the "Gas Consumers' Guide," "are too small, a greatly increased pressure is required to expel it, and the light derived is diminished just in proportion to that increased pressure. With burners constructed in this defective manner, the flame has a dull, blue tinge, which increases in intensity according to the augmented pressure; the jets forming the flame are more or less detached, and a large portion of the lower part of this is of a deep blue color. Defective burners are very common, and by their use the consumer frequently does not obtain more than one-half the available light to be derived from the gas." Lava-tipped burners are preferable to metal, because they will not rust.

Next to proper burners, a good *regulator* is an economizer of gas. This is a small self-acting instrument, generally attached to the outlet of the gas meter, at the entrance to the premises, and contains a suspended plug, or cone, which opens or closes the orifice through which the gas passes in direct accordance with the decrease or increase of the pressure in the company's pipes. By this means the pressure in the consumer's premises may always be maintained at one uniformity, so long as there is a sufficiency of supply. "The economy derived by the use of the regulator must depend on circumstances, such as the pressure of the gas in the locality, the care previously employed in adjusting the lights, the kind of burners employed before and after using the instrument; but it is by no means uncommon for a saving of from 25 to 40 per cent. being effected by its use, and still retaining the same amount of light. Professor Silliman gained even better results than these by using a regulator, thereby, as he stated, effecting a saving of nearly 50 per cent. In all large establishments of several stories high, a distinct regulator is essential for each floor, inasmuch as gas by its lightness has a tendency to ascend, so that in the absence of this instrument there is often an excess of gas in the upper portion of a building, whilst the lower premises are in comparative obscurity."

There is a method of enriching gas, by causing it to pass, just previous to combustion, through prepared oils which are rich in carbon. By this process the gas becomes loaded with the carbon of the oil, which is thereby carried to the burners, and produces a much larger amount of light at a comparatively small cost. The apparatus is called a *carbonizer*, and is attached to the meter.

The best way to regulate the flow of gas, and thereby economize it, to the burners, is not by the burner valves, but the main valve near the meter. When the gas jets are burning, this valve should be turned to regulate the flame to the proper length, with the burner valves freely open. The object of this is to reduce the total pressure in the pipe before the gas comes to the burners, so that some gas may not escape unconsumed, as is usually the case when the burner valve is used as the regulator.

How to Extinguish Fires and Prevent Conflagrations.

Science has deplorably failed as yet in teaching builders how to erect a perfectly fire-proof building. The great conflagrations in Chicago and Boston demonstrated that those buildings which were supposed to be fire-proof could not withstand a whirlwind of flame. They demonstrated that neither granite nor iron can arrest the progress of a great fire, and that the fire departments, as at present organized in American cities, are powerless to prevent conflagrations. Of all the safeguards that have been invented, and the ingenious plans that from time to time have been promulgated, not one remains, except the simple idea *that the only certain method of preventing conflagrations is to extinguish fires at their beginning.* Whenever a fire is allowed to destroy one building, it may destroy hundreds of others. In order to extinguish a fire at its beginning, it is necessary that every building should be provided with a suitable apparatus for the purpose, such as a small hand-pump, one or two buckets of water, and an axe or hatchet. The "Scientific American" recommends portable hand forcing-pumps, and remarks: "The rule is, that the beginnings of fires are small, and their progress comparatively slow. In most cases, a very little water judiciously applied will extinguish a fire within five minutes of its ignition. It is for this reason that small portable hand forcing-pumps have been approved by the most experienced firemen as the very best means, all things considered, for extinguishing fires."

Mr. Bird, the author of a valuable work on "Protection from Fire," recommends that every city and large town should reorganize its fire department, alter the present steam-engines so that they may throw steam into buildings where the flames have not burst from the doors, windows or roofs, and in addition thereto, place in every large building, store, stable or manufactory, a small engine, three buckets, and one axe, with a card of directions what to do in case of fire. Each family should organize its "Home Fire Brigade;" and in buildings where many persons are employed, there should be some of them trained to do duty as firemen.

[In order to prevent fires, the "London Builder" offers the following suggestions:

"Keep matches in metal boxes, and out of the reach of children; wax matches are particularly dangerous, and should be kept out of the way of rats and mice. Be careful in making fires with shavings and other light kindlings. Do not deposit ashes in a wooden vessel, and be sure that burning cinders are extinguished before they are deposited. Never put firewood upon the stove to dry, and never put ashes or a light under a staircase. Fill fluid or spirit (or kerosene) lamps only by daylight, and never near a fire or light. Do not leave a candle burning on a bureau or chest. Always be cautious about extinguishing matches or other lighters before throwing them away. Never throw a cigar stump upon the floor, or into a spit-box containing sawdust or trash, without being certain that it contains no fire. After blowing out a candle, never put it away until sure that the snuff has gone entirely out. A lighted candle ought not to be stuck up against a frame wall, or placed upon any portion of the woodwork in a stable, manufactory, shop, or any other place. Never enter a barn or stable at night with an uncovered light. Never take an open light to examine a gas-meter. Do not put gas or other lights near curtains. Never take a light into a closet. Do not read in bed.

"The principal register of a furnace should always be fastened open. Stove-pipes should be at least four inches from woodwork, and well guarded by tin or zinc; rags ought never to be stuffed into stove-pipe holes; openings into chimney-flues for stove-pipes which are not used, ought always to be securely protected by metallic coverings. Never close up a place of business in the evening without looking well to the extinguishment of lights and the proper security of the fires. When retiring to bed at night, always see that there is no danger from your fires, and be sure that your lights are safe."]

What to do when Clothing is on Fire.

To preserve life *when clothing has caught on fire* the first great requisite of safety is to preserve presence of mind. Mr. Bird says: "Throwing one's self upon the floor, and wrapping a rug or blanket or overcoat about one, will occupy two or three seconds, and the danger would be over.

The reason for lying down is, that then the flames burn quite slowly towards a vital part, but almost instantly while standing upright.

"If persons awake in the night, and find the room filled with smoke, they should get out of bed, and creep with the face as near the floor as possible to a door or window. A room may be so full of smoke as to suffocate any one standing up, and be perfectly safe to breathe in, a few inches from the floor."

With regard to the use of *kerosene lamps*, which so often cause fires and death by their explosion, he says: "Never blow down the chimney of a kerosene lamp to extinguish it. Never use great quart lamps. They are very dangerous. If you have them, throw them against a stone wall. Never buy the cheapest oil. Get the best. Lamps, when lighted in the morning without being filled, and taken quickly about the house, are very liable to explode." *

To Save a Person on Fire.

Seize a blanket from a bed, or a cloak, or a carpet, or any woollen material. Hold the corners as far apart as

---

* There are sellers of "patent burning oils" who claim you cannot explode them if you try all day. To show this they pour the oil on a tin plate or pan, apply a match to the fluid, and the fire is extinguished. The fallacy of this is explained, as follows: Benzine does not explode, but the vapor which rises from it does. When the benzine is poured upon the plate the vapor passes off into the air safely. When it is gone, the match is applied with the result as stated. But when the dangerous oil is in a lamp, the vapor cannot find its way to the air, but fills the lamp above the oil. Now we have the flame of the lamp over the vapor. If we blow the flame down to the vapor, or so shake the lamp as to force a tiny stream of the vapor up to the flame, or the vapor increases until it fills the lamp, and is forced up the side of the wick to the flame, the vapor takes fire, and burns its way back into the lamp, when the whole of the vapor explodes, setting fire to the oil, and often killing the person holding the lamp.

you can, stretch them out higher than your head, and rush boldly on the person, throwing the fabric around the upper part of the body. This instantly smothers the fire, and saves the face. The next instant throw the unfortunate person on the floor. This is an additional safety to the face and breath, and any remnant of flame can be put out more leisurely. The next instant immerse the burnt part in cold water, and all pain will cease with the rapidity of magic. Next get some common flour, remove from the water, and cover the burned parts with an inch thickness of flour; if possible put the patient in bed, and do all that you can to soothe until the physician arrives. Let the flour remain until it falls off itself, when a beautiful new skin will be found, and unless the burns are deep, no other application will be needed. The dry flour for burns is the most admirable remedy ever proposed, and the information ought to be imparted to every one. The principle of its action is, that like the water, it causes instant and perfect relief from pain, by totally excluding the air from the injured parts.

CHAPTER VII.

ABOUT EATING AND ARTICLES OF FOOD.

"Animals fill themselves, man eats. The man of mind alone knows how to eat."—BRILLAT SAVARIN.

ALL the inferior animals are endowed with instinct to direct them to the right food, that has been provided for them, and which requires no cooking or previous preparation; man, on the contrary, was predestined to exert not only his body in gathering his food, but his intellect in adapting it to the wants of a complicated organism. All the elements that compose the human body have corresponding elements in the animal and vegetable creation; but man is compelled to exercise his mind and reason to select from the various articles, those which are adapted to his peculiar and constantly changing circumstances. Food, that to the Esquimaux would be wholesome nutriment, would disgust and poison the inhabitant of the tropics, while the cooling fruits and vegetables of the equator would freeze or starve the sojourner in polar regions.

All food in ordinary use may be divided into four classes: heat-producers, of which the representative articles are, butter, lard, fat of meats, vegetable oils, fine flour, etc.; 2d, muscle-makers, of which the representative articles are, lean meats, cheese, peas and beans, etc.; 3d, brain feeders, represented by shell fishes, lean meats, active fishes, birds, etc.; and waste articles, or those containing little nutriment, but which are useful to modify and dilute concentrated food. As a general rule, that food is best and most economical which contains the proper proportion of heaters and muscle-producers, but all of these classes of food are needed, and every day; varying, however, in proportions, according to age, circumstances and temperature. Those who are ignorant of dietetic laws provide nearly the same kind of food in summer as in winter, for the young and for the aged, for the active and the sedentary; and the result is seen in the prevalence of bowel and liver complaints, gastric and typhoid fevers, dysenteries and dyspepsia. The great secret in the preparation of food that will prolong life in good health is to adapt it to the mental or muscular employments of those consuming it, and to provide a variety suited to the ages of the individuals and the season. Divine wisdom has in nature provided an infinite variety of articles adapted for food, but it requires some knowledge of their constituent parts, and a good deal of intelligence, to select and properly prepare them.

1. Grain as Food.

Of grains, the most extensively cultivated and most generally used is

Wheat. Of this the varieties are so numerous that the French Academy of Arts and Sciences has described no less than four hundred. All of them, however, contain the elements which correspond with the requirements of the human system, though differing in proportion and value, and it is possible to maintain life and health on wheat alone for an indefinite period, with good water and good air. The proper modes of preparing wheat, and baking bread, will be considered subsequently.

Rye is a valuable grain for persons predisposed to constipation, and with corn meal makes a nourishing and digestible bread.

Indian-corn is a heating grain, and, abounding in oil, it is more fattening than wheat. It is a food peculiarly well adapted to cold climates, and the meal when mixed with rye, makes a wholesome and excellent bread. The "large hominy," or the grain divided into two or three parts, is suited to both the active and the sedentary, but is especially valuable food for laborers, because it contains much of the muscle-making elements.

Oatmeal, though little used as food for man in this country, is a staple article of consumption in portions of Great Britain, particularly in the north of England, Scotland and Ireland. In porridge, or cakes, it greatly promotes muscular and mental activity.

Rice is one of the most popular articles of food, and its consumption is greater throughout the world than any other grain, except perhaps wheat. It is, however, only capable of supporting life feebly, has less than half the muscle-feeding properties of wheat, and a fourth of its elements for the brain and nerves. Its principal component is starch, and it should be eaten in conjunction with beefsteak and vegetables that contain no starch.

2. Vegetables as Food.

Of vegetables the most nutritious are *beans*, which contain a large proportion of casein. Like cheese, they are therefore less easily digested than the cereals, but are well adapted to active people whose digestive powers are strong. Two pounds of beans will do more muscular work than three pounds of wheat, and more brain work than three and one-half pounds. But, as they contain less by twenty per cent. of the requisite amount of heaters, they are appropriately eaten with fat pork or some other heat-making food.

Peas, which contain nearly the same elements as beans, and in similar proportions, are more easily digested, and require to be eaten with potatoes, and such heaters as pork, butter, or fat meats.

Potatoes, parsnips, turnips, carrots and green vegetables generally contain some nutritive elements, but with such an amount of water and *waste*, that the capacity of the human stomach is insufficient to hold the supply necessary to keep the body in good condition. Eaten, however, with lean meats or other concentrated food, they perform a useful office in distending the stomach, and facilitating digestion.

3. Animals as Food.

The flesh of animals, fat and lean together, like a grain of wheat, contains every one of the elements that compose the human system, but not in the same proportions.

The difference in the nutritive properties of five articles of animal food, in common use, is set forth in the following table. In one hundred parts are—

	Mineral matter, or food for brains.	Fibrin and albumen, or food for muscles and tissues.	Fat, or food for heat.	Water.
Veal	.5	16	16.5	62.5
Beef	5.0	15.0	30.0	50.0
Mutton	3.5	12.5	40.0	44.0
Lamb	3.5	11.0	35.0	50.5
Pork	1.5	10.0	50.0	38.5

It will be perceived that pork contains five times as much of the food for heat as of the food for muscles and tissues, and is therefore the best for cold weather, while veal is better suited to warm weather. In lean beefsteak, the muscle-making principles predominate, and consequently butter or potatoes, rice or Indian corn should accompany it, while with fat pork we require beans, peas, etc. Pork and beans contain the muscle and vital elements as well as the heaters, and are exceedingly wholesome diet for those who are active and exposed to the cold, while they are stupefying to the sedentary, and tend to produce inflammatory diseases or congestion if eaten in hot weather.

Fishes are found to contain, when chemically analyzed, about the same muscle-making elements as are found in lean beef and mutton, with a larger proportion of phosphorus or food for the brain. The active kinds of fish, as trout, pickerel, and shad, are more valuable as food than the common white fish, like cod and haddock. Containing a large proportion of phosphorus, or the vital element, they are especially suited to students and sedentary men, though fish pickelled in brine are more suitable for laboring men than others.

Chickens or poultry are not equal to fishes as a food for the studious, but they contain more of the muscle-making and heat-producing elements than beef or veal. This is especially true of the legs of a chicken or turkey, which are far superior to the breast as a valuable food. The breast is white, dry, and somewhat insipid, while the muscles that move the legs are dark, juicy and have a rich flavor. In birds which live on the wing, it is otherwise. Their breasts are rich in muscle-making and vital elements, while the meat on the thighs and side bones is poor and dry.

Oysters are unsatisfactory food for laborers, but will do very well for the sedentary, and to sup on. They contain but twelve and a half per cent. of solid matter, " in which are included fibrin, albumen, gelatine, mucus and osmazome."

4. Food Makes the Man.

It is unnecessary to pursue the analysis further, for "every moving thing that liveth shall be meat" for those who know how to appropriate it. Everything that has life can be used to sustain life in man, and some think that somewhere in the store-house of nature there is a remedy for every ill the flesh is heir to. It is believed by some eminent thinkers, that even mental and nervous power can be greatly increased by the use of proper food. This, if true, is one of the most important applications of science to dietetics ever made. If true, the cook and the caterer are as important agents in a scientific system of education as the schoolmaster, the one furnishing the brain with power to work, and the other training it to do work. Let any man observe his feelings and mental capacities, says Dr. Bellows, the author of the "Philosophy of Eating," "after a breakfast of white bread and butter, or griddle cakes and syrup, or any other such carbonaceous articles of food, and I am sure he will find himself unable to perform the same mental labor as he can on a breakfast of beefsteak, or fish and potatoes, or unbolted bread and milk, or any other articles abounding in the phosphates. Brains can no more be made or worked without phosphorus than Egyptian bricks can be made without straw. Why not then apply these plain laws to raising children, and cultivating their minds, as we do to the raising of wheat, and hens, and bees, and developing their properties and powers?

"No man who understands his business would expect to raise wheat in soil in which is no nitrogen, lime, or phosphorus, or make hens profitable on food containing no lime for egg-shells, or keep bees on a desolate island where no flowers could be found. Why, then, expect to develop brains on white bread, griddle-cakes and doughnuts?"

This is a theory that every one can test for himself, and if found valuable and practical, its application is very important. Is your boy, says the doctor, fat and stupid, having neither muscle nor brains? Feed him on lean meats, fish, oatmeal cakes, beans, peas, and food in which phosphorus abounds. Is your son, on the contrary, mentally active, thin in body and precocious in intellect? He is liable to dangerous diseases of the brain, and inflammations, and it will be well to confine his diet principally to cooling fruits and vegetables, with bread, milk, and articles containing starch and sugar. Is your daughter pale, feeble and undeveloped? Do not feed her on white bread, sweet cakes, puddings and confectionery, but give her lean meats, fish, milk, coarse bread and articles containing iron and phosphorus. Is your grandfather fat, stupid and dozy, disposed to sit by the fire, saying nothing, and caring for nothing? Change his diet from fat beef and pork, white bread and butter, buckwheat cakes and molasses, to fish, beefsteak, and potatoes. Is he, on the contrary, very restless and irritable? Let him eat of the fattest meats, and of butter, sugar, and molasses as much as he desires. Do you expect to spend the day in study or mental exercise? Take a breakfast of beefsteak, fish and potatoes, game, oatmeal or barley-cakes, or any other articles in which phosphorus abounds. Do you intend to spend the day in hard out-of-door work in the cold? Eat fat and lean meats, beans and corn bread. Do you wish to feel badly and be predisposed to fevers and inflammatory diseases? Eat in summer what you found wholesome in winter—pork and beans for breakfast, a side of pork for dinner, and have your vegetables cooked swimming in fat.

As a further corollary from the principles set forth, it may be stated that everything designed for food is wholesome under some circumstances, and unwholesome under other circumstances. Dr. Bellows forcibly remarks, "A rattlesnake, all but the head, would make a delicious and wholesome meal to a man who was starving and could get nothing else, while the most delicate woodcock would be poison to a man prostrated with typhoid fever. That abstract question, then, so often asked, Is this or that kind of food wholesome? is consummate nonsense."

Keeping Lent.

In Catholic countries it is the practice to fast for a season in early spring, especially to abstain from eating meat, and the practice seems founded on a wise physiology. "If all persons for a month in early spring," says Dr. Hall, "were to abstain from all meats whatsoever, as the spirit of the doctrine of Lent requires, it would add greatly to the health of communities by enabling the system to throw off the impurities of the body acquired by the hearty eating of winter, would cool off the heated blood, and thus destroy the germs of spring and summer diseases, and thus is it that the proper practice of the precepts of religion promotes not only the spiritual but the physical health of man. These are simple measures: they are practicable, cost no money, and are available to all, and if heeded in a rational manner, death would be kept from many a dwelling, and life-time sorrows would be lightened in many bosoms."

Digestibility of Foods.

With regard to the comparative digestibility of the various articles that are usually used as food, the nearest approach to accuracy which has hitherto been obtained was made by Dr. Beaumont, who had an opportunity to witness the operations of the stomach of a Canadian, which had been deprived of its outer coating, and laid bare by a musket ball. He discovered that boiled rice, raw sweet-apples, boiled sago, raw fresh eggs, boiled and fried trout, barley broth, boiled tripe and broiled venison were the most digestible of all the common articles of diet. Next to these were boiled tapioca, boiled beans, roasted or baked potatoes, raw cabbage, fresh and raw oysters, hash, broiled liver, boiled and roasted turkey, roasted goose, broiled lamb, fricaseed chicken and boiled beef, which were digested in three hours or less. The most indigestible of all were roasted and boiled pork, roasted wild ducks, fried heart, fried veal and fried beef, beef soup, boiled cabbage and boiled salmon. These required from four to five hours to digest. It is proper, however, to state that the value of articles as food does not depend altogether on their digestibility, except for very feeble stomachs. The stomach requires rest, it is true, but when it has nothing to do for long intervals, it is apt to become restless and enfeebled.

How and when to Eat.

To derive full nourishment from the food which is taken into the body, it is as important to know how and when to eat as what to eat. All the medical authorities concur in recommending people to chew their food well, so as not to give the stomach the work which the teeth ought to perform. Eat slowly, they all say, and at regular hours. Never eat when very tired, or heated, or angry, or the food will probably ferment instead of digesting. Take a hearty but not a heavy dinner, and rest, if possible, at least half an hour after a hearty meal. Eat light suppers: nightmares are generally occasioned by eating, before going to bed, heavy food which presses steadily on the great veins of the body, arrests the flow of the blood, dams it up in the vessels of the brain, and a man having nightmare is much nearer death than most persons suppose. If he cannot arouse himself instantly, and escape from his imaginary peril, he will probably never awake.

Physicians also concur in declaring that the quantity of food to be taken at a meal is even more important than its quality. Americans as a rule eat too much. Some one has said, "Our men are all gluttons, and our women are all slaves." A little food well assimilated, yields far more nutriment and vigor than quantities crudely digested. Lewis Cornarro, who brought himself by dissipation and gluttony to death's door, reversed his practice, and by limiting himself to twelve ounces of solid food per day, prolonged his life for sixty-three years, dying at an advanced age. The lightest and least of meat and drink, says Dr. Cheyne, "a man can be tolerably easy under, is the shortest and most infallible means to preserve life, health, and serenity."

CHAPTER VIII.

CHEAP LIVING AND ECONOMICAL FOOD.

"No charitable societies have ever done so much good to the poor by the distribution of food, as they could do by printing and putting into the hands of every family, a little tract containing practical lessons of economy in the art of living well and living cheap—an art that would prevent the waste of food, and lessen the expense of first purchases, and increase the nutritious qualities while it added immensely to the table enjoyment of every family."—ROBINSON.

AMERICANS are reproached not only for being great eaters, but the most wasteful and extravagant consumers of food on the face of the earth. The whole system of American cookery is based upon a state of things that existed when food was so plentiful as to have scarcely any money value. When wheat could be purchased for less than fifty cents a bushel, and corn was burned for fuel, as it has been in some of the Western States, there could be little or no inducement to economize in their use. But where thousands are on the brink of starvation, relying on public soup-houses for the means to sustain life, as has been the case in the Atlantic cities since the late financial panic, the waste of food becomes a crime against the well-being of society. How to get sufficient nourishment from food with the least expenditure of money, is therefore the question we propose to consider in this chapter.

The editor, in his "Opportunities for Industry," published some years ago, remarked: "The cost of what are absolute and actual necessaries of life is, in most countries, comparatively little—as is evidenced in cases where stern necessity affixes the bounds of possible expenditure. In France, for instance, there are tens of thousands of peasants and operatives whose daily earnings do not exceed ten cents, and yet they continue to live gayly on that sum. As a consequence, in no other country has the art of cookery made equal progress. In Paris an enterprising woman, Madame Robert, furnishes a dinner daily to six thousand workmen for two pence each, her bill of fare being cabbage soup, a slice of bouilli (boiled beef), a piece of bread, and a glass of wine. In our Southern States, the food of the chief laborers—the men who produce an export value of over two hundred millions of dollars per annum in cotton, sugar, tobacco and rice—does not probably cost their providers ten cents per day."

What may be done with ten cents a day, even in the extravagant city of New York, was illustrated by Solon Robinson, in his famous story originally published in the New York *Tribune* of "A dime a day." He told how a woman with four children, whose daily income for some time was only ten cents, managed to provide subsistence for all without charity from any one. Now this is the way she did it: she bought one cent's worth of corn meal, four cents' worth of white beans, and paid three cents for a scraggy piece of salt pork, half fat and half lean. With the meal, she made three dumplings, and these, with the pork, beans and a pepper-pod given her, she put into a pot containing plenty of water, for the pork was salt, and boiled the whole for two hours. For breakfast the family ate one of the dumplings, and each had a plate of soup; for dinner they ate half the meat, half the soup and one of the dumplings, leaving the same allowance for supper. For a change, she bought five cents' worth of scrap pieces of lean beef, which, with some potatoes and an onion and the meal worked up into round balls of stiff dough, she made into a stew or chowder that sufficed for the day. There are thousands placed in similar circumstances who, not knowing how to use a sum so small, would have invested their ten cents in some cheap poison and swallowed it. Some years ago a Yankee philosopher of the school of Diogenes, M. Thoreau, endeavored to ascertain by actual experiment how cheaply a man could live, and his experience is recorded in a volume entitled "Walden, or Life in the Woods." For eight months his food cost him in money twenty-seven cents a week; and for two years it consisted of rye and Indian meal (without yeast), potatoes, rice, a very little salt pork, and molasses; and his drink was water. He says, "a man may use as simple diet as the animals, and yet retain health and strength."

From experiments made some years ago, in five prisons in Scotland, where the habits of the prisoners were about alike, it was found that to supply the waste of the human system when not in active exercise, about four ounces of muscle-making and thirteen ounces of heat or fat-producing food were required daily; and that a lesser supply was insufficient to restore the waste of the tissues, and that the body consequently diminished in weight. About the same proportion is observed in the rations provided for soldiers by governments whose officers study the laws of dietetics. Now, assuming this to be the amount of nutriment daily required, we need only analyze the various articles of food and select those containing the requisite elements that cost the least. In other words, we need eat only one and three-quarter pounds of cracked wheat or unbolted flour daily, or one and a half pounds of maize and Southern corn mixed, a pound of beans or peas and rice, two pounds of barley, or two pounds of oatmeal and one of buckwheat, or three pounds of beef of average fatness, or about ten pounds of potatoes or sixteen pounds of turnips, carrots and parsnips. A bill of fare consisting of one pound of roast beef, one pound potatoes, one pound unbolted bread, one pound milk, and one pound apples, will contain the same quantity of muscle-making and heat-producing elements. The combinations by which the same end may be obtained are almost unlimited; but where cost alone is considered, the simplest and cheapest articles must be selected. Less than two pounds of unbolted flour, or beans or peas or Indian corn, are all a man need purchase and consume daily, to supply the waste of his system in ordinary circumstances. This statement furnishes a key to about all that can be said respecting economy in food.

Soyer's Cheap Soups.

Soyer, in his "Culinary Campaign," has given recipes for making palatable soups which he says will not cost more than *a cent a quart* in London. His directions for two of them are as follows:

No. 1. Take two ounces of drippings; quarter of a pound of solid meat, at four pence a pound, cut into pieces one inch square; quarter pound of onions, sliced thin; quarter pound of turnips (the peel will do, or one whole one cut into small slices); two ounces leeks—green tops will do—sliced thin; three ounces of celery; three quarters of a pound of common flour; half a pound of pearl barley, or one pound of Scotch; three ounces of salt; quarter of an ounce of brown sugar; two gallons of water. I first put two ounces of dripping into a saucepan, capable of holding two gallons of water, with a quarter of a pound of leg-beef without bones, cut into square pieces of about an inch; and two middling-sized onions, peeled and sliced; I then set the saucepan over a coal fire, and stir the contents around for a few minutes with a wooden (or iron) spoon until fried lightly brown. I had then, ready-washed, the peelings of two turnips, fifteen green leaves or tops of celery, and the green part of two leeks (the whole of which, I must observe, are always thrown away). Having cut the above vegetables into small pieces, I threw them into a saucepan with the other ingredients, stirring them occasionally over the fire for another ten minutes; then added one quart of cold water, and three-quarters of a pound of common flour, and half a pound of pearl barley, mixing all well together; I then added seven quarts of hot water, seasoned with three ounces of salt, and a quarter of an ounce of brown sugar, stirred occasionally until boiling, and allowed it to simmer very gently for three hours; at the end of which time I found the barley perfectly tender. The above soup has been tasted by numerous noblemen, members of Parliament, and several ladies, who have lately visited my kitchen department, and who have considered it very good and nourishing.

The soup will keep several days when made as above described; but I must observe, not to keep it in a deep pan, but within a flat vessel, where the air could act freely upon it. Stir it now and then until nearly cold, or otherwise the next day it will be in a state of fermentation. This does not denote the weakness of the soup, because the same evil exists with the strongest of stock, or sauce, if not stirred, or confined in a warm place—a fact known to every first-rate cook. The expenses may come to three farthings per quart in London; but as almost everything can be had at less cost in the country, the price of the soup will be still more reduced. In that case, a little additional meat might be used. By giving with this a small portion of bread or biscuit, better support would be given to the poor at a trifling cost; and no one, it is to be hoped, hereafter, would hear of the dreadful calamity of starvation.

No. 2. *Same Cost.*—Quarter of a pound of beef, cut into pieces one inch square; two ounces of dripping, or melted suet; quarter of a pound of turnips, or carrots, cut into fragments half an inch square; four drops of essence; one and a half pounds of maize flour; three ounces of salt; quarter ounce of brown sugar; one teaspoonful of black pepper, ground fine. Take two ounces of either dripping, American lard, or suet, to which add the turnips or carrots; fry for ten minutes; add one quart of cold water, and the meal, well mixing, and moisten by degrees with seven quarts of hot water; boil five hours, and season with three ounces of salt, one quarter ounce of brown sugar, one teaspoonful of black pepper, *two drops* of essence of garlic, *one drop* of essence of mint, a little celery; stir quickly, and serve directly.

By adding a pound of potatoes to this, a superior soup will be the result.

Grits, or Crushed Wheat.

Wheat has been analyzed and found to contain, as we have already remarked, all the elements that compose the human system, and in such proportions, that life and health can be continued on wheat alone for an indefinite period, with good water and good air. Ground or crushed into what are called grits, but unbolted, it forms a very valuable, cheap and palatable food. All the food for muscle or brain that is in wheat is found in the outer layer or crust and in the germ or "chit," the centre, which furnishes superfine flour, being simply starch. This flour or starch now constitutes the principal food of children, while the outer coat or bran is fed to animals, or, in the language of Dr. Bellows, "So perfectly ignorant are people generally of the laws of nature, that they give to their pigs the food which their children need to develop muscle and brain, and give their children what their pigs need to develop fat."

Crushed white wheat is now made, by a superior process, at the "Atlantic Mills" in Brooklyn, so that it can be cooked in half an hour, and used in every way that rice, oatmeal, barley, tapioca, sago or any similar article can be used. Boiled and eaten with milk and sugar, it is very palatable, and when cold, sliced and fried, it is an excellent dish.

Beans and Peas.

Of these the venerable agricultural philosopher before quoted remarks:

Every family should eat beans and peas, because of all articles they afford the most nutriment for the least money.

One pound of cheap meat, say at ten cents, and one pound of split peas, say five cents, will give a fuller dinner to a family than a dollar expended for beefsteak and white bread. This is a kind of economy that should be known and rigidly practised.

One bushel of white beans will feed more laboring men than eight bushels of potatoes. The beans will cost two dollars, potatoes six.

A single quart of beans costs nine cents; a half pound of salt pork, six cents; a pound of hominy, five cents; and that will give a meal to a larger family than a dollar's worth of roast beef, white bread, potatoes and other vegetables.

Peas are a little more costly than beans, but some think they will go further.

How to Cook Pork and Beans.

Pork and beans has long been a favorite article of food in New England. This dish is made, according to Professor Blot, as follows:

Soak a quart of beans, if old, for twenty-four hours in cold water, then boil gently till tender. Never put any salt to boil dry beans, but as soon as boiled tender, drain them. Cut in dice about half a pound of bacon, and put it in a saucepan on the fire; when about half fried, add the beans, mix and stir for one minute, then put in a warm oven for twenty minutes, stirring occasionally; when done, sprinkle over it some parsley chopped fine, pepper and salt to taste if not salt enough.

Another Method.—Two quarts of middling-sized white beans, two pounds of salt pork, and one spoonful of molasses. Pick the beans over carefully, wash, and add a gallon of boiling hot soft water; let them soak in it over night. In the morning put them in fresh water, and boil them gently till the skin is very tender and about to break. Take up dry and put them in your dish; stir in your molasses, gash the pork, and put it down in the dish, so as to have the beans cover all but the upper surface; turn in boiling water till the top is just covered; bake with a steady fire four or five hours. Watch them, and add more water from time to time as it dries away. The molasses may be omitted.

Indian Corn.

This is another article that furnishes a large amount of nutriment for little money. It has always been a favorite dish in the Southern States, where the cooking of it is best understood. The first great error usually made in preparing corn meal is in grinding it too fine, and the next in not cooking it enough. Coarse corn meal makes the sweetest mush. Corn meal for mush should boil two hours; it is better if boiled *four,* and not fit to be eaten if boiled less than one hour.

To make Corn Bread.—Put a quart of Indian meal into a wooden bowl, with as much salt as can be taken up with the thumb and fingers, that is, about a teaspoonful; then add as much sweet milk as will make it up into adherent dough, of which take up a double handful, laying it over on one hand and thus carry it to the pan or skillet for baking; turn it in with one pat of the hand, and so on, until the vessel is full; and with a good heat, let it remain until the crust is a yellowish brown; put it on the table piping hot, press it open, lay in a large lump of grass butter, just made, and it is ready for demolition. Corn bread is best if eaten while hot; it becomes sodden if it cools. The milk supersedes the use of lard or butter; no water is needed, although many use butter and water instead of milk; but the true constituents of a pone of bread are meal, milk, salt, nothing else. If you add eggs, it becomes Johnny-cake, and is no longer a pone of bread.

A more simple, healthful, nutritious, and agreeable article of bread, is, in our opinion, never made. The roughness of the meal particles gives the advantage of brown bread; its natural sweetness makes sugar or molasses unnecessary; while the sweet milk answers all the purpose of soda or cream of tartar.

A Receipt for Indian Pudding.

Three and a half pounds of corn (Indian) meal and a handful of salt, one teaspoonful or not, we would prefer not, of carbonate of soda. Mix well, and pour over it a sufficient amount of *boiling* water to soften the whole, then pour on a quart of cold water; sprinkle over it three-quarters of a pound of dry flour, and stir it well. Divide into five puddings; put each into a floured cloth, tie tight, put in boiling water, and boil three hours; eat it hot, or cold, or fried. It is said that this will give a family of twelve persons two hearty meals, at a cost of twenty-five cents. It is eaten with syrup.

How to Cook Hominy.

By hominy is meant grains of white corn from which the hull and chit, or eye, have been removed, leaving the grains almost whole. Solon Robinson says, that not one person in a hundred knows how to cook hominy, and gives this as the proper way, which he learned in the land where "hog and hominy" are understood.

Wash slightly in cold water, and soak twelve hours in tepid, soft water; then boil slowly from three to six hours in same water, with plenty more added from time to time, with great care to prevent burning. Don't salt while cooking, as that or hard water will harden the corn; so it will peas or beans, green or dry, and rice also.

When done, add butter and salt; or a better way is to let each one season to suit the taste. It may be eaten with meat, in lieu of vegetables, or with milk, sugar, or syrup.

It is good, hot or cold, and the more frequently it is warmed over; it is like the old-fashioned pot of

> "Bean porridge hot, or bean porridge cold,
> Bean porridge best at nine days old."

So is hominy. It is good always, and very wholesome, and, like tomatoes, only requires to be eaten once or twice to fix the taste in its favor.

Rice and Lentils.

Two-fifths of the human family it has been calculated make rice their principal article of food, but like superfine flour, it is almost entirely starch, and therefore for mental or muscular strength it is one of the poorest of the common articles of nutritive food, and those who live exclusively upon it are generally weak and effeminate. It is useful, however, to eat with meat, or in case of sickness, where little sustenance is required, and when properly prepared, it is very palatable.

Rice may be boiled in various ways, or rather with several ingredients. In Italy they boil it with ham, sausage, and sometimes Parmesan cheese, and it may be made into cakes, croquettes, fritters, or into pudding. The following is a recipe

To Make a Rice Pudding Without Eggs.

Wash a half pound of rice, and put it in a broad shallow tin pan holding four quarts, with a large teacupful of sugar and a half teaspoonful of salt. Fill the pan up with milk, fresh from the cow is best, and set in the oven or stove to bake, stirring it occasionally, and trying the rice. When the latter is soft, and begins to thicken the milk, the pudding is done. If it boils too long, or there is too much rice in it, it will be too thick to be good.

Lentils are not much known in America, but in the East they are used largely in connection with rice, supplying the muscle-making elements in which rice is deficient. Professor Blot pronounces them an excellent vegetable, and says they are prepared like dry beans in every way. Many persons think them much dearer than beans or peas, not knowing that they swell three or four times their size when soaked in water before cooking them. A *purée* of lentils is excellent with almost every kind of meat, and it also makes a good soup.

A good supper or dinner may be had from a bowl of

Farmer's Rice.

Take a quart of milk, and put it on to boil in a pot of sufficient size. Mix two eggs thoroughly in a pint of flour, and when the milk has begun to boil, sprinkle this into the milk, and stir constantly. When well boiled, transfer to a deep dish, and make it very sweet with brown sugar. Grate some nutmeg over the surface.

A Plum Pudding for the Million.

Soyer gives the following receipt for a pudding, which, he says, will cost only sixteen pence to make one large enough to supply ten or twelve people.

Put in a basin a pound of flour, half a pound of stoned raisins, ditto of currants, ditto of chopped suet, two tablespoonfuls of treacle, and half a pint of water. Mix all well, put in a cloth or mould, and boil from four and a half to five hours. For sauce, take melted butter, sugar, and juice of lemon, if handy. A little spice, or a few drops of any essence, or lemon peel chopped, and a little brandy or rum will be an improvement.

Oatmeal.

Oatmeal is especially rich in food for muscles and brains, and this may explain the reason of the fact that Scotchmen, who are raised principally on oatmeal porridge and oatmeal cakes, are remarkable for mental and physical activity. It is said to contain the most material for hard work of any known grain, while, at the same time, it is about the cheapest of foods. In the form of cakes, Oatmeal, it is claimed, is as good as buckwheat, and in the form of porridge it is especially healthy for children.

The best way to make *porridge* is to mix the oatmeal with warm water; strain the batter, pour it into a farina-boiler (a tin utensil enclosed in a larger one, with space between the two for boiling water), and then leave it on the fire for an hour and a half. It needs no stirring, and will be found cooked to a perfect jelly, free from lumps.

Economical Meats.

When the best beefsteak is selling at twenty cents a pound, the butchers are glad to sell the "rein" piece at eight or ten cents a pound. It has no bone or fat, and three pounds of it for twenty-five cents will make soup enough for a family of eight or ten persons two days, besides furnishing enough meat for a dinner.

Of all the parts of *corned beef*, that is the most nutritious and cheapest which is called the round, for it has neither bone nor gristle, nor waste fat worth naming. Both in the purchase of meat and fish, persons are generally falsely economical in choosing an article with bone in it, at two or three cents a pound less than a piece which has none. They purchase porgies, blue fish, flounders, and the like, at six or eight cents a pound, instead of halibut at twelve cents (wholesale), but the halibut is the cheapest, and also the safest, where there are children.

Beef Stew.

A very economical and most savory and delicious dish, says some one, can be made with two or three pounds of chuck steak (a cheap kind of beef), which infinitely surpasses the tasteless, insipid, eating-house stuff, called *beef à la mode*. Cut the steak into pieces two inches square; put them into a saucepan, with a large breakfast cup of cold water; put it on the fire; as soon as it boils up, stand it on the hole to simmer, for two hours, until perfectly tender. While simmering, put in, tied up with a bit of thread or cotton, a bunch of herbs, composed of knotted marjoram, winter savory, and a little thyme; take this out just before the dish is served. Of course the stew must be occasionally shaken, as all others are; the more fat there is, the better is the stew. This dish is of Italian origin, and in that country is eaten with plain boiled maccaroni and Parmesan cheese, or with salad, and with either is "a dainty dish to set before a king."

A good and economical breakfast dish is made of

Fried Rashers of Bacon and Poached Eggs.

Cut the bacon into thin slices; trim and cut off the rind. Put it into a *cold* frying-pan—that is to say, do not place the pan on the fire before the bacon is in it. Turn it two or three times, and dish it on a very hot dish. Poach the eggs, and slip them on to the bacon without breaking the yolks, and serve quickly. Time, three or four minutes. Allow six eggs for three persons.

An excellent family dish, very savory, and which can be recommended also for its cheapness and economy, is

Roasted Oxheart Stuffed.

Put the heart into warm water to soak for two hours; then wipe it well with a cloth, and, after cutting off the lobes, stuff the inside with a highly seasoned forcemeat, made, for instance, from six ounces of bread crumbs, two eggs, two ounces of ham or lean bacon, quarter of a pound of suet, the rind of half a lemon, one teaspoonful of minced parsley, one teaspoonful of minced sweet herbs, salt, cayenne, and mace to taste. Fasten this stuffing in with a needle and coarse thread; tie the heart up in buttered paper, and set it before a good fire, being very particular to keep it well basted, or it will eat dry, there being but very little of its own fat. Two or three minutes before serving, remove the paper, baste well, and serve with good gravy, and red-currant jelly or melted butter. If the heart is very large, it will require two hours, and covered with a caul, may be baked as well as roasted. Cost of heart, twenty cents, and sufficient for six or eight persons. Seasonable all the year.

A Genuine Pepper Pot.

This soup, which is of West Indian origin, should be made in an *earthen pot*, which always remains by the side of the fire, where the contents simmer, but do not boil. These should consist of an equal admixture of fish, flesh, fowl, and vegetables, seasoned with chilli, or Cayenne pepper and salt, the only attention it requires being occasional skimming, and the addition of a little water when it gets too dry. As it should at all times be simmering by the fire, a good meal is always ready for any guest that may chance to come uninvited.

A Scotch proverb says, They hae need o' a canny cook wha hae but *ae egg* to their dinner.

Cold Meat Cookery.

This is a field that offers many resources for economical living to those that understand the art of thrifty housekeeping. In the opinion of most American housekeepers, roast or boiled meat left over is good for nothing except to be eaten cold or thrown to the dogs. A few of them know that it can be made into a plain hash, but this is the extreme limit of their knowledge in this particular. Those who would learn what savory dishes can be made of cold roast or boiled beef, mutton, veal, and poultry, should consult Mrs. Beeton's "Englishwoman's Cookery Book." No other work that we know of is so complete in its directions for cooking cold meats, and with its aid a thrifty housekeeper, who could secure from her more ignorant or lavish neighbors a supply of cold meats at a small expense, could support a family of three or four persons for a trifle per day.

What can be done with cold roast *beef?* It can be broiled with mushroom or oyster sauce; it can be made into beef fritters, beef rissoles, beef rolls, into hashed beef, minced beef, potted beef, and beef ragout. Cut into slices, and with some herbs and vegetables and mashed potatoes, it can be baked into a pie. Cold boiled beef, fried in a little butter, and covered with fried greens, constitutes the hereditary English dish known as "bubble and squeak." Cold *mutton* can be broiled, and with tomato sauce, makes an excellent dish, if served hot. Cold mutton may be made into very fair pies, if well seasoned, and mixed with a few nerbs, or it can be made into "hodge podge," "toad-in-the-hole," ragout, or baked minced mutton. Cold *veal* can be made into Scotch collops, or veal cake, or pie, or fried patties, or ragout, or rissoles, or rolls, or minced with vegetables or maccaroni. Cold *poultry* can be made into French chicken cutlets, chicken salad, curried fowl, hashed, fricasseed, fried, minced, into a ragout of fowl, or fowl sauté with peas, or croquettes. Even cold *pork* may be cut into nice-sized cutlets, put into a stew-pan with butter, and chopped onions, and fried, and when properly seasoned, will make a savory and economical dish.

Soyer's Thirty Receipts in One.

Put a pound of the crumbs of bread to soak in cold water, or better, in milk; take the same quantity of any kind of boiled or roasted meat, a little fat, which chop in dice rather fine; press the water out of the bread; put in the pan two ounces of butter, lard, or dripping, with two teaspoonfuls of chopped onions; fry two minutes; add the bread; stir with a wooden spoon until rather dry; then add the meat; season with a teaspoonful of salt, half of pepper, a little grated nutmeg, if handy; stir till quite hot; then add two eggs, one at a time; mix very quick, and pour on dish to cool. Then roll it into the shape of small eggs, then in flour; egg them and bread crumb; fry a nice yellow color, and serve plain, or with any sauce you may fancy.

Anything eatable, the remains of meat, poultry, game, or fish, may be used up in this way.

While considering the subject of economy in food, we may as well here allude to one or two other points; as, for instance,

Coffee Substitutes.

French cooks, who are celebrated for making good coffee, mix three or four different kinds, and recommend as a good proportion, to add to one pound of Java about four ounces of Mocha and four ounces of one or two other kinds. It is said that from three parts of Rio, with two parts of Old Government Java, a coffee can be made quite as good, if not superior, to that made of Java alone.

Wheat coffee, made of a mixture of eight quarts of wheat to one pound of real coffee, is said to afford a beverage quite as agreeable as the unadulterated Rio, besides being much more wholesome. It is probably known to many that a very large per cent. of the *ground* coffee sold at the stores is common field peas roasted and ground with genuine coffee. There are hundreds of thousands of bushels of peas annually used for that purpose. Those who are in the habit of purchasing ground coffee can do better to buy their own peas, burn and grind them, and mix to suit themselves.

Sturgeon Veal Cutlets.

There are few persons so poor that they will consent to eat sturgeon, yet this fish, if properly cooked, affords it is said a luxurious meal. Get a few slices, moderately thick, says Mather, put them in a pot or pan of water, and parboil them to get rid of the oil; then roll in crumbs of cracker and egg, just as you would a veal cutlet, and fry. This makes a veal cutlet that beats the original by far, and you are sure that it is full "six weeks old," as the butcher always certifies in regard to the veal

Vegetable Beefsteaks.

Dr. Badham, of England, thinks he has discovered a large supply of excellent and cheap food in the mosses and fungi that grow upon trees. He says, "I have indeed grieved when I reflected on the straitened condition of the poorer classer, to see pounds innumerable of extempore beefsteaks growing on our oaks in the shape of *fistulina hepatica*—puff balls—which some of our friends have not inaptly compared to sweetbread for the rich delicacy of their unassisted flavor. It varies in size from that of a small kidney to an irregular mass of many pounds weight. When grilled, it is scarcely to be distinguished from broiled meat. No fungus yields a richer gravy. It is to be found in England, principally on the old oak trees, throughout the summer in great abundance. But we spurn the vegetable beefsteak, as we have spurned the horsesteak and the ass steak. And so the ignorant and poor *are left hungering in the midst of plenty, praying against famine in the village church, with plenty rotting in the woods and meadows round about the parish.*"

CHAPTER IX.

VALUABLE SECRETS KNOWN TO GOOD COOKS.

"Bad cooking is waste—waste of money and loss of comfort. Whom God has joined in matrimony, ill-cooked joints and ill-boiled potatoes have very often put asunder."—SMILES.

"There is a great deal of good eating and drinking in seven hundred a year, if people knew how to manage it."—MACAULAY.

MRS. WARREN, in one of her works, relates an interview she had with a friend, who expressed deep regret that she had not learned the art of cookery before she had married, and who wished that all the time she had wasted in illuminating texts of Scripture had been spent in *illuminating instructions to promote household comfort.* This suggestion stimulated her imagination, and she saw, or fancied she saw, that very great benefit might be derived both to mistresses and the "help" if handsomely printed cards were hung up in the kitchen, containing general directions for cooking meats, soups, fish, game, and poultry, for boiling vegetables and making pastry, in a word, the points that constitute good cookery. The idea is a valuable one, and in our researches among the works of the masters of the art, we have had in view the preparation of a code of standard rules, or what might be called *Family Kitchen Maxims.*

How to Boil, Fry, Roast, etc.

All the essential operations in cookery are comprised in BAKING, BOILING, BROILING, FRYING, ROASTING, STEWING, SIMMERING, and SEASONING; the rest are all fancy, though the French have what they call BRAISING, in which they have a fire both above and under the braising-pan; and sautéing, which is frying in a very small quantity of butter or fat.

In BAKING meats or fish, it is important not only to keep the bottom of the pan covered with broth or water, but to place a piece of buttered paper over the object in the pan, which keeps the top moist and juicy, and acts as a self-baster. Soyer recommends in using dishes for the oven, if of metal, that they may be made of galvanized iron, and to have separate ones for meat and fish.

In BOILING meats it is the general practice to put all, whether fresh or salted, into nearly boiling water, and from those that are very salty, careful cooks throw off the first water, and fill up again with boiling water. But the modern theory is, that fresh meat, if intended for soup, should be put into cold water, and if not intended for soup, into boiling water; and that salt meat should be put into warm, or, if very salt, into cold water, in order that by its slow cooking the salt may be extracted. After the water has boiled up rapidly, the pot should be drawn back, and its contents allowed to simmer gently. Simmering is simply slow boiling.

Always boil cabbages in two waters, and to prevent the disagreeable odor which arises from boiling cabbages, cut the head in half, and pour boiling water on it before cooking.

In boiling peas and potatoes do not bury them in water, nor allow them to remain in water after they are done.

In BROILING, it is important to grease the bars of the gridiron first, and have the fire brisk and clear. A layer of coke or charcoal over a pretty strong fire is a good plan. There is a great difference of opinion among professional cooks, whether in broiling a beefsteak it should be turned only once, or often, but the weight of authority is in favor of frequent turning. Soyer says, "My plan is to turn it often, and my reason is, that, if turned but once, the albumen and fibrine of the meat get charred, and the heat throws out the osmazome, or gravy, on the upper side, which, when turned over, goes into the fire; by turning it often, so as at first only to set the outside, the gravy goes into the centre, and it becomes evenly done throughout. As regards the thickness of the meat to be broiled, that depends on the intensity of the fire (three-quarters of an inch is a good thickness for rump steak), but the quicker the better, and also the sooner it is eaten after taken from the fire the better."

[Macbeth's receipt for broiling a beefsteak is a very good one.

"When 'tis *done*, 'twere well
It 'twere *done quickly.*"]

Broiling and roasting are essentially the same, though properly roasting is done before the fire and broiling over the fire.

FRYING, as understood by professional cooks, is to immerse the article in boiling grease; in other words, they take a pan, say six inches deep, nearly fill it with fat, and when boiling, insert in this the article to be fried, so that it is completely covered with the fat. "Those articles to be fried," says Soyer, "are generally those that have a coating of materials (such as bread crumbs and batter), which are quickly carbonized, and thus form a crust, which prevents the grease penetrating, concentrates the liquids, and preserves the flavor of the article; the carbonization once effected, the fire should be immediately moderated, particularly if the article is large, in order that the interior may become properly solidified. All articles properly fried are generally much liked, as they are agreeable to the eye and afford a pleasing variety."

American cooks, however, understand by frying what the French call sautéing: that is, cooking an article in a shallow pan, with a small quantity of fat, one side at a time. The secret of doing this well consists in doing it quickly, to keep the gravy and succulence in the meat which a slow process would nullify, and is of course confined to small articles of food.

It is important in frying that the pan be perfectly clean, that the oil or drippings be sweet and fresh, and that the fat be boiling before the meat or fish is put into it. A good way to test the heat of your fat is to throw a little bit of bread into the pan: if it fries crisp, the fat is of the right heat; if it burns the bread, it is too hot. When the articles are done, care must be taken to drain all the fat from them most thoroughly.

The grand point in frying is to get the boiling fat to *seize the article fried, i. e.,* to form a brown crust all over its surface at the very instant of immersion. The *seizing* cannot take place unless the fat has been over a sharp fire a sufficient time. When once the seizing is properly effected, the pan may be raised or withdrawn a little, to let the article cook through without burning outside. Articles properly fried are not greasy, while badly fried things are the reverse. A well-fried fish will hardly soil a napkin;

potatoes properly fried may be eaten like a biscuit, without soiling the fingers.

Careful cooks save their frying fat and use it repeatedly, keeping that used for meats and fish in separate jars. Economical cooks seldom buy fat; generally there is enough left from skimming broth, sauces and gravies for every purpose. When they do make it, they use beef suet, the part around the kidneys, or any kind of fat, raw or cooked, chop it fine, boil for fifteen minutes, skim well, strain, and put in stone jars. This fat, for frying, it is claimed, is better than lard. and it does not fly over the pan like lard.

In ROASTING meats, slow roasting, like slow boiling, is the best. The more meat is basted, the less time it will require to roast. When the meat is half done, the fire should be stirred to burn brightly and clearly for browning. Nearly all the writers on Cookery think fifteen minutes for each pound is a proper time to allow in roasting, but a great deal depends upon the nature of the fire and the meat. A good cook will be particular to place a pan so as to catch the dripping. [See the English method of roasting beef, in next chapter.]

Veal, fowls and rabbits, when roasted, should always be covered with bacon fat, and then be well floured before putting to the fire; by so doing, all the juices of the meat or poultry are kept in, and it does not become dry. One of the secrets of the excellence of French cookery is, to cut up shreds of bacon and tie them around the article to be roasted.

In STEWING, it is necessary to have a moderate fire, and as even as possible. A brisk fire causes the steam to evaporate, and this steam is the flavor of the article stewed.

Soyer says stewing should be done slowly, the pan partly uncovered and frequently skimmed.

In SEASONING, the senses of tasting and smelling must be employed, and the art consists in so proportioning the flavors, that no one may predominate or be tasted more than another. Consult, in seasoning, the tastes of those for whom you cook rather than your own. Be moderate in the use of salt, for it is easy to add salt to a dish which is too fresh, but if once made too salt it cannot be remedied.

Beef and mutton are best when rather underdone, but pork, veal, poultry, beef's tongue, tripe, and young meats generally, must be thoroughly well cooked. Vegetables, when not sufficiently cooked, are exceedingly unwholesome and indigestible.

Wash greens carefully, first in warm water, to remove dirt and insects, and then plunge them into cold water, which will immediately restore their crispness. Mrs. Warren astonished her cook by doing this.

For all vegetables have *plenty of boiling water* and salt. Make them boil up *very quickly*. Take all greens out of the water the instant they are done. Mash all vegetables with a wooden spoon.

In addition to some of the foregoing, the ILLUMINATED FAMILY KITCHEN MONITOR should contain the following points of

Good Advice to Hired Cooks.

1. Accustom yourself to look upon your business as akin to a profession. The kitchen is a family laboratory, and a good cook should be a chemist. Read all the best books on the art of Cookery, select and adopt what seems to you good in each, and especially study "HOME COMFORTS."

2. Cleanliness, not only in the kitchen utensils, but in your dress and person, is the first lesson in cookery. Dough-boards and rolling-pins should be well scoured in hot water, but no soap, or sand or stone dust of any kind should be used. Do not allow food to become cold in any metal vessel, especially no liquid food, in any brass or copper pot or pan, after it is cooked, or it may absorb rust and poison the family. Do not clean bottles with lead shot for the same reason.

3. A good cook regards the appearance as well as the quality of the dishes she sends to the table. A beefsteak trimmed oval, surrounded by nicely browned fried potatoes, and garnished with parsley, is really more digestible as well as sightly than a rough, scraggy steak dished without regard to appearance. Veal cutlets should be cut round, about three inches in diameter, and done very quickly.

4. Not only should meats, etc., look well on the table, but they should be hot. Nothing can be more repugnant to the taste than lukewarm soup or meat, while fish is made utterly worthless by being allowed to become cool.

5. Punctuality in having meals at the appointed hours is a sterling virtue. Having things ready that can be prepared beforehand prevents hurry and secures punctuality. By stuffing a fowl overnight (except in very hot weather), and trussing it, not only can it be put to the fire at a minute's notice, but the flavor of the stuffing will have time to penetrate to the flesh.

6. Guard against unnecessary waste. A good cook has very few waste articles. The clippings and trimmings of fresh meat will make soups and gravies; the fat can be

melted for dripping, which will save lard in frying; the bones can be made into soups and gravy; the bacon fat will come useful in pastry, while pieces of stale bread can be made into excellent puddings.

7. Before cooking meat or vegetables, a good cook understands what kind of fire is required, and prepares accordingly. Half an hour before broiling a steak stir up the fire, clear away the ashes, rake out all dead cinders from the bottom, and secure a good, clear fire for the gridiron.

8. Provide yourself with serviceable cooking aprons, made with bibs. These will save your gown, and keep you neat and clean. Have them made large enough, so as to nearly meet behind.

9. Do not scrub the inside of your frying-pans, as after this operation any preparation fried, is liable to catch or burn to the pan. If the pan has become black inside, rub it with a hard crust of bread and wash in hot water, mixed with a little soda.

10. Few cooks make really good, quick biscuit. The common fault is to use soda too freely, and to "guess at" the quantities instead of measuring them.

To Neutralize the Acid in Fruits.

A large quantity of the free acid which exists in rhubarb, gooseberries, currants, and other fruits, may be judiciously corrected by the use of a small quantity of *carbonate of soda*, without the least affecting their flavor. To an ordinary sized pie or pudding take as much soda as, piled up, will cover a shilling, or even twice such quantity, if the fruit be very sour. If this little hint is attended to, many a stomach-ache will be prevented and a vast quantity of sugar saved, because, when the acid is neutralized by the soda, it will not require so much sugar to render the pie sweet.

There is a French motto, *Ne touchez pas a la broche*—Do not touch the spit; which probably means "Leave the making of cookery books to cooks." We concede the wisdom of the advice, and do not propose to touch the spit; but in our researches among the writings of these learned professors, we have discovered some things which promise to improve the methods of preparing common articles, as practised in American and English households; and so great is the need of improvement, that it would be rank injustice to withhold them. First,

How to Make Good Family Bread.

The books abound in directions for making bread, and all the authors agree that good flour, and good yeast, and plenty of kneading, are essential; yet probably nothing was ever published on the subject so comprehensive, minute, and practical as the following directions, taken from Marion Harland's new work on Common Sense in the Household. She says:

[Chiefest among the conditions to good bread, I place good "family" flour—dry, elastic, and odorless. Next in importance to the quality of the flour is that of the yeast. This should be light in color and lively, effervescing easily when shaken, and emitting an odor like weak ammonia. If dull or sour, it is bad. In cities it is easiest, perhaps cheapest, to buy yeast from a brewery or bakery, exercising your discrimination as to quality. Unless you can satisfy yourself in this respect, you had better make your own from the following receipt for

Hop Yeast.

Four large potatoes, or six small.
Two quarts cold water.
Double handful hops, tied in a coarse muslin bag.
Four tablespoonfuls flour.
Two tablespoonfuls white sugar.

Peel the potatoes, and put them, with the hop-bag, into a saucepan containing two quarts cold water. Cover and boil until the potatoes break and fall apart. Take these out with a perforated skimmer, leaving the water still boiling, mash them fine with a potato-beetle, and work in the flour and sugar. Moisten this gradually with the *boiling* hop tea, stirring it to a smooth paste. When all the tea has been mixed in, set it aside to cool. While still warm, add four tablespoonfuls of lively yeast, and turn all into a large open vessel to "work." Keep this in a warm place until it ceases to bubble up, or until next day. In summer it will work well in a few hours. When quite light, put in earthen jars with small mouths, in which fit corks, or bottle it, and remove to ice-house or cellar. It will keep good for a fortnight—longer in winter. When you wish to use it for baking, send a small vessel to the cellar for the desired quantity, and re-cork at once. A half-hour in a hot kitchen may spoil it.

Potato Yeast.

Six potatoes, two quarts cold water, 4 tablespoonfuls of flour, two of white sugar. Peel and boil the potatoes until they break. Leaving the water on the fire, take them out and mash fine, with the flour and sugar, wetting gradually with the hot water, until it is all used. When lukewarm, add a gill of good yeast, and set aside in an open vessel and warm place to ferment. When it ceases to effervesce, bottle and set in ice-house. This yeast is very nice and white, and is preferred by many who dislike the bitter taste of hops. It is also convenient to make when hops cannot be obtained.

Potato Bread Sponge.

Six potatoes, boiled and mashed while hot; six tablespoonfuls baker's yeast, two of white sugar, two of lard, one teaspoonful soda, one quart of warm (not hot) water, three cups of flour.

Mash the potatoes, and work in the lard and sugar. Stir to a cream, mixing in gradually a quart of the water in which the potatoes were boiled, which should have been poured out to cool down to a blood warmth. *Beat* in the flour, already wet up with a little potato-water to prevent lumping, then the yeast, lastly the soda. Cover lightly, if the weather is warm; more closely in winter; and set to rise overnight in a warm place.

Bread Sponge (Plain).

One quart of warm water, six tablespoonfuls baker's yeast, two of lard, two of white sugar, one teaspoonful of soda, and flour to make a soft batter. Melt the lard in the warm water, add the sugar, then the flour by degrees, stirring in smoothly. A quart and a pint of flour will usually be sufficient, if the quality is good. Next comes the yeast, lastly the soda. Beat up hard for several minutes, and set to rise as above. Bread mixed with potato sponge is more nutritious, keeps fresh longer, and is sweeter than that made with the plainer sponge. But there are certain seasons of the year when good *old* potatoes cannot be procured, and new ones will not do for this purpose. The potato sponge is safer, because surer, for beginners in the important art of bread-making. After using it for fifteen years, I regard it as almost infallible—given the conditions of good flour, yeast, kneading and baking.

Family Bread (White).

Having set your sponge overnight, or, if you bake late in the afternoon, early in the morning, sift dry flour into a deep bread tray, and strew a few spoonfuls of fine salt over it. The question of the quantity of flour is a delicate one, requiring judgment and experience. Various brands of flour are so unequal with respect to the quantity of gluten they contain, that it is impossible to give any invariable rule on this subject. It will be safe, however, to sift two quarts and a pint, if you have set the potato sponge; two quarts for the plain. This will make two good-sized loaves. Make a hole in the middle of the heap, pour in the risen sponge (which should be very light, and seamed in many places on the top), and work down the flour into it with your hands. If too soft, add more flour. If you can mould it at all, it is not too soft. If stiff, rinse out the bowl in which the sponge was set with a little lukewarm water, and work this in. When you have it in manageable shape, begin to knead. Work the mass into a ball—your hands having been well floured from the first; detach it from the tray, and lift it in your left hand, while you sprinkle flour with the right thickly over the bottom and sides of the tray. Toss back the ball into this, and knead hard—*always towards the centre of the mass*, which should be repeatedly turned over and around, that every portion may be manipulated. Brisk and long kneading makes the pores fine and regular. Gaping holes of divers sizes are an unerring telltale of a careless cook. Spend at least twenty minutes—half an hour is better—in this kind of useful gymnastics. It is grand exercise for arms and chest. This done, work the dough into a shapely ball in the centre of the tray, sprinkle flour over the top; throw a cloth over all, and leave it on the kitchen table to rise, taking care it is not in a draught of cold air. In summer it will rise in four or five hours—in winter, six are often necessary. It should come up steadily until it at least trebles its original bulk, and the floured surface cracks all over. Knead again for ten or fifteen minutes. Then divide it into as many parts as you wish loaves, and put these in well-greased pans for the final rising.

In a large household baking, it is customary to mould the dough into oblong rolls, three or four, according to the number of loaves you desire, and to lay these close together in one large pan. The second kneading is done upon a floured board, and should be thorough as the first, the dough being continually shifted and turned. Set the pans in a warm place for an hour longer, with a cloth thrown over them to keep out the air and dust. Then bake, heeding the directions set down in the article upon bread in general. If your ovens are in good condition, one hour should bake the above quantity of bread. But here again experience must be your guide. Note carefully for yourself how long a time is required for your first successful baking, as also how much dry flour you have worked into your sponge, and let these data regulate future action. I have known a variation of two quarts, in a large baking, over the usual measure of flour. I need not tell you that you had better shun a brand that requires such an excessive quantity to bring the dough to the right consistency. It is neither nutritious nor economical. When you make out the loaves, prick the top with a fork.

Novices in bread-making, and many who should have learned better by long experience, fall into a sad mistake in the consistency of the dough. It should be mixed as soft as it can be handled. Bread will rise sooner and higher, be lighter and more digestible, and keep fresh much longer, if this rule be followed. Stiff bread is close in texture, often waxy to the teeth, and after a day or so becomes very hard. Set the dough to rise in a moderately warm place, and keep it at an even temperature. There is force in the old lament, "My bread took cold last night." Cold arrests the process of fermentation. There is a chance, should this occur, that a removal to a more genial atmosphere and careful nursing may cure the congestion, should it be only partial. Too much heat carries forward the work too rapidly. In this case, you will find your dough puffy and sour. Correct the latter evil by dissolving a little soda or saleratus in hot water, and working it well in.

Knead your bread faithfully, and from all sides, until it rebounds like india-rubber after a smart blow of the fist upon the centre of the mass. The oven should not be too hot. If you cannot hold your bare arm in it while you count thirty, it is too quick. Keep the heat steady after the bread goes in. Too much fire at first, and rapid cooling, produce the effect upon the bread which is technically called "slack-baked," *i. e.*, the inside of the loaf is never properly done. Practice and intelligent observation will, in time, make you an adept in the management of your ovens. If the bread rises rapidly while baking, and the crust begins to form before the lower part of the loaf is baked, cover the top with clean paper, until you are ready to brown it.]

Miss Leslie recommends, as soon as the bread is quite done, to wrap each loaf lightly in a clean coarse cloth, damped by sprinkling it with water, and *stand it on its edge*. This will prevent the crust from becoming too hard. Keep the loaves wrapped up after they are deposited in the bread box, which should be of *tin*.

How to Make Stale Bread, or Cake, Fresh.

Plunge the loaf one instant in cold water, and lay it upon a tin in the stove ten or fifteen minutes. It will be like new bread without its deleterious qualities. Stale cake is thus made as nice as new cake. But bread or cake heated over thus, should be used immediately.

Various Uses of Bread Dough.

In the winter, dough may be kept sweet many days in a place where it will be cold, without freezing, and it will grow better to the last.

It should be raised light, then kneaded a little, then covered with a damp cloth, so that a dry crust will not form on the top.

Fresh bread can thus be furnished for the table every day, without extra work. Doughnuts, bread, cake, or rusks can be made of it by adding butter, sugar, or spice; tea biscuit, also fried biscuit, crust for apple dumplings, and for pan-pie.

The dough should be made, at least in part, with milk, when it is to be used for these purposes. These directions are particularly recommended to persons who do their own housework, and of course wish to save time and labor.

How to Make Good Buttered Toast. A. Soyer.

Take remnants of a loaf that have become too dry to be eaten as bread, dip them in warm water, place a slice of the bread upon the toasting-fork, about an inch from the sides, hold it a minute before the fire, then turn it, hold it before the fire another minute, by which time the bread will be thoroughly hot; then begin to move it gradually to and fro until the whole surface has assumed a yellowish-brown color, when again turn it, toasting the other side in the same manner; then lay it upon a hot plate, spread a piece of butter, rather less than an ounce, over it, and cut into four or six pieces. Cut each slice into pieces as soon as buttered, and pile them lightly upon the plate or dish you intend to serve it on.

This way you will find a great improvement upon the old system, as often, in cutting through four or five slices with a bad knife, you squeeze all the butter out of the upper one, and discover the under one, at the peril of its life, swimming in an ocean of butter at the bottom of the dish.

How to Fry Ham and Eggs.

Cut thin slices, and take off the rind; if very salt, pour hot water upon them, but do not suffer them to lie long in it, as the juices of the meat will be lost. Wipe them in a cloth; have the spider ready hot, lay in the pieces, and turn them in a minute or two. They will cook in a very short time. The secret of having good fried ham is in cooking it quick, and not too much. The practice of cutting thick slices, and laying them in a cold spider and frying a long time, makes ham black and hard. It needs nothing added, but to be laid upon a hot covered dish.

After you have fried ham, drop in the eggs, one at a time. In about a minute, dip the boiling fat with a spoon over them, again and again. This will prevent the necessity of turning them, which it is difficult to do without breaking the yolks. Take them out in about two minutes and a half, with a skimmer. The fat that roasts out of a ham that is browned in an oven is good for frying eggs.

French Beef Broth and Soup. Prof. Blot.

Take three pounds of good, lean, fresh beef, from any part except the shin. There must not be more than two ounces of bone to a pound of meat, and the less bone the better. Place the meat in a soup-kettle or saucepan, lined with tin, with three quarts of cold water, and salt, and set it on a good fire. After about thirty minutes, the scum or albumen of the meat will gather on the surface, and the water will commence boiling. Now place the kettle on a more moderate fire, add one gill of cold water, and begin to skim off the scum, which will take only a few minutes. Then add one middle-sized carrot, half of a turnip, one middle-sized leek, a stalk of celery, one of parsley, a bay-leaf, one onion with two cloves stuck in it, and two cloves of garlic. Keep the kettle between simmering and boiling heat for about five hours. Dish the meat with carrot, turnip, and leek around it, and serve it as a *relevé*. Strain the broth, and it is ready for use. I do not put parsnips or thyme in broth, the taste of these two vegetables being too strong. They really neutralize the fine aroma of broth.

The French use broth previously prepared in making *potages* or soups; as, for instance, soup *à la Julienne*.

Scrape two carrots and two turnips, and cut them in pieces about an inch and a half long; cut slices lengthwise, about one-eighth of an inch thick, then cut crosswise so as to make square strips. Put them in a saucepan, with about two ounces of butter, three tablespoonfuls of cabbage, chopped fine, and half a middling-sized onion, also chopped; set on the fire, and stir till about half fried. Add broth to make it as you wish, thin or thick; boil gently till done; salt to taste, skim off the fat, and serve. It takes about two hours.

How to Boil Eggs.

The ordinary way is to put them into a cup or saucepan of boiling water and boil steadily for three minutes, if you want them soft, and ten, if hard. But gourmands like them best if put into *cold* water and left until it comes to a boil, which will be in about ten minutes. The inside, both white and yelk, will then be of the consistency of custard.

Always drop hard-boiled eggs into cold water as soon as they are done to prevent the yelks from turning black.

How to Boil Potatoes.

An English attorney used to say that a woman who could boil potatoes and melt butter *well* was a good cook, and he never required any other proof of the capabilities of a cook.

The Irish, with whom potatoes are the national diet, may reasonably be supposed to know the best method of cooking them. This is their process:

The potatoes, after being washed, are put into a cast-iron pot of cold water, slightly salted, which is placed on the fire. When the water boils, a small quantity of cold water is added to check the boiling; this is once or twice repeated. When the potatoes are done, or nearly done, the water is poured away from the potatoes, which are subjected to the fire to let the steam evaporate and make them mealy. They are served up in the usual way. During the meal only a portion of the potatoes are put on the table at a time, and before it is finished, you will have two or three supplies of hot potatoes, the last being better than the first, for those at the bottom of the pot become partially roasted.

Whether it is better to put potatoes into cold or boiling water is a mooted point among good housekeepers. The result of experiments seems to be that Garnet, White Mountain and Early Rose potatoes are apt to dissolve in cold water, while Peach Blows, Prince Alberts and other late varieties are best cooked in cold water, *always* pouring off the hot water the instant they are done, and letting the potatoes dry for a few minutes.

Potatoes should be boiled with just enough water to cover them. Old potatoes are best steamed; new ones boiled.

Cold potatoes left over from dinner make an excellent dish for breakfast by covering them with milk or cream in a frying pan, adding butter and salt, and let them remain until the milk thickens, say fifteen minutes.

Sweet potatoes should be boiled until done, then peeled and cut into longitudinal slices. Then pour upon each slice as you lay it in the sauce-dish, gravy made in the following manner: Of sugar and butter take one cup of each; add half a cup of hot water, and boil until it is thick. This sauce is a great improvement to the sweet potato, and removes the dryness of that vegetable.

How to Boil Turnips.

Pare them not too thickly, and instead of cutting them in quarters, you should cut across the turnip in thin round slices, not a quarter of an inch thick; wash them well and put them in plenty of boiling water, with a lump of salt, a little piece of dripping the size of a walnut, and make them boil very fast; in a quarter of an hour or less they will be ready; then drain them in a colander, mash them with a wooden spoon, turn them into a basin and add some milk, heat them hot in a covered basin in the oven, and serve them while hot in a warm dish. By this method eight or ten roots will go as far as double the quantity in the ordinary way. By adding milk instead of butter, the turnips are made creamy and richer, and are not liable to produce indigestion as when butter is used with them.

To Cook Onions Without Smell.

Select those that are alike in size and not very large. Boil half an hour and pour off the water. The offensive oil is thus liberated by the heat and most of it goes with the water. Now make a dressing by adding a lump of butter the size of an egg to a pint of milk; put in a little chopped parsley and a bit of mace. When it boils, put in the onions and let them steam slowly until done. When you take them up, open the top of each and drop in a small lump of butter; eat while warm and you need have no misgivings about your breath; for thus dressed they are as mild as baked apples and far more nutritious.

How to Make Macaroni Cheese.

Weigh six ounces of macaroni and break it into short pieces; wash it in hot water, and then scrape well the outer part of a crust or rind of cheese and grate six ounces of this with a coarse grater. Put the macaroni in *boiling water* in which a piece of butter the size of a hazelnut has been placed, and about an ounce of salt. Boil about twenty minutes, when the macaroni will be soft. Prepare some melted butter sauce by mixing an ounce of butter with a little milk, water and flour. Place a layer of cheese in the *bottom* of a well-buttered, shallow pie dish, then a layer of macaroni; over this pour a little of the butter sauce, then a layer of cheese and again of macaroni and butter until the dish is full; lastly, a thick layer of the grated cheese and then the butter sauce and some tiny bits of butter on the top. Bake the whole in an oven for three-quarters of an hour until the cheese is of a light golden brown. Do not serve at table *too hot*. Thus for a very small sum, a handsome and always welcome dish is obtainable. The crust of cheese cannot be made use of in any other way.

Mrs. Lyman's Method of Cooking Salt Mackerel.

Soak for two days, after coming out of the brine, in cold water. Lay in a small tub, *with the flesh side down*, and change the water several times. Just before cooking lay it in a shallow vessel and cover with hot milk. The effect of the milk is to remove the strong taste so unpleasant when this dish is carelessly cooked. Take out of the milk, pour water over it to rinse, and wipe dry with a napkin. Then lay in a wire gridiron and broil in the same manner as fresh shad, or fresh mackerel, and eat with lemon juice for sauce.

What Good Cooks do with Cold Veal.

They chop it very fine, and put a layer in the bottom of a buttered pudding dish, and season with pepper and salt. Next they put a layer of finely powdered crackers, and strew some bits of butter upon it and wet with a little milk. Then more veal, seasoned as before, and another round of cracker crumbs with butter and milk. When the dish is full they wet well with gravy or broth, diluted with warm water, and spread over all a thick layer of cracker seasoned with salt, wet into a paste with milk and bound with a beaten egg or two, if the dish be large. Then they stick butter-bits thickly over it, invert a tin pan so as to cover and keep in the steam, and bake half an hour, or three-quarters if the dish be large. They remove the cover ten minutes before it is served, and brown.

This is called "veal scallop," and is liked by children exceedingly, and by all who are fond of veal in any form. *Do not get it too dry.*

How to Boil Bacon.

Dr. Kitchiner remarks: The boiling of bacon is a very simple subject to comment upon; but our main object is to teach the art of dressing common food in the best manner. Cover a pound of nice streaked bacon with cold water, let it boil gently for three-quarters of an hour; take it up, scrape the under side well, and cut off the rind; grate a crust of bread not only on the top, but all over it, as you would ham, put it before the fire for a few minutes, not too long or it will dry and spoil it. Bacon is sometimes as salt as salt can make it, therefore before it is boiled, it must be soaked in warm water for an hour or two, changing the water once; then pare off the rusty and smoked part, trim it nicely on the under side, and scrape the rind as clean as possible.

Cabbage with Milk.

Those who usually find cabbage an unpleasantly indigestible article of food, will be gratified with the result of the following mode of cooking it:

Cut half of a solid head of cabbage fine as for slaw.

Have a deep spider on the fire and hot. Put in your cabbage, pour quickly over it a pint of boiling water, cover close, and cook for ten minutes; then pour off the water that remains and add half a pint of rich milk. When the milk boils up, stir in a teaspoonful of flour moistened with a little cream or milk, a sprinkle of salt, and cook the flour a minute, then dish up.

This closely resembles cauliflower, and is much cheaper.

Novel Mode of Making Coffee.

Soyer strongly advises his readers to give a trial to coffee made in this way:

Put two ounces of ground coffee into a stewpan, which set upon the fire, stirring the powder round with a spoon until quite hot, when pour over a pint of boiling water; cover over closely for five minutes, when strain it through a cloth, rinse out the stewpan, pour the coffee, which will be quite clear, back into it, place it on the fire, and when nearly boiling serve with hot milk.

When the milkman fails to bring the milk or cream in the morning, a very good *substitute* for it may be made by beating the white of an egg to a froth, putting in it a very small lump of butter, and mixing well. If perfectly mixed, it is said to be an excellent substitute for cream.

It is well known that the Turks excel in making coffee. They never grind the berry, but beat or crush it with wooden pestles in mortars. When the pestles have been long used, they become precious and are sold at high prices.

Brillat Savarin says he determined to examine and test the question whether grinding or beating in a mortar produced the best coffee; and having taken equal weights of each and treated them precisely alike, he found that the coffee that had been beaten in a mortar was far better than that which had been ground. Any one may repeat the experiment for his or her own satisfaction.

How to Make Tea.

There are many ways of making Tea, but Professor Blot says, after many experiments and much information, he has found the following to be the best:

Warm the teapot, either by pouring boiling water in and emptying it, or by placing it on a corner of the range. Then put good tea into it (the quantity to be according to the strength and the quantity you want), and pour boiling water on the leaves, just enough to wet them; leave thus about one minute, then pour on all the water you want.

Let it steep no longer *than six minutes and not less than four minutes* before drawing it. If allowed to steep longer than six minutes, all the astringency of the tea is extracted and it acts, with bad effect, on the nervous system, besides losing most of the aroma.

Chemists and physiologists generally recommend black tea for not affecting the nervous system so much as green tea.

Other authorities on cookery recommend *boiling black tea* for about fifteen minutes, and state that it greatly improves the flavor.

Soyer has a somewhat different method of making tea. He says: Pour the dry tea into the pot a quarter of an hour before you are ready to use it, warm both tea and pot for that length of time, then fill with boiling water and leave it draw from three to five minutes, when it is quite ready.

Points about Chocolate.

Chocolate deserves a higher place in the regard of the American people than it has obtained, and is especially suitable for literary men, lawyers and persons with feeble stomachs. A French authority says, to make it fit for immediate use, about an ounce and a half should be taken for each cup, which should be slowly dissolved in water while it is heated, and stirred from time to time with a spatula of wood. It should be boiled a quarter of an hour in order to give it consistency, and served up hot.

"Monsieur," said Madame d'Austel, "when you wish good chocolate, make it the evening before in a tin-pot. The rest of the night gives it a velvet-like flavor that makes it far better. God will not be offended at this little refinement, for in himself is all excellence."

How to Prepare Salads, etc.

Mrs. Warren's method of washing greens, etc., will astonish other cooks beside her own. She says:

"First, I had a pan of warm water rather more than tepid, and a second of cold water. After having carefully picked the refuse leaves from some cabbages which the rain and hot sun intervening had covered with insects, I first took the worst part of the leaves and put two or three in the warm water to show the girl how readily the insects fell off, leaving the leaf clean. Her eyes dilated as if I had been a conjurer. So fresh hot water was had for the cabbages, *each small head was washed singly,* and then put into cold water; and in the warm water each worm and snail and grub found instantly a watery grave. I would here remark that if greens or lettuces are washed in a mass, and not *each singly,* the process is of little avail, yet better than washing them in cold water. No vegetables lose their crispness, or if for a moment they do, it is instantly restored by the necessary act of plunging them into cold water. Who has not had their teeth set on edge by eating gritty spinach, sea-kale, celery, or leeks, which need not have happened if the cook had only known that to wash these things *in two waters that are warm* and *then immediately to lay them in cold for an hour,* much trouble and time would have been saved. This is one bit of comfort, a knowledge of which cannot be too widely known."

Remember always to boil greens with a small piece of baking soda, in plenty of boiling water and salt.

Garnishes.

Much of the palatableness of food depends on the style in which it is served up. Parsley is the general garnish for all kinds of cold meat, poultry, fish, etc.; and slices of lemon for boiled fowl, turkey, fish and roast veal.

Carrots in slices should accompany boiled beef, hot or cold.

Fried sausages or forcemeat balls are placed around roasted turkey, capon or fowl.

Currant jelly is the garnish for game, and mint, either with or without parsley, for roast lamb, either hot or cold.

> Always have lobster sauce with salmon,
> And put mint sauce your roasted lamb on;
> In venison gravy, currant jelly,
> Mix with old port—see Francatelli;
> In dressing salad, mind this law,
> With two hard yelks, use one that's raw;
> Roast veal, with rich stock gravy serve,
> And pickled mushrooms, too, observe;
> Roast pork, sans apple sauce, past doubt
> Is "Hamlet," with the Prince left out;
> Boiled turkey, gourmands know, of course
> Is exquisite with celery sauce;
> The cook deserves a hearty cuffing
> Who serves roast fowls with tasteless stuffing.

Drawn or Melted Butter.

The foundation of many of the principal sauces is melted butter; and an English lawyer, it is said, in hiring a cook, asked but one question—how she made melted butter; and if her answer was satisfactory, she was engaged; if not, she was rejected. Where expense is not considered, this is made of two-thirds butter and one-third of cream, warmed gradually with a box spoon; but for families in ordinary circumstances, Soyer gives the following recipe:

Take two ounces of butter, and two ounces of flour, half a teaspoonful of salt, a quarter that of pepper, mixed together with a spoon, put into a quart pan, with a pint of cold water; place it on the fire and stir continually until it begins to simmer, then add one more ounce of butter and stir till melted. This melted butter is fit to serve at the best tables, by adding three ounces of butter. Take as a guide, that the back of the spoon, on being removed, should always be covered with the butter or sauce.

Many good housekeepers are sorely puzzled at times to know what to cook for a variety; they are tired of the same things everlastingly boiled, stewed and fried, and it would be a good plan to have on the reverse side of the Illuminated Kitchen Monitor before recommended, a comprehensive list of food articles, or Bill of Fare that would suggest something that would relieve their perplexity. It is often difficult to know what to cook for children and for delicate and sick persons; and a list like the following would often be useful for reference:

Food for the Sick.

Beef tea, oatmeal or Indian gruel, chicken, mutton, veal or calves' feet broth, arrowroot custard, milk toast, boiled rice, sago or tapioca milk, baked apples, panada, breast of partridge or pigeon, minced fine and stewed. Beef, rumpsteak, broiled ten minutes or less.

Food for Young Children.

Milk, scalded or boiled, mixed with farina or barley; rusks or stale bread warmed, pressed and mixed with sugar; crushed white wheat; Graham bread or crackers; rare beef, and well-boiled mutton; tender roast or boiled chicken, minced fine; mealy old or dry sweet potatoes; young onions boiled in two waters; simple custard, and rice or farina pudding; inner part of a well-roasted apple; soft-boiled eggs. No veal or pork, or fried meats generally.

Food for Sedentary and Delicate Persons.

Eggs, fried or poached, or soft boiled, or in omelet. Beef, veal, chicken, guinea fowl; boiled or hashed calf's head; veal cutlets broiled in papers or with cauliflower, or broccoli; roast fowl, with water-cresses; broiled partridge; asparagus, with drawn butter; green peas, macaroni, julienne or hare soups; boiled rice, oysters, roast apples, boiled fish, except eels, skate or cuttle fish. No pork, sucking pig, ducks, geese, smoked or salted meats, or fat and greasy things generally.

Standard Breakfast Dishes.

Dry or milk toast, toasted muffins, rolls, hot cakes, buns, and rusks, corn bread, fried mush, fried hominy, waffles and catfish, mackerel salt or fresh, haddock, small whitefish, boiled, fried or poached eggs, ham and eggs, omelet, beefsteak, pork and mutton chops, sausages, frizzled beef, hashed kidneys on toast, bacon, sausages, potatoes and cream, fried potatoes, fried or broiled chicken.

Dishes for Sunday Dinners, to Save Cooking.

Pea, spring, white or tapioca soup; cold roast beef with horseradish, or roast mutton with salad, or broiled fowls with mushroom sauce; hashed duck and green peas; giblet soup and calf's-head pie; macaroni and cheese; baked cod or boiled pike stuffed; fruit fritters, apple tart, boiled custard; pudding, cold; apple pie, cheese cakes, Welsh rare-bits; creams, syllabubs, tipsy cake, trifles. Many of these dishes can be entirely or partly prepared on the preceding day.

There is such a lamentable lack of brains among all classes in the world, that if there be any food which will make brains, it is very important that all of us should know of it and partake of it. Dr. Lambort asserts that all of the following articles contain brain-making elements, and has outlined a bill of fare to show that a dinner may be prepared from them alone, which epicures would not disdain.

Relish (Russian Fashion):
Toasted Crackers and Toasted Cheese.
Second Course:
Oysters on Half-shell and Cold Cabbage.
Third Course:
Sardines.
Fourth Course:
Cod-fish and Cream.
Fifth Course:
Oyster-Salad.
Sixth Course:
Stewed Tripe and Green Peas.
Seventh Course:
Calves' Brains on Toast.
Bread:
Graham, French Rolls, Oat, Graham Meal Crackers, and Milk Biscuit.
Dessert:
Oat Groats and Cream.
Pancakes:
Oat, Buckwheat, and Graham Meal.
Boiled Custard.

Fruit:
Apples and Oranges.

Drinks.
Coffee, Buttermilk.

CHAPTER X.

DAINTY DISHES FOR DAINTY PALATES.

"The art of cookery consists in exciting the taste. To excite a stomach of papier-maché, and enliven vital powers almost ready to depart, a cook needs more talents than he who has solved the infinitesimal calculus."—SAVARIN.

1. DOMESTIC COOKERY.

WE are now approaching that mysterious realm known as "high-class cookery," but we do not propose to enter very far within its precincts. It is surmised by some, that many of the dishes prepared by the French professors of the culinary art are not what they seem, and that often rich and highly-flavored sauces disguise what in itself is not very savory or palatable. But before we approach the great oracles of this branch of cookery, to inquire what foundation of truth this suspicion rests upon, or to ask those who compound the dishes that grace banquets and astonish epicures to disclose some of the secrets of their art, we propose to dwell for a while in still more pleasant company, and inquire how the most skilful of American and English wives and mothers prepare those familiar yet dainty dishes that are among the most valued of HOME COMFORTS.

First of all, as the English are celebrated for their roast beef, we have requested Mr. BOYCE, of London, to tell our readers

How to Roast Beef, English Style.

Roasting—that is, cooking by the direct heat of the fire (in front of, and not over the fire, which constitutes broiling)—is characteristic of English cooking, as much as stewing or sautéing is of French cookery, or frying and baking of American, and though the interchange of ideas is breaking up the old distinctions, we can still enjoy the idea that the Englishman looks down upon French dishes as kickshaws and messes, while the French cook still boasts, that

> From an old shoe,
> He could make a *ragoût*,
> That should beat the roast beef of Old England.
> The glorious old English roast beef.

The first point of importance is to select beef of the very best quality, and, whether it be the fillet, ribs, or sirloin, see that the fat and lean are mingled, so that the clean cut seems marbled, that it is free from much sinew, which would indicate age, and that the outside fat show of a rich color, which denotes good feeding and proper maturity.

Beef for roasting should be kept some days before being used, or as long as it is possible to keep it without salting, for no salt should touch beef until it is cooked; and then the first thing to notice is, that the fire must burn perfectly clear and bright. In England, bituminous coal is used, and ranges are made capable of being widened or contracted, with the bars running horizontally, and the fire usually extends beyond the meat, so that the ends of the joint may be properly cooked. A Dutch oven is most generally used, the spit passing through, and receiving its motion from machinery, as previously described in the

American tin kitchen, a flap at the back giving access for basting.

Having a good fire, burning bright and close up to the bars of the grate, proceed to spit the sirloin, exercising caution to spit it evenly, so that it balances, or the spit will turn more quickly at one time than another, and the meat not be cooked evenly. A cradle spit is sometimes used to obviate this. Pin some thin writing paper over the outside fat, and pour some water in the dripping-pan to commence basting with. Push the meat up close to the fire for a few minutes, until a slight crust forms, which will tend to keep the rich juices from escaping; then draw about ten or twelve inches away until nearly done, when the paper is removed, and the joint brought near the fire to brown it.

The length of time required for cooking thoroughly averages a quarter of an hour to each pound in weight: a sirloin weighing fifteen pounds requiring three hours and a half; but meat from an old animal takes longer to cook, and in winter longer time must be allowed, and very fat meat requires time to cook it thoroughly.

Rub a little butter or fresh dripping over the meat before spitting, in order to supply dripping to baste with—water alone not being sufficient—and baste very often, as on this much of the success of roasting depends. When the meat is nearly done, dredge over it some flour that has been browned by baking, and a little salt, and as soon as a rich brown is obtained, and steam rises from the joint, it is sufficiently cooked.

Perfection in roasting is very difficult, and only by observation and experience can success be attained to, as many things, such as age, size (especially the thickness) of the joint, the kitchen conveniences, the time of serving, etc., have to be considered, and only when everything favors can the cook expect the praise that "it was done to a turn."

Roast beef should be sent to the table as soon as it is done; the dish should be very hot, and only a small quantity of rich and rather thick gravy should be made, for as soon as the joint is cut, the juices will add sufficient to the gravy to supply all the diners. A dish with a well for the gravy should always be used. The under side of the sirloin is sometimes called the *lumbar*, and is the most delicious part; it is usually served to the ladies, a good carver reserving some for the lady of the house.

Roast Canvas-back Ducks.

Nearly all wild ducks are liable to have a fishy flavor, and, when handled by inexperienced cooks, are sometimes uneatable from this cause. Before roasting them, guard against this by *parboiling them, with a small carrot, peeled*, put within each. This will absorb the unpleasant taste. An onion will have the same effect; but unless you mean to use onion in the stuffing, the carrot is preferable.

After parboiling as directed, throw away the carrot or onion, lay in fresh water half an hour, stuff with bread crumbs seasoned with pepper, salt, sage, and onion, and roast until brown and tender, basting half the time with butter and water, then with the drippings. Add to the gravy, when you have taken up the ducks, a tablespoonful of currant jelly and a pinch of Cayenne pepper. Thicken with browned flour, and serve in a tureen.

Game, as a general rule, is best if kept for about three days; but when time cannot be afforded, some persons think that, by burying it in the ground for a few hours, it becomes more tender. Most cooks roll game in strips of bacon before roasting it, but buttered paper is preferable, as bacon spoils the flavor of delicate birds like woodcock. A hare or rabbit, when roasting, should be basted with cream and dredged with flour.

Barbecued Rabbit or Squirrel. HARLAND.

Clean and wash the rabbit, which must be plump and young, and having opened it all the way on the under side, lay it flat, with a small plate or saucer to keep it down, in salted water for half an hour. Wipe dry and broil whole, with the exception of the head, when you have gashed across the backbone in eight or ten places, that the heat may penetrate this, the thickest part. Your fire should be hot and clear, the rabbit turned often. When browned and tender, lay upon a very hot dish, pepper and salt and butter profusely, turning the rabbit over and over to soak up the melted butter. Cover and set in the oven for five minutes, and heat in a tin cup two tablespoonfuls of vinegar, seasoned with one of made mustard. Anoint the hot rabbit well with this, cover, and send to table garnished with crisped parsley.

The odor of this barbecue is most appetizing, and the taste not a whit inferior. Squirrels may be barbecued in the same manner.

Broiled Pigeons or Squabs.

Young pigeons, or "squabs," are rightly esteemed a great delicacy. They should be cleaned, washed, and dried carefully with a clean cloth; then split down the back, and broiled like chickens. Season with pepper and salt, and butter liberally in dishing them. They are in great request in a convalescent room, being peculiarly savory and nourishing.

Broiled Beefsteak, Wakefield Style.

Cut a steak an inch thick; score it on each side crosswise. Put into a tart-dish two teaspoonfuls of salt, one of pepper, one of sugar, a teaspoonful of chopped tarragon, a tablespoonful of some good relish or sauce, two tablespoonfuls of vinegar; put the steak in it for six hours; turn it now and then. This seasoning is called *marinade*. Previous to broiling, dredge it slightly with flour while doing, and serve with butter in very small pieces under the steak. Some raw potatoes, cut into very thin slices and nicely fried, and served as a garnish, renders it a dish fit for the most fastidious epicure.

Roasted Guinea Fowls

are a dainty dish, very little known to American farmers, who keep them chiefly for their plumage and their eggs, which are far richer than those of chickens. For roasting, they should not be more than twelve months old. They are trussed like common fowls, larded, and served plain roasted, rather well done. Season the gravy with a chopped shallot, parsley, or summer savory, not omitting the minced giblets, and thickened with browned flour. Currant, or some other tart jelly, is a suitable accompaniment for this fowl.

Veal Cutlets, with Tomatoes or Oysters.

Wash the cutlets, season them with pepper and salt, dip in cracker dust and fry in equal portions of lard and butter until they are of a nice brown on both sides, and when done, take them up on a dish.

Also, stew about a quarter of a peck of tomatoes, drain, mash, and season with red pepper and salt. Pour the tomatoes into the pan with the gravy, after the cutlets have been dished, and stir well together. Pour this over the cutlets, and send to table hot. This dish is very much liked by many persons.

In the place of tomatoes, some take oysters, pan them, season with salt and Cayenne pepper, and pour them over the cutlets, which are served hot, in a covered dish.

How to Cook Sweetbreads. WIDDIFIELD.

Take one or more sweetbreads, wash, and put them into a stew-pan, and let them boil five or ten minutes; then put them in cold water, and when cool, skin, but not break, them; then season with salt and pepper, dredge over a little flour, and fry slowly in butter a light brown on both sides. For persons slightly indisposed, these may be served with potatoes, mashed with a little cream, and seasoned with salt to taste.

The French cooks prepare sweetbreads as above; then place them on a dish, remove all the brown particles from the pan, retaining the butter, and pour over them a gravy made by dredging in a gill of boiling water a dessert-spoonful of browned flour, stirring all the time, seasoning to taste, and adding gradually two tablespoonfuls of Madeira wine. While boiling hot, this is poured over the sweetbreads, which are sent to the table in a well-heated covered dish.

Baked Salmon Trout. HARLAND.

Marion Harland becomes rapturously enthusiastic when she thinks of the salmon trout she ate in the Adirondacks, *baked with cream.* Her recipe for cooking the fish in this way, when divested of its "bathos," is as follows:

Handle the beauty carefully and lay in a baking-pan, with just enough water to keep him from scorching. Bake slowly, basting often with butter and water. By the time it is done, have ready in a saucepan a cup of cream—diluted with a few spoonfuls of hot water, lest it should clot in heating—in which has been stirred cautiously two tablespoonfuls of melted butter and a little chopped parsley. Heat this in a vessel set within another of boiling water, add the gravy from the dripping-pan, boil up once to thicken; and when the trout is laid in state in a hot dish, pour the sauce around him. Salt him lightly, should he need it, but let no sharply-spiced sauces come near him. Eat, and be happy.

Brook trout form a rarely delightful breakfast or supper dish. They should be fried quickly in hot fat or fine olive oil, without seasoning, and taken out instantly they are a delicate brown, and placed for a few seconds upon a hot folded napkin, to absorb whatever grease may cling to their speckled sides. This simple dish, says Savarin, duly sprinkled with slices of lemons, is worthy to be offered to a cardinal.

Roasted or Broiled Rail or Reed Birds

are a dainty dish. Skilled cooks roll an oyster in melted butter, then in bread crumbs seasoned with pepper and salt, and put this into each bird before roasting. Then baste with butter and water three times, put layers of toast underneath, and, while roasting, baste freely with melted butter. About twelve minutes will be required to cook these birds in this way, and they will be found a dainty dish indeed.

Roast Pig and Apple Sauce.

Charles Lamb claims that, of all the delicacies in the eatable world, the most delicate is a young tender suckling of a pig roasted. It must be *roasted*, not seethed or boiled. He says: "There is no flavor comparable, I will contend, to that of the crisp, tawny, well-watched, not over-roasted, *crackling*, as it is well called; the very teeth are invited to their share of the pleasure of this banquet in overcoming the coy, brittle resistance, with the adhesive oleaginous—oh, call it not fat—but an indefinable sweetness growing up to it, the tender blossoming of fat—fat cropped in the bud—fat and lean so blended, and running into each other, that both together make but one ambrosial result or common substance."

For very young roast pig, the best sauce is probably a few bread crumbs, done up with the liver and brains, and a dash of mild sage. For roast pork, *browned flour* is said to be the best for gravies. *Apple sauce* is the proper accompaniment.

To Make a Haunch of Mutton Eat like Venison.

Mix two ounces of bay salt with half a pound of brown sugar; rub it well into the mutton, which should be placed in a deep dish for four days, and basted three or four times a day with the liquor that drains from it; then wipe it quite dry, and rub in a quarter of a pound more sugar, mixed with a little common salt, and hang it up, haunch downwards; wipe it daily till it is used. In winter, it should be kept three weeks and roasted in paste, like venison. Serve with currant jelly.

Oysters Broiled on the Shell. LYMAN.

Perhaps no dish is able to give more epicurean delight than this, if well managed. It is just the thing for a night supper, or for an elegant breakfast.

Select as many dozen as you have guests. They should

be large, and the shells of good shape. Clean them with a stiff brush, and open, saving the juice. Throw the oysters into boiling water, and let them remain a minute or two, according to size. Take out, and lay at once on one half of the shell, and place on a gridiron over a brisk fire. As soon as the oyster begins to broil in the shell, season with butter, pepper, and a drop of lemon juice. Serve hot on the shell.

French Stewed Oysters. Leslie.

Wash fifty fine large oysters in their own liquor; then strain it into a stewpan, putting the oysters in a pan of cold water. Season the liquor with a large glass or half a pint of white wine (sherry or Madeira), the juice of two lemons, six or seven blades of mace, and a small grated nutmeg. Boil the seasoned liquor, and skim and stir it well. When it comes to a boil, put in the oysters. Give them one good stir, and then immediately take them from the fire, transfer them to a deep dish, and send them to table. They are not to boil.

Many persons consider this the finest way of cooking oysters for company.

Chicken Dressed as Terrapin.

Boil a fine, large, tender chicken; when done, and while yet warm, cut it from the bones into small pieces, as for chicken salad; put it into a stewpan, with one gill of boiling water; then stir together, until perfectly smooth, one-quarter of a pound of butter, one teaspoonful of flour, and the yelk of one egg, which add to the chicken, half at a time, stirring all well together; then season with salt and pepper. After letting it simmer about ten minutes, add half a gill of Madeira wine, and send to table hot.

This is liked by many who are not fond of terrapins.

French Pot-au-Feu. SOYER.

In France, no dinner is served without soup, and no good soup is supposed to be made without the *pot-au-feu*, it being the national dish of the middle and poorer classes of that country. The following is Soyer's receipt for making it:

Put into an earthen pipkin six pounds of beef, four quarts of water; set near the fire; skim. When nearly boiling, add a spoonful and a half of salt, half a pound of liver, two carrots, four turnips, eight young or two old leeks, one head of celery, two onions, and one roasted, with a clove in each, and a piece of parsnip; skim again, and let simmer four or five hours, adding a little cold water now and then; take off a part of the fat, put slices of bread into the tureen, lay half the vegetables over, and half the broth, and serve the meat separate, with the vegetables around.

Eggs and Cheese

are a favorite dish in Italy, and also in Switzerland, where the recipe originated. Beat well six eggs, and put them in a stewpan, with two ounces of well-grated Gruyère cheese and about one ounce of butter; set on a brisk fire, and leave till it becomes rather thick, stirring all the time with a wooden spoon; take from the fire, add pepper, and stir a little; turn over on a warm dish, and serve.

French Omelets,

mixed with sliced apples fried, or with asparagus boiled and chopped fine, or chopped parsley, were so much of a favorite with General Washington, that he often had them served on his table when he gave presidential dinners.

The following is Prof. Blot's recipe for making a plain omelet:

Beat well, say eight eggs, with salt and pepper, by means of a fork; then put about two ounces of butter in a frying-pan; set on a brisk fire and toss gently, to melt the butter as evenly and as quickly as possible, else some of it will get black before the whole is melted. As soon as melted, turn the beaten eggs in, and stir continually with a fork or knife, so as to cook the whole as nearly as possible at the same time. If some part of the omelet sticks to the pan, add a little butter, and raise that part with a knife, so as to allow the butter to run under it and prevent it from sticking again. It must be done quickly, and without taking the pan from the fire. When cooked according to taste, either soft or hard—that is, when only about two-thirds of the eggs are solidified, or nearly the whole—turn or fold one-half of the omelet over the other, and serve warm.

When it is ready to be folded, you may pour on the middle of it five or six tablespoonfuls of cooked kidney, and you have omelet with kidney; or spread the surface with stewed tomatoes, or two or three tablespoonfuls of any kind of jam or sweetmeats, then fold and serve. By using different kinds of sweetmeats, a great variety of omelets can be made.

The adding of milk to the eggs makes an omelet soft.

To make a *sweet omelet*, beat four eggs in a basin, add a tablespoonful of milk, a teaspoonful of sugar, a pinch of salt, and beat them well up; put some nice butter into a pan, put in the eggs, and fry as above described. Serve with sugar sifted over.

A very good omelet may be made of two yelks of eggs and one white, a tablespoonful of cream, a little minced parsley and shallot, and a very little nutmeg. Whisk all well together, and fry in as little butter as possible.

A Swiss Rare-bit. M. TROLLET.

Take as many eggs as you wish, according to the number of your guests, and weigh them. Then take a piece of cheese weighing a third of the weight of the eggs, and a slice of butter weighing a sixth. Beat the eggs well up in a saucepan, grate the cheese, or chop very small, and place the saucepan, with the eggs, cheese and butter in it, over a good fire, stir with a flat spoon until the mixture becomes sufficiently thick and soft, add a little salt and a large proportion of pepper—this being one of the principal points of the rare-bit—and serve it up in a warm dish.

A Welsh Rare-bit. ENGLISH RECIPE.

A genuine Welsh rare-bit is made of Welsh cheese—a certain kind only, and prepared for that purpose—melted to a certain degree, and then spread on toast of Welsh bread. The nearest approach to the genuine that can be had here is the following:

Grate some Gloucester or Gruyère cheese, and pepper it with Cayenne pepper. Fry some slices of bread with a little butter, but on one side only, until perfectly yellow; then spread a thick coat of grated cheese on the fried side of the bread, place the slices in a baking-pan, put them in a pretty warm oven, take off when the cheese begins to melt, and serve warm.

How to Cook Mushrooms. SOYER.

Mushrooms are regarded by some as the choicest of delicacies, while others denounce them as "a contemptible, rank-smelling fungus." Soyer calls them the pearl of the fields, and says, if Apicius had known of them, he would not have gone to Greece for crawfish, or committed suicide. His recipe for cooking them is as follows:

Toast slices of bread, cut half an inch thick, and large enough to cover the bottom of a plate, and spread over these some rich cream, or milk boiled until it is reduced to the consistency of cream. Remove all the earthy part from the mushrooms, and lay them gently on the toast, head downwards, slightly sprinkle them with salt and pepper, and place in each a little of the clotted cream, cover with a basin, and place in the oven for half an hour.

Another recipe for *stewing* mushrooms is:

Rub them white, stew in water ten minutes, strain partially, and cover with as much warm milk as you have poured off water; stew five minutes in this; salt, pepper, and add some veal or chicken gravy, or drawn butter. Thicken with a little flour, wet in cold milk, and a beaten egg.

A Good Sauce for Every Kind of Fish,

baked, boiled, or roasted. Prof. Blot's recipe:

Boil hard two eggs, take the yelks and pound them well, and place them in a bowl. Have boiling water on the fire, and put in it four or five sprigs each of civès, burnet, chervil, tarragon, and parsley; boil five minutes, take off, drain, and pound them well; then strain them on the eggs, add two tablespoonfuls of cider vinegar, two of French mustard, salt, pepper, and four tablespoonfuls of sweet oil, which you pour in, little by little, at the same time mixing the whole well with a boxwood spoon, and it is ready for use.

A Clam-Chowder. HARLEM RIVER BOATMEN.

Clam-chowder is made in a hundred different ways, but it is generally admitted that the boatmen on the Harlem river make the best:

Put in a pot some small slices of fat salt pork, enough to line the bottom of it; on that a layer of potatoes, cut in small pieces; on the potatoes a layer of chopped onions; on the onions a layer of tomatoes in slices, or canned tomatoes; on these a layer of clams, whole or chopped (they are generally chopped), then a layer of crackers. Season with salt and pepper, and other spices if desired. Then repeat this process, layer after layer, in above order, seasoning each, until the pot is nearly full. When the whole is in, cover with water, set on a slow fire, and when nearly done, stir gently, finish cooking, and serve.

When done, if found too thin, boil a little longer; if found too thick, add a little water, give one boil, and serve.

Fish-chowder is made exactly as clam-chowder, using fish instead of clams.

Clam-Bake. RILEY.

The experienced Harlem river clam baker, Tom Riley, is the authority for the following recipe:

Lay the clams on a *rock*, edge downward, and forming a circle; cover them with fine brush; cover the brush with dry sage; cover the sage with larger brush; set the whole on fire, and when a little more than half burnt (brush and sage), look at the clams by pulling some out, and if done enough brush the fire, cinders, etc., off; mix some tomato or cauliflower sauce or catsup with the clams, minus their shells; add butter and spices to taste, and serve.

Done in sand, the clams, on opening, naturally allow the sand to get in, and it is anything but pleasant for the teeth while eating them.

A Wholesome Summer Salad.   Soyer.

Cut up a pound of cold beef into thin slices, and half a pound of white fresh lettuce; put in a salad bowl, season with a teaspoonful of salt, half that quantity of pepper, two spoonfuls of vinegar, and four of good salad oil; stir all together lightly with a fork and spoon, and when well mixed, it is ready to serve.

Chaptal, a French chemist, says the dressing of a salad should be saturated with oil, and seasoned with pepper and salt, before the vinegar is added. It results from this process, that there can never be too much vinegar; for from the specific gravity of the vinegar compared with the oil, what is more than useful will fall to the bottom of the bowl. The salt should not be dissolved in the vinegar, but in the oil, by which means it is more equally distributed throughout the salad. A Spanish proverb says, To make a perfect salad, there should be a miser for oil, a spendthrift for vinegar, a wise man for salt, and a madcap to stir the ingredients up and mix them well together.

Strawberries, with Orange Juice.   Parkinson.

Place a layer of strawberries into a deep dish; cover the same with a liberal supply of very finely pulverized sugar; add another layer of berries; then the same quantity of sugar. Now another layer of fruit and sugar, alternately, until you have the desired quantity. Express over the whole the juice of half a dozen sweet oranges. Let the whole stand for half an hour. Now serve, and let the partaker thank the gods!

To those who have never tried this method, it will afford a delightful surprise to note how much more fully it brings out the fine flavor of the strawberry; and much of which effect is due to the delicate flavor of the orange.

I will now give another expedient for heightening the flavor of strawberries and cream. Prepare in every respect as above described, as to alternate layers of berries and sugar, and substitute for the orange juice half a pint of pure claret wine. In default of claret of known purity, use the same quantity of our best native or home-made wines. Our home-made currant wine is admirable for bringing out in fuller force the delicious native flavor of the strawberry.

An Excellent Custard. Mrs. Freedley.

Take a pint of milk, four eggs, and a cup of sugar. Put the milk on to boil, and beat together the yelks of the eggs and the sugar until very light. When the milk has boiled, pour it by degrees over the eggs and sugar, stirring constantly and return to the fire. Watch carefully, so as to remove when it has just begun to boil, and set off to cool. Flavor to suit the taste. Beat up the whites of the eggs into a light froth, and pour it over the custard.

Very Fine Cold Cup Custard. Widdifield.

One quart of new milk, one pint of cream, a quarter of a pound of fine white sugar, three large tablespoonfuls of wine in which rennet has been soaked.

Mix the milk, cream and sugar together, stir the wine into it, pour the mixture into custard cups, and set them away until the milk becomes a curd. Grate nutmeg on the top, and eat them with cream that has been kept on ice.

The Queen of Puddings. HARLAND.

One and a half cups of white sugar, two cups fine dry bread-crumbs, five eggs, one tablespoonful of butter, vanilla, rose-water or lemon flavoring, one quart fresh rich milk, and one half cup jelly or jam.

Rub the butter into a cup of sugar, beat the yelks very light, and stir these together to a cream. The bread-crumbs, soaked in milk, come next, then the flavoring. Bake in a buttered pudding dish—a large one and but two-thirds full—until the custard is "set." Draw to the mouth of the oven, spread over with jam or other nice fruit conserve. Cover this with a méringue made of the whipped whites and half a cup of sugar. Shut the oven, and bake until the méringue begins to color. Eat cold, with cream. You may, in strawberry season, substitute the fresh fruit for preserves. It is then truly delightful.

An Elegant Bread Pudding.

Take light white bread, and cut it in thin slices. Put into a pudding mould a layer of any sort of preserve, then a slice of bread, and repeat until the mould is almost full. Pour over all a pint of warm milk in which four beaten eggs have been mixed, cover the mould with a piece of linen, place it in a saucepan with a little boiling water, let it boil twenty minutes, and serve with pudding sauce.

A Pleasant Fruit Dessert. PROF. BLOT.

Beat well the white of an egg with a little water, dip the fruit—whether currants, blackberries, or other fruit—in, and roll it immediately in some fine crushed sugar, place it on a dish, and leave it thus five or six hours, and serve.

A more sightly and exquisite dessert, he says, than a plate of currants dressed thus, cannot be had.

An Excellent Dish of Apples.   Frost.

Take two pounds of apples, pare and core them, slice them into a pan, add one pound of loaf sugar, the juice of three lemons and the grated rind of one. Let these boil about two hours, turn it into a mould, and serve with custard or cream.

An Improved Apple Sauce.

Take sweet cider, as soon as it comes from the press, boil it down nearly one-half, then pare and quarter as many of the best sour apples as you wish to "do up," cover them with the cider when boiling hot, and cook until well done, but not so as to lose their shape. Most of the cider will be absorbed by the apples; what remains can be bottled for future use. When done, put into jars, and cover or cement. This makes not only a most delicious sauce, but it is also very healthful, as all the nourishment of the apples from which the cider is made is retained, while we lose the sharp, biting taste of the old *apple butter* made from boiled cider.

A Nice Breakfast Dish.

Grate some cold tongue or beef, put it into a stewpan with a little pepper and salt, and four tablespoonfuls of cream or milk; when quite hot, put in four well-beaten eggs, stir all the time till the mixture is quite thick; have ready some nicely toasted bread, well buttered, and spread the tongue or beef over it; send to the table hot.

A Farmer's Dainty Dish.

Peel and slice thin potatoes and onions (five potatoes to one small onion), take half a pound of sweet salt pork in thin slices to a pound of beef, mutton or veal, cut the meat in small pieces, take some nice bread dough and shorten a little, and line the bottom of the stewpan with slices of pork, then a layer of meat, potatoes and onions, dust over a little pepper, and cover with a layer of crust; repeat this until the stewpot is full—the size of the pot will depend on the number in the family; pour in sufficient water to cover, finish with crust. Let it simmer till meat, vegetables, etc., are done, but do not let it boil hard. Serve hot. This, we are assured by one who knows, is a dish fit to set before a king, or his peer—a farmer.

Green Corn Fritters or Cakes. HARLAND.

Grate green corn from the cob, and allow an egg and a half for every cupful, with a tablespoonful of milk or cream; beat the eggs well, add the corn by degrees, beating very hard, salt to taste, put a tablespoonful of melted butter to every pint of corn, stir in the milk, and thicken with just enough flour to hold them together—say a tablespoonful for every two eggs. You may fry in hot lard, as you would fritters, or cook upon a griddle, like batter cakes. Eaten at dinner or breakfast, these always meet with a cordial welcome.

The same authority also commends, as a most delicious accompaniment to a meat course, the annexed

Green Corn Pudding.

Take one quart milk, five eggs, two tablespoonfuls melted butter, one tablespoonful white sugar, and a dozen large ears of green corn.

Grate the corn from the cob; beat the whites and yelks of the eggs separately. Put the corn and yelks together, stir hard, and add the butter, then the milk gradually, beating all the while; next the sugar, and a little salt; lastly the whites. Bake slowly at first, covering the dish for an hour. Remove the cover, and brown finely.

Buckwheat Shortcakes.

Take three or four teacups of nice sour milk, one teaspoon of soda-saleratus dissolved in the milk; if the milk is very sour, you must use saleratus in proportion, with a little salt; mix up a dough of buckwheat flour *thicker* than you would mix for griddle cakes, say quite stiff; put into a buttered tin and then directly into the stove oven, and bake about thirty minutes, or as you would a shortcake from common flour.

Dr. Chase, of Ohio, writes strongly in favor of the excellence of this cake, and says he could eat it while dyspeptic, when he could eat no other warm bread. He is also the authority for saying that the following is

The Nicest Pie Ever Eaten.

Peel sour apples, and stew until soft and not much water left in them, then rub them through a colander, beat three eggs for each pie to be baked, and put in at the rate of one cup of butter and one of sugar for three pies; flavor with nutmeg. Bake as pumpkin pies, which they resemble.

Strawberry Shortcake. BEECHER.

Rub into a pint and a half of prepared flour one teacup of butter; beat one egg very light; add milk to make a soft dough; divide in three parts; roll out lightly, lay one portion on a pie plate or tin, sprinkle a little flour on the top, then add the second cake, a little flour on the top of that, and cover with the third. Bake quickly, but not too brown. Let the berries stand with sugar sprinkled over them till the cake is baked, then pull the thin portions of cake apart; spread half of the berries over the bottom cake, adding more sugar and a little butter, lay the second over them, and put on the remainder of the berries, with more sugar and butter, placing the top cake over all. Put it in the oven for a few minutes to heat through, and send to the table.

National French Cake. SOYER.

In Paris it was formerly the fashion, and perhaps is yet, for men and women, as well as children, after having witnessed a melodrama, to rush to the shops where a delicious puff-cake, called *Galette*, was sold. This celebrated cake was made as follows:

Work lightly in a basin, or on a table, one pound of flour with three-quarters of a pound of fresh butter; add two eggs, a gill of cream, and a little milk if too stiff; then add a quarter of a teaspoonful of salt, two of sugar; work all well to form a good stiff paste; throw some flour on the table, mould the paste round, roll it three-quarters of an inch thick and quite round; egg over, score it with a knife in diamonds or any other shape, bake for about half an hour in a rather hot oven, sprinkle sugar over, and serve.

A cheaper kind of *Galette* may be made by taking one pound of flour, a teaspoonful of salt, and six ounces of butter, moisten with milk, and bake as above, adding a teaspoonful of sugar.

Imperial Southern Cake. Mrs. Powell.

Mrs. J. C. Powell, skilled in the Southern style of cookery, and who has promised to revise the proof-sheets of this chapter, has contributed for the benefit of our readers the following recipes for making Imperial Southern Cake, Baltimore Tea Cake, and Southern Corn Bread and Pone.

Take one pound of sugar, one pound of flour, one pound of butter, ten eggs, one wine-glass of apple brandy, three pounds of blanched almonds, two of raisins, one pound of citron—the almonds put in whole, and the citron cut in large pieces. It will take from five to six hours to bake.

Baltimore Tea Cake.

Melt a tablespoonful of butter in a pint of milk, two spoonfuls of yeast (home-made), and flour sufficient to make a soft paste; let the dough stand three or four hours to rise, split it open, then butter, close it, slice it, and send to table hot. Grease the pan before putting in to bake.

Southern Waffles.

Take a pint and a half of flour, three eggs, two tablespoonfuls of *lightened* corn-meal dough before adding the ingredients for corn bread, or pone, one large tablespoonful of butter in milk (warmed) to make a thin batter, one teaspoonful of baking powder (Durkee's). Bake in genuine *waffle-irons*, which are *smooth* iron of a jet black, which is very hard to find, even at the foundries.

Grease the waffle-irons well. I recommend a baking powder, but the old mode was to beat the batter one hour with a ladle before putting all of the milk in it. This recipe, if followed, will make waffles that cannot be excelled.

Southern Corn Bread.

Take one pint of corn meal, pour half pint boiling water over it, then add a little salt, and with cold water reduce it to the consistency of muffin batter; place in a cool, dry cellar for twenty-four hours to lighten, for if kept in a warm place, it will sour.

Then beat three eggs, melt a piece of butter the size of a walnut, then lard the size of an egg, a cup of sweet cream, then a tablespoonful of flour; grease the pan thoroughly, bake a half hour. White corn is far preferable to yellow, and in the South is expressly cultivated for table use, and ground by water, not by steam power, as the latter mode destroys the sweetness and vitality of the grain.

The same batter may be used in rings, which will give you corn muffins, or on the griddle, which are the genuine corn cookies.

This is the best recipe known for corn bread, and next to the old Virginia Corn Pone, stands unrivalled.

Virginia Corn Pone.

Quadruple the quantities above. The material difference is in the baking, as the pone requires a longer time, and then must stand, after baking, *eight* to *ten* hours in the oven (moderately warm). *Wood embers* and a Dutch oven are requisites to a perfect Virginia pone.

An Exquisite Marmalade.

Take large ripe oranges, quarter them, remove the rind, seeds and the strings or filaments, taking care to save all the juice. Put the pulp, with the juice, into a porcelain kettle, and mix with it an equal quantity of strained honey, adding sufficient powdered loaf sugar to render it very thick and sweet. The honey alone will not make it sweet enough. Boil it uncovered, and skim till very thick, smooth and clear. Taste it, and if necessary add more sugar and boil it longer. When cold, put it up in tumblers or whiteware marmalade pots, and cover it securely. This marmalade is said to be superior to any other, and can be made when the season for other fruits is over.

Saratoga Fried Potatoes.

At the "Lake House," in Saratoga, thousands of packages of fried potatoes are sold every summer, to be carried away and eaten as a dainty. The following is said to be the method of preparing them: Wash the potatoes clean, slice with a potato-slicer very thin, throw into cold water long enough to take out some of the starch, then wipe dry and put into boiling lard, a few pieces at a time; be sure and keep the lard boiling; as soon as the potatoes are of a clear, golden brown, skim out, and drain in a colander or sieve.

[In Philadelphia potatoes are fried in the following manner:

The tools are a common cabbage-cutter, two wire sieves, and a "spider." Take say eight large potatoes, pare them and slice very thin with the cutter, soak the slices for two hours in cold water, stir into it one teaspoonful of salt to a quart, and let them remain half an hour in that. Pour them into the sieve to drain, and when well-drained wipe the slices dry; put a pound of lard into the spider, and when it becomes smoking-hot put in the potatoes. They must be constantly stirred to prevent the pieces from adhering to one another, and until they are sufficiently browned to make your mouth water, when they should be served at once.]

Delicious Mince Pies.

Take a pound of the undressed under-cut of a sirloin of beef, boil and mince it fine; drain off the fat from it thoroughly, and mix in two ounces of fresh butter, half an ounce of finely-ground allspice, four large apples pared, cored and chopped fine, half a pound raisins washed and chopped fine, half a pound currants well washed, three tablespoonfuls of moist sugar, three ounces of candied orange peel (not lemon); mix the whole of these ingredients well together, then place a half-pound preserve jar of raspberry jam in boiling water, and let it remain without uncovering the jar until the jam is dissolved; then strain the jam over the ingredients, taking care not to let the slightest portion of the seeds escape. Make paste and bake in a very quick oven. When the pies are nearly cold, lift the corner of each, and pour over the mince a small quantity of brandy. These will keep good for three weeks.

The peculiarity of these pies is, that no suet is used, which agrees but with few persons, and that the juice of the raspberries gives them an indescribable but delicious flavor.

Superior Vanilla Ice-Cream. CARVER.

The manufacture of ice-cream, as a branch of household economy, is increasing every year. The essential ingredients of all kinds are cream or rich milk, sugar, and some flavoring material, as vanilla, lemon, strawberry, or pineapple. Where milk is used, eggs are necessary, about four to two quarts of milk, and generally a tablespoonful of arrowroot, rubbed smooth in a cupful of milk, is added. The yelk of eggs is also stirred into boiled cream, where the richest quality of ice-cream is desired. But to make, say four quarts of superior vanilla ice-cream, take two quarts of pure cream, and add two-thirds of a pound of granulated white sugar; boil about half a vanilla bean, cut in small pieces, in a small quantity of milk or cream, taking care not to let it burn; after the flavor is thoroughly extracted, add the whole to the sweetened cream, and when all is thoroughly incorporated, strain into the can of the freezer, of which the best for family use is one of those patent-geared freezing apparatus turned by a crank. Full directions for their use accompany these machines, which are quite inexpensive.

Put the can into the wooden part of the freezer, and fill the space between the can and pail with broken pieces of ice about the size of a walnut, adding a handful of coarse rock salt to each layer of ice. Turn the crank until the whole is frozen, which will take about twenty minutes. Draw off the water from the pail, fill up with ice and stand away to harden. One quart of good, pure cream will make very nearly two quarts of ice-cream.

For lemon ice-cream, add the juice and grated rind of one lemon to each quart of cream, instead of the vanilla bean. For strawberry, one quart of bruised berries to four quarts of cream.

CHAPTER XI.

DAINTY DISHES FOR DAINTY PALATES.

"Among all the arts known to man there is none which enjoys a juster appreciation, and the products of which are more universally admired, than that concerned in the preparation of our food. Led by an instinct, which has almost reached the dignity of conscious knowledge, as the unerring guide, and by the sense of taste which protects the health, the experienced cook, with respect to the choice, the admixture and the preparation of food, has made acquisitions, surpassing all that chemical and physiological science has done in regard to the doctrine or theory of nutrition. In soup and meat sauces he imitates the gastric juices; and by the cheese which closes the banquet, he assists the action of the dissolved epithelium of the stomach."—LIEBIG.

2. HIGH CLASS COOKERY.

WE are now prepared to approach the professors of "high class cookery," and learn what they choose to impart to us respecting the mode of preparing those wonderful dishes of which even the names are mysterious. In some of the hotels and club-houses in the large cities, where costly banquets are often served, the chief cooks earn, in salaries and perquisites, sums greater than the salaries paid to the Judges of the Supreme Court or members of the Cabinet. In some of the fashionable restaurants in New York, dinners have been served where the flowers alone placed upon the table to garnish the viands cost fifteen hundred and even two thousand dollars. The kitchen and storehouse for provisions, in one of these hostelries, extends for a square, and so methodically arranged that, it is said, the *chef*, without a spark of light, could descend into the kitchen and lay his hand at the first trial upon any cut of meat that may be ordered, and it would be found in readiness to place upon the fire. There is as much discipline among the subordinates as on board a man-of-war, and so complete is the system that the responsibility for a bad roast, or any other error, can be fixed with absolute certainty. The dinners prepared in these places are marvels of culinary skill, as may be supposed from their cost, which sometimes exceeds fifty dollars for each person. At a famous banquet given on New Year's day by the Owl Club in New York, plates were laid for twenty persons, and the total cost was $1000, or fifty dollars per plate. The bill of fare or *menu*, consisting of a little book containing fifteen leaves, partly printed in gilt, alone cost five dollars each. But the most costly bill of fare probably ever used at a dinner, was that which a Senator from the Pacific coast, largely interested in silver mines, placed before his guests, consisting of slabs of silver on which the courses had been engraved, and each of which was worth forty-five dollars by weight. These *menus* the guests were permitted to take home with them as mementoes of their banquet.

Mr. CHARLES RANHOFER, now President of one of the societies of chief cooks in New York, and until recently the *chef* in Delmonico's celebrated restaurant, has written out for this work the recipes of some of the dishes that were invented in that establishment; and, to make the matter plain to the dullest comprehension, he has given a Bill of Fare or *menu* of a dinner for twelve persons, and then shown how some of the principal dishes were compounded:

MENU DINER POUR 12 PERS.
Potage.
Crème d'Asperges.
Poisson.
Truites de Rivière, Sauce Colbert,
Salade de Concombres,
Pommes de terre Duchesse.
Relevé.
Filet de Bœuf Salvandy.
Entrées.
Escaloppes de Volaille a l'Aquitaine,
Petits pois au beurre.
Brissotins de Ramiers au Suprême,
Haricots Verts Sautés.
Sorbet au Kirch.
Bécassines Rôties.
Letuce Salade.
Ananas Bagration,
Parfait au Café.
Fruits and Dessert.

How to Make Creme d'Asperge.

Break the stalks of one hundred green asparagus; cut them in small pieces; cook them in boiling water, with salt, in a copper sugar-pan. After they are perfectly cooked, drain them, and mash them, with a piece of butter, and pass through a sieve. Then mix a quarter of pound of flour, with quarter pound of butter, and one quart broth; stir the liquid until ebullition, with the asparagus; immediately remove it back, let it boil for about fifteen minutes. Skim the butter coming to the surface; add one quart of cream, let it come near boiling; thicken with liaison of six yelks of eggs and about a quarter pound of butter; season with salt and a pinch of sugar. Serve separately a plate of small croutons or crusts of bread cut in small dice, fried with butter.

If you want the soup to be green, pound a half peck of spinach, strain through a towel, put the liquor in a saucepan on the fire until it comes near to a boil; pour the liquid on a fine sieve, the water will pass through, and the solid part may be used to color the soup.

Truite de Riviere, Sauce Colbert.

Lay enough trout in a fish-kettle for twelve persons; put on them two carrots, four onions, all sliced, two bay-leaves, a little thyme and parsley, a few cloves, salt and pepper, and a bottle of white wine (Bordeaux) and a quart of water. Set it on the fire and boil it for a few minutes, remove it back and keep it nearly boiling for about half an hour, according to the size of your trout. Strain half the liquor and put it into another saucepan; stir the liquid to ebullition, until it is reduced to a half pint, add a little brown sauce, gradually introduce into it a half pound of fine butter divided in little bits; finish the sauce with the juice of four lemons and a spoonful of chopped parsley. At serving time drain the fish, place them on a long dish, the bottom of which is covered with a napkin; garnish all round with parsley.

Serve the sauce separately.

Pommes de terre Duchesse.

Peel some potatoes, cut them in slices, wash them, salt them, and let them boil on a brisk fire; as soon as they are nearly done, drain the water; let them remain about ten minutes in the oven; pass them through a sieve; put this purée in a sauté pan, with a little butter, salt and nutmeg; add some yelks of eggs and a little cream; make some moulds about the shape of an egg, flatten them down a little; beat one egg and spread some with a brush over the potatoes and brown in a brisk oven a few minutes before serving.

Filet de Bœuf Salvandy.

Choose a well-shaped fillet of beef, of tender, streaky flesh; after having taken away the superfluous skin and fat, the upper part is larded from one end to the other; the fillet is then placed in a baking dish, and after having been cooked it is to be placed in a long dish for serving, having underneath it a support made with a piece of bread same length and width as the fillet, and about two inches in height, fried in butter or lard. Garnish the fillet all round with stuffed tomatoes, stuffed cucumbers, and some little patties; fill with spinach; pour a little gravy on the bottom of the dish.

A good reduced brown sauce, with Malaga wine, should be served up in a sauce boat.

FILLETS OF CHICKENS, PARTRIDGES, ENGLISH PHEASANTS OR QUAILS.

Fillets of Chickens a l'Aquitaine.

Select six tender middle-sized chickens; take up the fillets, carefully trim them round on one side and pointed at the other; range them on the bottom of a sauté pan, which must be covered with clarified butter; place the fillet, in the same direction, the pointed side on the centre. Trim the *minion* fillets, make some incisions in them transversely; slip into the incisions some slices of truffles, cut slantwise; put those fillets minion on the large fillets.

Force Meat.

To make the force meat, you will use the trimming of the fillets and the legs of the chickens; trim the skin, bone and sinewy part to get about one pound; cut them into small pieces, pound them and pass through a fine sieve; put your meat in the mortar, with a half pound of panada (see panada), and pound well and add a half pound of butter and yelks of four eggs, and a half pint of cream, salt, white pepper and nutmegs.

Butter a tin or copper border mould which is flat on the top, fill it with the forced meat; set the mould on a sauté pan with warm water a half hour before serving; put your sauté pan on a slow fire without boiling; at serving time turn the border out on a dish, dress the fillet on the border and garnish the centre with Ragoût a l'Aquitaine.

Ragout a l'Aquitaine.

Put a pint of Madeira into a middle-sized saucepan, with a few pieces of Ceylon cinnamon, add one quart of brown sauce; let it boil slowly a few minutes; skim well, pass through a sieve, add some scollops of duck liver, cockscombs, fresh mushrooms, cocks' kernels, and truffles.

Panada.

Put into a small stewpan a half pint of water, and a half ounce of butter; let it boil, and then introduce enough rice-flour so as to get a rather consistent batter; dry it on the fire till it can disengage itself from the stewpan; let it cool before using it.

English Snipe.

When the snipe have been picked for trussing them, press the legs close to the side and pierce the beak through them, tie a slice of bacon over each bird, run a long skewer through the sides and tie them to the spit; roast them on a good fire for about ten minutes; in the meantime cut twelve slices of bread, fry them of a fine brown color in butter; chop fine a few chickens' livers, with a little bacon;

season with salt, pepper, nutmeg, and chopped parsley; garnish one side of the crust, bake them in a hot oven for a few minutes.

Serve them with the bread under, and some gravy.

Lettuce salad should be served at the same time with the snipe.

Sorbet au Kirch.

Make a lemon ice in the following manner: One quart syrup at 32 degrees; add the rinds of two lemons; the third part of a pint of lemon juice, a little piece of vanilla bean; and add water enough to reduce it to 20 degrees; let it macerate about two hours; strain through a fine sieve and freeze; after being frozen, add a wineglassful of kirch; mix all well together, and serve in glass.

Ananas a la Bagration.

Pare all the skin and pith of one large pine-apple; divide it first into two pieces crosswise, then in slices not too thick; put them into a kitchen basin, and cover them with boiling syrup one hour; afterward pour the pine-apple through a sieve.

Blanch a half pound of rice; boil it with milk, keeping it consistent; when it is at the degree requisite, mix into it a few spoonfuls of raw cream and a little orange peel, chopped very fine; when the liquid is absorbed, take it off the fire, introduce into it a quarter pound of butter, then dish it up in the centre of the dish; surround it with slices of pine-apple, and keep the dish warm.

Add a jar of peach marmalade to the syrup, and a little maraschino; serve the sauce separately.

Parfait au Cafe.

Whip eight yelks of eggs with a half pound of sugar; when the preparation is frothy, dilute it with a glassful of a very strong infusion of coffee; put the liquid into a copper basin tinned inside; set it on the fire, stir the liquid until it is thickened, but without allowing it to boil; pass through a fine sieve; put it again in the basin, and whip it on ice until very light; mix about one quart whipped cream which is firm and well drained; line parfait mould with a white paper inside, pack it with pounded ice and salt, pour the preparation into the packed mould, which must be covered with white paper and with the lid; spread over the lid a thick layer of salted ice, pack the preparation for one hour and a half; at serving time, dip the mould into cold water, wipe it and turn the parfait out on a folded napkin.

August Valadon, *Chef* at the St. James Hotel, New York, contributes the following original recipes:

Salad Dressing.

This sauce is made in many different ways; but the best and shortest way to make it is:

Take the yelks of two raw eggs to a pound of sweet-oil; put the yelks in a small bowl, with a little salt, white pepper and the juice of half a lemon; stir with a whip or a wooden paddle, adding little by little the sweet-oil; if it becomes too thick, soften with a drop of vinegar, and continue until the oil is exhausted. This serves for dressing any kind of salad or cold fish.

Sauces, Croquettes, etc.

Cream Sauce.—Take a half pound of butter, four ounces of flour, salt and pepper to taste; mix thoroughly; add to these one pint of cream and one pint of milk; put the mixture on the fire, and stir till it boils; add a little grated nutmeg. This is a good sauce for halibut, cod, scollops, etc.

Currie Sauce.—Take five ounces of good butter, two ounces of flour, two teaspoonfuls of India currie, Cayenne to taste, also a little nutmeg. Stir well in a saucepan, and pour in a little of the broth from the meat you want to have in currie.

Maitre d'Hotel or Steward's Sauce, Cold.—Take about a pound of good butter, put it in a bowl, mix with it some parsley and chives chopped fine, also the juice of a lemon. Serve under or on top of broiled meat or fish.

English, or Bread Sauce for Game.—Take crumbs of fine white bread, stew them in equal parts of milk and cream, well seasoned with salt, pepper and nutmeg. In fifteen minutes the sauce will be done.

Piquante Sauce.—Take a handful of shallots, chopped fine; put them in a stewpan, wet them with strong vinegar, and boil it on a hot fire until nearly dry; add some capers, pickles, parsley, chives chopped very fine. Then take another pan, and put into this four ounces of butter, and two ounces of flour; mix well, wet with a little broth, and boil for a few minutes. Mix the contents of the two pans together, and boil twenty minutes, and serve.

Rice Croquettes.—Take half a pound of rice well washed, soak in a pint of milk, season with lemon or vanilla flavor, add half a pound of sugar, a little salt, and a piece of butter the size of a walnut; cook on a slow fire; as soon as it is cooked, throw in six yelks of eggs, stir up well, pour out into a flat pan, and when cold, roll into convenient shapes, cover with egg and bread crumbs, and fry quickly in hot fat. Serve well-powdered with lemon or vanilla sugar.

Cream fried.—Take a quart of milk and boil it. Then put in another pan half a pint of cream, two ounces of corn starch, half a pound of sugar, flavor to taste, and six yelks of eggs; mix well and pour this into the boiling milk; stir all well together, and quickly pour into a flat pan to cool; cut it up into round or square pieces; bread as rice croquettes; fry and serve hot, well-powdered with sugar.

Omelette Soufflée.—Take four eggs, separate the yelks and whites; take the yelks and three ounces of powdered sugar, with some grated orange or lemon peel, beat well. Take the whites, beat them to snow, and mix the two together. Shape in a silver dish any form you like. Bake in a hot oven for twelve minutes. Sugar over and serve.

[It may be true, as the French say, that "cooking is all pleasure and no trouble;" but we apprehend that our readers will not take the same view of reading French recipes. A dainty chapter of such dainty dishes will satisfy their curiosity, as to what High Class cookery means.]

CHAPTER XII.

PRACTICAL SUGGESTIONS ON CLOTHING.

"All affectation in dress implies a flaw in the understanding."—CHESTERFIELD.

"If there is one thing in which the schoolmaster or the reformer is more wanted than in another it is in our dress. From our birth to our death we are the slaves of fashion, of prejudice, and of circumstances. The tender, unresisting infant, the delicate girl, the mature woman, alike suffer from these evil influences. Some fall victims to them; others suffer during life."—MERRIFIELD.

CLOTHING constitutes so large an item in the comfort of families and the expenses of many households, that it deserves more consideration in a work of this kind than we have space to give to it.

Nearly three centuries ago the most renowned of English dramatists wrote:

> "Costly thy habit as thy purse can buy,
> But not expressed in fancy; rich, not gaudy;
> For the apparel oft proclaims the man."

And this advice is as good and as practical to-day as when Shakspeare gave it. Thrifty housekeepers know, that to purchase materials of inferior quality for clothing because they are cheap, is not only a want of economy but gross extravagance. A rich man or woman may afford to make a mistake in the quality of a piece of cloth, but a poor man cannot afford to buy any but goods of superior quality, handsome and durable.

Buying Cloth.

"In purchasing cloth for family wear," says Lyman, "and especially for its adult members, regard should be had to the various uses to which the fabric may be put when the wearer has done with it. In this way a serviceable piece of goods may be kept on duty until it no longer hangs together, and even then its parts may be made to contribute to the family comfort in the form of a quilt, a rug, or a carpet. With this in view, it will be found that cloths of a gray or neutral color can be converted to more numerous and various uses than either black or blue. Clothing of this color will bear washing, and it cuts up for boys at a better advantage than any other. In choosing cloth for a gentleman's coat, and deciding on its cut, it is well to remember that a frock coat, while suited to a greater number of occasions than a dress coat or a sack, affords larger pieces for the pattern when it is cut up for smaller garments. For instance, the skirts of any frock coat in tolerable preservation will furnish an ample pattern for a business vest, which will be of almost as much service as though made of new cloth. The linings of the skirt, if not badly worn, will make the back of the vest; and the body, if ripped in pieces, pressed, and cut down, will make a boy's jacket. The unworn parts of a fine silk or velvet vest will give a number of pieces, which, properly fitted together, will make a handsome cap for a boy; and almost the whole may be used in trimming children's clothing."

In a general way it may be stated, that in a family of the average size, and disposed to a thrifty economy, no article of dress should be thrown away. From the rim of a common felt hat double soles may be cut which will protect the feet from the cold and damp of the winter. It may be worth while to remember that felt makes the best of gun-wads. From pieces left in cutting broadcloth, pincushions, caps and slippers may be manufactured.

How to Clothe Children.

It should never be forgotten that the temperature of children is some degrees lower than that of adults, and that of all ages which resist cold the least, and suffer from its ill effects the most, is early childhood. From early childhood to adult age the capability of resisting cold increases, remains nearly stationary during the prime of life, and diminishes towards old age in about the same ratio as it increases in early life. There are certainly some old men who apparently resist the effects of cold as well as the young, but such cases are rare.

The covering next to the skin of very young children should be of *cotton;* never, except in peculiar cases, of *flannel.* Over the cotton a fine flannel may be placed. When the child arrives at an age to take vigorous exercise, the flannel may be put *under* the cotton shirt, but not till then. The clothing of young children should be loose and free, and absolutely devoid of any tight ligatures around the throat, chest, or knees. Every joint must have full room for play, and no artificial support or bandage should on any account, except in special cases under medical supervision, be applied to any portion of the body of a healthy child. Bandages around the abdomen or stays around the waist are not to be tolerated, and the folly of exposing the limbs of children to the rigors of winter weather is almost inconceivable. "I never see a **poor** child dressed as a young Highlander," says an eminent medical authority, "or in any fancy dress, with its uncomfortable look and naked appearance, its poor bare knees and open neck, but that I prophesy for that child a future of colds, coughs, and throat disease, and a probable death of consumption."

Men's Clothing.

While all eccentricity or affectation in dress should be avoided by both sexes, it is not good policy to carry the idea of plainness and uniformity to the extreme adopted by some men, of having only one suit at a time, which is worn until it is shabby in appearance and then replaced by another. This is decidedly an expensive custom. A very short period of constant wear will cause the new look to leave the surface of the cloth, the button-holes and faces of the lapels will show wear, and it is impossible to appear well-dressed in that suit. Few are aware, or if they are, ever practise the plan of carefully folding and laying their clothes away for a while in a trunk or drawer. All woollen goods, when kept in darkness, renew their lustre, and the dingy look produced by exposure to a great extent disappears. The insensible perspiration from the body, no matter how wholesome or cleanly a person's habits, will linger in any woollen garment. When they are temporarily laid aside they should be well aired and brushed, and folded so as not to show wrinkles, then placed where they will be free from dust and light. If the location is somewhat damp, so much the better; for when wool is kept very dry the fibre becomes brittle and will not render good service. Two suits bought at the same time and worn alternately, following the above suggestions, the one not in service will last a third longer than one suit purchased and worn without intermission until not presentable, and then another one procured and served in the same manner.

Black and dark shades of blue cannot retain their lustre unless protected at intervals from the blanching effect of sun and wind.

A gentleman who confines himself to two suits—one for full dress and one for daily wear—will, in the usual course of life and business, find himself unsuitably attired. It should never be forgotten that sailing, sporting, and travelling cannot be separated from roughness and dust, and garments will suffer more from a day of that kind of usage than a week's ordinary wear, not speaking of the luxury of commanding a change.

The wardrobe of a gentleman who mingles in society and indulges in the above-mentioned pastimes, should consist of, first, a full dress suit, and a medium dress suit for church, calling, or ordinary evening wear; usually made a frock coat, vest to match, and light pants. Then a business or travelling suit, for which the most proper material is Cheviot or mixed goods.

For gunning, velveteens, fustians or corduroy are best adapted, as they resist the briars, and stand any amount of hard usage. Sailing costumes are generally made of blue Cheviot or flannel, and coats cut double-breasted sack.

Two overcoats are indispensable; one for winter and one for spring and fall. The materials suitable for these are so varied that it is simply a matter of taste.

Gentlemen provided with an outfit like the above can safely consider themselves prepared for any emergency requiring appropriate dress, and in wearing garments suited to the occasion lies the great secret in the economical management of clothes.

If colored trowsers are worn, those patterns should be selected which conform to the rules of taste. Bars running across the legs should be avoided, and also all large staring patterns. Stripes down the side, or stripes of any sort, should be worn only by those who are tall and whose legs are straight, or else the eye, running along the stripe, will quickly detect any deviation from the perpendicular.

How to Cleanse Broadcloths.

The following mode has been tried repeatedly with uniform success by Miss Beecher:

Take one beef's gall, half a pound of saleratus, and four gallons of warm water. Lay the article on a table, and scour it thoroughly in every part with a clothes brush dipped in this mixture. The collar of a coat and the grease spots (previously marked by stitches of white thread) must be repeatedly brushed. Then take the article and rinse it up and down in the mixture. Then rinse it up and down in a tub of soft cold water. Then, without wringing or pressing, hang it to drain and dry. Fasten a coat up by the collar. When perfectly dry, it is sometimes the case with coats that nothing more is needed. In other cases it is necessary to dampen the parts which look wrinkled with a sponge, and either pull them smooth with the fingers or press them with an iron, having a piece of bombazine or thin woollen cloth between the iron and the article.

How to Treat Wet Clothes.

Handle a wet *hat* as lightly as possible. Wipe it as dry as you can with a silk handkerchief, and when nearly dry use a soft brush. If the fur sticks together in any part, dampen it lightly with a sponge dipped in beer or vinegar, and then brush it till dry. Put a stick or stretcher into a damp hat to keep it in proper shape.

When a *coat* gets wet wipe it down the way of the nap with a sponge or silk handkerchief. Do not put wet boots or shoes near the fire.

How to render Cloth Water-proof.

There are various processes for water-proofing cloth, but the following is a very simple and inexpensive method:

Take of powdered alum and of sugar of lead each one ounce, and stir them into a gallon of rain water, and when the mixture is clear pour off the upper liquid. Choose Scotch tweed, or any light, closely-woven cloth, and immerse it in this liquid for twenty-four hours; then dry and press it. The cloth will be uninjured in color or texture, and will turn any amount of rain to which the wearer is likely to be exposed.

Buying Boots and Shoes.

With regard to *boots* and *shoes*, which are a source of much trouble, pain, and annoyance to most persons who have not secured for themselves an accurate last, it may be said in general, that to secure ease it is a good plan to put on *two pairs of thick socks before being measured*, and to remind the bootmaker that in walking the foot elongates fully half an inch, and to allow accordingly, or callosities and ingrowing nails may be the result. Of the thousands of boot and shoemakers in the country there are very few who have at all studied the principles of their trade, or know anything of the anatomy of the foot. The upper leather should be soft and pliable; the soles should be as broad as the foot when the weight of the body rests on it, and the heels neither high nor narrow. It is also economical to purchase boots some time before they are wanted, in order to allow the leather to season; and to have two pairs, to be worn on alternate days.

How to Preserve Boots and Shoes.

F. Maceroni, in a communication to the London *Mechanics' Magazine*, says: "I have only had three pairs of boots for the last six years (no shoes), and I think that I shall not require any for the next six years to come! The reason is, that I treat them in the following manner: I put a pound of tallow and half a pound of rosin in a pot on the fire; when melted and mixed, I warm the boots, and apply the hot stuff with a painter's brush, until neither the soles nor upper leathers will suck in any more. If it is desired that the boots should immediately take a good polish, dissolve an ounce of beeswax in an ounce of spirits of turpentine, to which add a teaspoonful of lamp-black. A few days after the boots have been treated with the tallow and rosin, rub over them the wax and turpentine, but not before the fire. Thus the exterior will have a coat of wax alone, and shine like a mirror.

"Tallow, or any other grease, becomes rancid, and rots the stitching as well as the leather; but the rosin gives it an antiseptic quality which preserves the whole."

To cure boots and shoes of *squeaking*, which is a great annoyance, especially in entering a sick-room, or a church after the services have commenced, the remedy is to boil linseed oil and saturate the soles with it well and thoroughly.

Women's Clothing.

Woman's dress has been the subject of so much discussion without practical result, and is so intertwined and interlaced with the caprices of fashion that at first glance it would seem there were no laws regulating it. To the blind votaries of fashion, the willing dupes of milliners and dress-makers who change styles to make work for themselves, nothing need be said; but in every community there are many sensible women who would dress with taste if they knew what constitutes good taste in dress, and for their use and benefit we have read many criticisms and disquisitions, and digested the following points:

1. Never buy an article of dress *unless it be suitable to your age, style and the rest of your wardrobe.* Nothing can be more objectionable in taste than to wear costly laces with a common delaine, or cheap lace with expensive brocades. Women, while shopping, are frequently tempted to buy what pleases the eye upon the counter, forgetting what they have at home to wear with it. "That parasol may be pretty, but it will kill by its color one dress in the buyer's wardrobe and be unsuitable for the others."

2. Whatever the material may be, *let the quality be good,* for it is never economy to purchase anything of an inferior kind, no matter how cheap it may be. "A good, strong, though coarse gingham," says Mrs. Lyman, "will be far more serviceable for a working dress than a cheap though showy calico; and one handsomely printed calico, in fast colors, tastefully made and neatly fitting, is of far more real value to the wearer than those of a low grade, carelessly made and ill-shaped. For the mother of a family, whose duties frequently call her into the kitchen and who is surrounded by children, there is no dress so suitable as a calico, for none other is so easily cleansed of spots and odors contracted in the ordinary routine of her family life. Every time it is thoroughly washed, starched and ironed it is a new dress, fresh and sweet. To choose calico, rub it

and see that there is not much *dress*, as it is called, in it. If a quantity of white powder falls out do not buy it, however cheap, for it is a poor article and will not wear well. It is well for a mother to consider, when purchasing for herself, whether, after she has done with the garment, it can be wrought over for her family, and if she is in moderate circumstances it will be economy to buy goods that will answer to make over for her little girls. Children should always wear small figures or goods of a solid color, trimmed with braid or some other material of a contrasting hue. A neutral tint may be brightened by a crimson or scarlet trimming, while for bright, decided colors white or black trimming is most suitable."

3. In buying an expensive dress it is advisable for those of limited means to *select such as will be serviceable under the greatest variety of circumstances.* Black silk is of this description, as it may be worn appropriately to a wedding, a party, a funeral, or to church. It is nowhere out of taste, except in the kitchen. It may be made gay with bright trimmings, or sombre with those of the same color. It can be worn with hat and wrappings of every hue, and is never out of fashion. If the silk is figured, let the figure be small, the same on both sides, with no up or down to it, so that when worn at the bottom it can be turned upside down, and when soiled outside it can be turned inside out. Figured silks do not generally wear well if the figure be large and satin-like. Black and plain-colored silks can be tested by procuring samples and making creases in them; fold the creases in a bunch and rub them against a rough surface of moreen or carpeting. Those which are poor will soon wear off at the creases.

A chemist has discovered that hydrochloric acid is a powerful solvent of silk, though it has little effect on cotton or wool, at least for a long time. The practical value of this discovery to women is very great. The purchaser of a silk has only first to buy or obtain a few inches of it and drop a little hydrochloric acid, which can be obtained at any druggist's, on the centre of the piece; if it be of *pure silk*, a hole will be made; if there is cotton in it, those threads will remain.

Next to a black silk is a good black alpaca for service and gentility; and for warm weather the different thin black fabrics are capable of great variety and utility. To wear white tastefully a woman must either be very young or quite pretty, and no stout lady can appear in it to advantage. Its very purity suggests a contrast in complexion that is hard to bear in florid faces, or in those which have lost youth's downy freshness.

4. In purchasing dress goods, ladies should not forget their own shape or figure. A pretty, delicate, spotted linen that would make a little lady look charmingly sweet and simple would have a contrary effect on a tall, large one. *Plaids* are becoming for tall women, as they shorten the appearance of the figure. *Stripes* look becoming on a large person, as they reduce the apparent size. *Flounces* should be worn only by those of a tall, graceful figure, and then they should be made of a light material, so that they fall in gracefully with the outline of the dress; when made of any rich stuff which stands out stiffly they break the graceful flow of the dress. Flounces, by marking the height at regular intervals, take away from it and make a short figure look shorter.

A sensible writer on perfect taste in dress says:

"Shawls are only properly worn by women of the camelopard form. A short, squat figure, with the finest camel's hair shawl that ever left India, never looked really well.

Some are bold enough to say that none but a French woman can ever fold herself gracefully in a shawl. Be that as it may, a stout American female does not shine in one. In a velvet circular she will look grand and impressive; in a good cloth sacque comfortable and cozy; but in an astrachan, or sealskin, she will remind you of an overgrown Newfoundland, for fat women will not bear furry wrappings.

"A large face should never bulge out of a small bonnet, nor be surmounted by a coquettish hat. A double-chin is solemnly opposed to butterfly head-gear, and only looks well under a pretty, plain, sensible kind of bonnet. Too many feathers make short forms look topheavy; one long, handsome plume will improve any one who can carry it gracefully; but a mingling of artificial flowers, feathers and ribbons, is too much—fashion notwithstanding."

5. To dress with taste a woman must *know her own face and select colors that harmonize with her complexion.* The great art, as regards color of dress, is to modify the tints of the complexion, care being taken to let the flesh appear of a healthy, natural hue, and to avoid wearing those colors which give the complexion a sickly or unnatural appearance. In this lies the secret of dressing well, but so abstruse is the problem, so multifarious the considerations involved in its solution, that we wonder any woman's brain ever mastered it.

Writers on the combinations of color in dress, divide complexions into the "fair and ruddy blondes" and the "pale and florid brunettes." In the fair blonde we find a delicate white skin, light hair—in all the shades from a golden hue to yellow or orange brown; light blue or gray eyes; a slight tinge of rose on the cheek, and a richer tint on the lips. In all such complexions the rose color is not decided enough, and the hair would be improved by a deeper hue —and these changes can be made, in a good degree, by a suitable mingling of color in the dress. One of the most favorable colors for the fair blonde is a delicate green, as it imparts to the flesh-white of the skin a tint of red, which mingling with the natural hue forms an agreeable rose-tint —a good contrast both to the face and hair, especially if the hair is golden, inclining to orange.

The most complete summary of what blondes should wear as trimmings for bonnets that we have seen has been made by MRS. H. W. BEECHER, and is as follows:

[The best colors to mingle with green, as trimmings, are red, orange and gold. Green and gold form a rich harmony, peculiarly becoming to the fair blonde. Scarlet, blended with green, harmonizes better than red; but if red, inclining to crimson, is used, then orange and gold must also be combined with it. There are some shades of green that are not becoming, unless blended with and enlivened by other harmonious colors. A green bonnet, with rose-color and white, with a white feather, will always be becoming for this complexion. Be careful that too much white is not used, else it will have a cold effect, and therefore will not aid the fair complexion so much. Orange or gold may be substituted for the pink or rose—also red, in a small bonnet, but neither should be placed close to the face. Orange in a green bonnet, in small quantities, is becoming, if the wearer's eyes are blue. A few autumnal shades of red, orange or yellow-green are also in harmony with the fair complexion; but dark-green is not at all desirable.

Blue is very suitable, giving an orange tint, which harmonizes finely with the delicate white and flesh hues of the complexion. There is always a natural trace of orange color on the skin, and this color, by intensifying this natural tint, is very pleasing; but the blue must be light, and not too positive. Blue being the perfect contrast of orange, it agrees finely with golden or orange-brown hair. This is the reason that light-blue head-dresses are so very becoming on light hair. To give a good effect to blue by gaslight, a little white or very pale blue is necessary to be in contrast, or very near the face. If there are green leaves with the blue flowers of a head-dress, they should be placed as near the face as possible.

White, black, a very little yellow, orange, straw or stone color, may either of them be used in the trimmings of a light-blue bonnet, with good effect; but not if there are pink or purple flowers on it, as these colors mingled with blue are unsuitable. The colors to be used carefully or avoided altogether, with fair complexions, are yellow, orange, red and purple. The light shades of lilac may be sometimes used; but it is very trying to, and must always, if used, be separated from the flesh by an edging of tulle or some similar trimming—or be associated with its harmonizing colors—cherry, scarlet, light crimson or gold color, and then they will in part overcome the bad effects; but green and lilac should never be coupled, as it will form a positive discord. A very little light purple is agreeable for a head-dress on light hair, but must be placed near the skin.

Neutral colors, if not too dark, accord well with fair blondes—gray, fawn, drab, and some few shades of brown are the best. Black is good for the fair blonde who has some healthy color, because it increases the rose in the complexion; but it is bad for pale skins, as it bleaches them by the painful contrast. No delicate color can be blended with black without seeming of a lighter tone.

Unless used for mourning, black must be mingled with either blue, cherry, mulberry, drab or lilac, to remove the sombre effects; but cherry and lilac must be used sparingly. Red must not be used at all with black for fair blondes, as it gives a rusty tinge. White is suitable with black, if some other color is added; otherwise it is too cold. A black bonnet looks well with a fair complexion, but a little white and rose color should be added, keeping the rose away from the skin. White is pleasant for all complexions, but more so with the fair blonde who has some color than for any other. Bright colors with white bonnet may be added, but must be kept low and well grouped. White increases the paleness of a pale skin; but this effect may be neutralized by a blue or green wreath brought well on the face.

The ruddy blonde has a full-toned complexion, inclining to a positive rose-red, or carnation; dark blue or brown eyes and brown hair. All the colors suitable for the fair blonde are generally suitable for the ruddy blonde, but the tones, and in some cases the hues, must be changed. As a rule this type may use more freedom in the selection of colors than the fair; her complexion, not being so delicate, is less sensitive. The hair being the medium between gold and black, and the complexion higher toned and more positive, rich and moderately dark colors may be used.

For brunettes purple and dark maroon and yellow and orange are suitable colors. Among brunettes there are a few who are so pallid that to wear stone-gray will render them almost ghastly. For such there is drab of the creamy or pinkish order that is singularly becoming. A tiny band or two of scarlet velvet around shining black hair has a very fine effect.]

Lastly. Follow fashion so far as it is *in consonance with good taste*, but avoid extremes.

Hints to Wearers of Kid Gloves.

It is not generally known, or does not appear to be known, even by those who wear kids almost exclusively, that the durability and set of these articles depend very much upon how they are put on the first time. Two pairs may be taken from one box, of exactly the same cut and quality, and by giving different treatment when first putting the hands into them, one pair will be made to set much better, and to wear doubly, or nearly that length of time longer than the other. When purchasing gloves, people are usually in too much of a hurry; they carelessly put them on, and let them go in that way then, thinking to do the work more completely at another time. When this is the case a person is sure to meet with disappointment, for as the glove is made to fit the hand the first time it is worn, so it will fit ever after, and no amount of effort will make a satisfactory change. Never allow a stretcher to be used, for the gloves will not be likely to fit as well for it. All of the expansion should be made by the hands. If the kids are so small as to require the aid of a stretcher, they should not be purchased, as they will prove too small for durability, comfort, or beauty. When selecting gloves, choose those with fingers to correspond with your own in length; take time to put them on, working in the fingers first, until ends meet ends; then put in the thumb, and smooth them down until they are made to fit nicely. A glove that sets well will usually wear well, at least will wear better than one of the same kind that does not fit well. When the ends of the gloves do not come down right, or when they are so long as to form wrinkles upon the sides of the fingers, they will chafe out easily. Where the stretcher has to be used to make the fingers large enough, the body part will be so small as to cramp the hand so that it cannot be shut without bursting the seams of the kids. Some recommend putting new kid gloves into a damp cloth before they are put on, and allowing them to remain until moistened. With this treatment they can be put on much easier than otherwise, and will fit very nicely until they get dry; but on second wearing there will be an unnatural harshness about them, wrinkling in spots, and they will not set so perfectly as at first.

How to Dress to Sit for a Photograph.

Very few women, except actresses and singers, know how to dress so as to secure the most pleasing photograph. Some photographers have written manuals of instruction on this point, and they state that the best materials for ladies to wear are such as are not too glossy and will fold or drape nicely, as reps, poplins, satins and silks. A black silk dress looks well on almost everybody, and if not bedecked with ribbons, or lace which will take white, will photograph satisfactorily. So garnet, cherry, wine color, sea or bottle-green, light and dark orange, light Bismarck, and slate color are all excellent colors to photograph. But pure white is bad, and lavender, lilac, sky blue, purple, and French blue take very light, and are even worse than pure white. Striped goods, or goods having bold patterns in them, should never be worn for a picture. Avoid anything that will look streaky or spotty.

The dressing of the hair is also a matter of importance. If the forehead be high, which is not a mark of beauty in any woman, it should be partially concealed by the hair or curls; so on a long, stork-like neck a few drooping curls will add to the effect agreeably.

Children should not be dressed in startling plaids and gaudy colors, or a variety of colors; nor do they photograph well in white or very dark dresses.

To Wash Chintz.

Many ladies will be glad to know how chintz may be washed so as to preserve its gloss and beauty. The following are the directions:

Take two pounds of rice and boil it in two gallons of water till soft; when done, pour the whole into a tub; let it stand till about the warmth you use in general for colored linens; then put the chintz in and use the rice instead of soap; wash it in this till the dirt appears to be out; then boil the same quantity as above, but strain the rice from the water and mix it in warm, clear water. Wash in this till quite clean; afterwards rinse it in the water you have boiled the rice in, and this will answer the end of starch, and no dew will affect it, as it will be stiff as long as you wear it. If a gown, it must be taken to pieces, and when dried be careful to hang it as smooth as possible. After it is dry rub it with a sleek stone or agate, but use no iron.

How to Wash Summer Dresses.

In the washing of summer suits a few useful hints may be appreciated. Nearly all are made of white or buff linen, pique, cambric or muslin, and the art of preserving the new appearance after washing is a matter of the very greatest importance.

Common washerwomen spoil everything with soda, and nothing is more common than to see the delicate tints of lawns and percale turned into dark blotches and muddy streaks by the ignorance of a laundress. It is worth while for ladies to pay attention to this, and insist upon having their summer dresses washed according to directions, which they should be prepared to give their laundresses themselves. In the first place, the water should be tepid, and the soap should not be allowed to touch the fabric. It should be washed and rinsed quickly, turned upon the wrong side, and hung up in the *shade* to dry. It should then be starched in thin boiled, but not boiling starch, and after again drying, should be nicely and evenly dampened and ironed upon the wrong side as soon as possible. Buff linen should be washed in water in which hay has been boiled, or a quart bag of bran will answer as well. The latter is perhaps best, for it will be found to do for starch as well, and is excellent for print dresses of all kinds. A handful of salt is very useful also to set the colors of light cambrics and dotted lawns. Beef's gall will not only set, but will heighten yellow and purple tints, and has a good effect upon green.

How to Detect Cotton in Linen.

In buying linen seek for that which has a round, close thread, and is perfectly white; for if it be not white at first it will never afterward become so. Much that is called linen at the stores is half cotton, and does not wear so well as cotton alone. Cheap linens are usually of this kind. It is difficult to discover which are all linen; but some housekeepers take a sample from a lot presumed to be good, wash it and ravel it. If this be good, they conclude the rest of the same lot will also be good. If they cannot do this they draw a thread each way, and if both appear equally strong it is probably all linen.

To detect cotton in linen one of the best methods is microscopic examination; for when flax is magnified three hundred times, it appears like long, compact tubes, with a narrow channel in the centre; while cotton appears to be flattened, ribbon-like cylinders, with a wide channel, and mostly in spiral windings.

The test with oil of vitriol is reliable in an experienced hand, but every trace of weaver's gum must have been previously removed by boiling with water. The fibres are laid on a plate of glass, and oil of vitriol dropped on it. A single lens is sufficient to observe the effect. In a short time the cotton fibre is dissolved, while the flax is unaltered, or only the finest fibres attacked.

The oil test is also a good one, and convenient in execution. When flaxen fibres are rubbed up with olive oil, they appear translucent, like oiled paper; while cotton, under similar circumstances, remains white and opaque. Dyed goods exhibit the same, if previously bleached by chloride of lime.

Flannels.

Flannel is the most healthy and serviceable article for underclothing that can be worn by every one except very young infants. Its peculiar merit, in which it excels all other materials, is that it keeps the vessels of the skin constantly open, stimulates them to free perspiration, and protects them from the chilling effects of external moisture. All persons who lead lives of exposure should adopt flannel undergarments, and especially farmers, who perform their work under wide differences of temperature, and who are peculiarly liable to diseases that result from a sudden check to copious perspiration.

Those women who, like cats, are not fond of water on their skin, and who do not take much physical exercise, will be especially benefited by wearing flannel. The objection made to this fabric, that it irritates the skin, is in fact an advantage; for the irritation is healthful, and may be entirely allayed by friction of the skin when woollen garments are removed upon retiring, as they invariably should be. A little persistence in this practice will inure the skin to its new covering, after which no inconvenience will be felt.

Many persons fall into serious disease by changing their winter flannels too soon. The first of May is quite early enough to lay them aside for a thinner material, south of Virginia, Tennessee, and Kentucky; but the people of those States, and north of them, should not make the change earlier than the last of May. An old physician, when asked what was the proper time to take off flannels, said the thirty-first day of July; and when to put them on again, said the first day of August.

How to Wash Flannels.

One of the great difficulties that an inexperienced housekeeper meets with, is in the discoloration and shrinkage of flannels, and few indeed know the best methods of washing them. Mrs. Lyman has summarized the directions in the following rules:

1st. Never apply *soap directly* to any woollen fabric. Make a strong hot suds, and plunge the garment in it.

2d. Never dip a flannel in cold, or even cool, water, but always hot. Wash first in hot suds, and rinse in hot water made very blue.

3d. Dry flannels as *quickly as possible.* Wring dry from the second water, and hang either in the hot sun, or before a brisk fire. When nearly dry, press with a hot iron. It may also be remarked that none but *soft water* should be used upon flannels, and resin soap is much inferior to common soft soap, as it hardens the fibres of woollens.

To Soften Hard Water.

It is said that half an ounce of quicklime put in nine quarts of water, and the clear solution put into a barrel of hard water, will make it soft. It is also said that a teaspoonful of sal-soda will soften from three to four pails of hard water. This is a valuable recipe for housekeepers if true, and one which can easily be tested.

An Easy Way to Wash Clothes.

The night before washing day, put the clothes to soak in water, and also place on the hot stove, in a suitable vessel, two pounds of soap cut small, one ounce borax, and two quarts water. These may be left to simmer till the fire goes out; in the morning the mixture will be solid. On washing day operations are commenced by setting on a stove or furnace the wash-kettle nearly filled with cold water. Into this put about one-fourth of a pound of the compound, and then wring out the clothes that have been soaking, and put them into the kettle. By the time that the water is scalding hot, the clothes will be ready to take out. Drain them well, and put them into clean cold water, and then thoroughly rinse them twice.

Refined Borax, in the proportion of one large handful of the powder to ten gallons of boiling water, is said to save nearly one-half of the soap, and make the clothes beautifully white and clear. It is a neutral salt, and will not injure the fabric. The washerwomen of Belgium and Holland, so famous for the beauty of their work, use borax instead of soda.

How to Keep Silks.

Silk articles should not be kept folded in white paper, as the chloride of lime used in bleaching paper may impair the color of the silk. Brown or blue paper is better than white, and the yellowish smooth India paper better than any other. Silk intended for a dress should not be kept in the house long before it is made up, as lying in the folds will have a tendency to impair its durability by causing it to cut or split, particularly if the silk has been thickened by gum.

To Secure Woollens, Furs, etc., from Moths.

Carefully shake and brush woollens early in the spring so as to be certain that no moth eggs are in them; then sew them up in cotton or linen wrappers, putting a piece of camphor gum, tied up in a bit of muslin, into each bundle, or into the chests and closets where the articles are to lie. When the gum has evaporated it must be renewed. A lady put up her blankets and carpets in this way before going to Europe, and on her return, three or four years after, found every article safe from moths.

Furs should not be hung out in the sun in the spring before being put away for the season. The moth miller will be likely to visit them when thus exposed. They should be put in a close box with a piece of camphor, and the box tied up in a pillow-case or bag. Blankets that are in use occasionally during the summer should be laid, when not wanted, under a mattress in constant use, or in a trunk where there are pieces of camphor gum, tobacco, or cedar chips. Boxes lined with ordinary roofing felt are said to be equal to cedar for keeping out moths, and much cheaper. It is more difficult than it used to be, to preserve woollens, carpets, furs, and furniture from being injured by moths. Thirty years ago it was regarded as an indication of very negligent housekeeping to have a moth-eaten carpet. Now the utmost care will not preserve carpets from being injured in this way. Perhaps the reason may be that, in general, warehouses and dwellings are warmed throughout, during the winter, by furnaces. New stuffed and cushioned furniture is sometimes found to contain moths. To destroy them pour burning-fluid plentifully upon the cushions, sofas, etc. If it is fresh, it will leave no stain, and the disagreeable odor will soon pass away.

To preserve a carpet that cannot be shaken often, draw out the tacks twice a year, turn back the edges a quarter of a yard all around, brush out the dust, and then with a painter's brush put new spirits of turpentine upon the boards as far as the carpet is turned back; then return it immediately to its place, and put in the tacks.

The floors of some houses have moths in the cracks. In this case cedar sawdust, sprinkled over the floor before laying the carpet down, will protect it from these diligent mischief-workers. If this cannot be had, use tar-paper.

How to Judge Furs.

In purchasing furs, a sure test of what dealers call a prime fur is the length and density of the down next to the skin. This can readily be determined by blowing a brisk current of air from the mouth against the set of the fur. If the fibres open readily, exposing the skin to view, reject the article; but if the down is so dense that the breath cannot penetrate it, or if at most but a small portion of the skin is shown, the article may be accepted.

CHAPTER XIII.

THE SECRETS OF THE TOILET.

"It has been affirmed, and I think correctly, that from the relative attention paid in any country to *cleanliness, the cosmetic arts, dress* and *hygiene*, and from the respective prevalence, influence and mutations of custom and fashion, may its claims to civilization, refinement and luxury be vindicated."—COOLEY.

THE end and aim of superior skill in housekeeping is to increase the comfort and promote the health of families. Now health is the fountain of personal beauty, and the direct and intimate connection between health and beauty leads us to consider what science has to offer for the improvement of the form and complexion, and the preservation of the hair, the teeth, the hands, the feet, and other members of the body.

How to Reduce Corpulence.

With respect to beauty of form, its two greatest enemies are excessive corpulence and excessive leanness. " Corpulence," says Dr. Clark, " is a disease that sometimes proves fatal. The difficulty of breathing with which very corpulent people are oppressed, is caused by an accumulation of fat on the kidneys, which obstructs the motion of the diaphragm; whilst the heart and large blood-vessels being equally encumbered, a slowness of pulse is produced, and possibly apoplexy and death." It is remarkable that the cure for this disease is comparatively a modern discovery. Remedies, it is true, have been proposed, such as violent physical exercise, rowing, boating, riding on horseback, Turkish baths, natural waters, fasting; but none of them have proved effectual in preventing the accumulation of fat in those inclined to obesity.

Modern science, however, has discovered that to prevent or reduce corpulence you must, besides taking active and regular exercise, not indulge in much sleep, and especially *abstain from those articles of food which contain starchy and saccharine matter.* Stock-raisers have long known that certain foods will fatten animals and others will not, and it is inexplicable that medical men have been so slow in applying this principle for the benefit of the human family. William Banting, Sr., is entitled to the credit of making known what can be done by attention to diet, as illustrated in his own personal experience. He was a short, fat Englishman, five feet five inches high, who weighed 202 pounds, when, according to Hutchinson's tables, a healthy man of that stature should not weigh more than 142 pounds. Under advice of his physician, Dr. Harvey, of London, he commenced a system of diet to reduce corpulence, and succeeded in taking off forty-six pounds of fat in a year, without detriment to his health. He was permitted to eat any kind of meat, except veal and pork; any kind of fish, except salmon, herrings and eels; any vegetables except potatoes, parsnips, beets, turnips and carrots; any kind of poultry and game, a little cheese or boiled rice; and to drink tea without milk or sugar, and claret, sherry or Madeira wines. He was forbidden to eat *bread*, except in the form of toast or biscuit, and *butter*, *milk*, *sugar*, *potatoes*, and the other vegetables above excepted, or to drink *ale* or *beer*, *champagne* or *port wines*. After two years' experience he writes: "In my humble judgment the dietary is the principal point in the treatment of corpulence, and it appears to me, moreover, that properly regulated, it becomes in a certain sense a medicine."

How to Cure Leanness.

To cure excessive leanness the practice must be exactly the opposite of that just related, that is, indulge in sleep, take but little exercise, eat bread and butter and potatoes, oily fish and pork, take milk and sugar in your tea and coffee, and drink beer and champagne and port wines. A lean dog, however, being the best for a long chase, unless the leanness is excessive it would be advisable to trust to nature and advancing years for an increase of avoirdupois.

Many ladies who are not troubled with general obesity of the system have a superabundant development of the breast. The modern mode of reducing this is by a preparation of iodine; but as this is a dangerous internal medicine in unprofessional hands, we, says a physician, shall recommend its external use, thus: Take

Iodide of zinc........................1 drachm,
Hog's lard............................1 ounce;

mix well, and rub daily into each breast a piece about the size of a nutmeg; a linen bandage so placed as gently to compress the breast without pressing upon the nipple, will assist its operation. We need scarcely say, this must not be done during lactation.

Some of the old practitioners recommend pounded mint applied to the breasts, accompanied with bandages, to check their exuberant growth.

For those whose breasts participate in their general leanness, the only remedy that science seems to furnish is to have the bosom loosely clothed, avoiding all pressure; and Sir James Clark advises that friction with the hand for an hour or two every day will assist much in its development.

How to Beautify the Complexion.

Beauty of complexion is valued by many even more than beauty of form, and some ladies will spend more time and money to improve the appearance of the face than for any other object. Even young men have been known to use pearl powders and rouges, and to pinch their cheeks until red, to give them a delicate tint.

The clearness or beauty of the complexion is so intimately dependent upon the state of the stomach and liver, that unless these have their proper action, all external applications can be but temporary expedients. In addition to a healthy condition of the stomach and liver, the pores of the skin must have free and undisturbed action. The skin of the face, as well as of all the other parts of the body, is full of little pores or holes, so minute that it is said a grain of sand will cover 25,000, and if these be clogged, the skin will commence to wither and fade, and the beauty of the face will depart. Hence the importance of daily washing, frequent bathing, and the danger of the constant use of powders, balms, blooms, enamels, which fill up the pores and dry the skin.

There are many articles that may be used for the face which are not in the least injurious, but, on the contrary, may be of great advantage to it.

The following elegant and serviceable lotion any lady can keep as an article of her toilet, and make free daily use of it, as it will be of great benefit in enhancing the healthy condition of the skin:

R.—Glycerine............................ 2 oz.
　　Rose water..........................12 oz.
　　Camphor water....................... 1 oz.
　　Alcohol or bay rum.................. 1 oz.

Jockey club, oil of rose, or any perfume may be added that may be desired.

This lotion will be found to impart a very soothing and pleasant effect. Should any one prefer not to have the glycerine in it, the following can be substituted:

R.—Bay rum............................. 5 oz.
　　Rose water.........................10 oz.
　　Camphor water....................... 1 oz.

Soap should not be very frequently used; it is better for the face not to make too free use of that article. Instead of using soap so often, use freely the following harmless wash, which will take the place of soap to a great extent, and keep the skin nice and clean, and not in any way obstruct the free action of the pores, but will remove obstructions and prevent clogging:

R.—Powdered borax.....................6½ drachms.
　　Rose water .... ½ pint.
　　Water.............................. ½ pint.

Dissolve together, and use daily.

How often is a well-defined face, with all the lines perfect, made completely unattractive from being incumbered with pimples, blotches, or a chronic impurity or defect of the skin! For these Dr. Bateman prescribes what is known as his Sulphur Wash:

Break one ounce of sulphur, and pour over it one quart of boiling water; allow it to infuse for twelve or fourteen hours, and apply to the face two or three times a day, for a few weeks. This application is equally useful in removing that roughness of the skin which generally succeeds pimples. A more powerful application is sometimes prepared with vinegar and the acetated liquor of ammonia, or the spirit of mindererus. Or the following, which will be equally effective, and known as Sir William Knighton's Lotion:

Half a drachm of liquor of potassa, three ounces of spirits of wine; to be applied to the pimples with a camel's-hair brush, and if too powerful, add half an ounce of cold water, which has been boiled and strained; distilled water is better.

When the face is to be exposed to a hot sun or a high wind, wash it, previous to and after exposure, with a little pure water, in which pour a teaspoonful of liquor of potassa and a few drops of cologne water. This it is said will prevent sunburn.

Freckles are by no means an easy thing to cure, especially in persons having red hair, but almond paste, made of an ounce of bitter almonds, honey and barley flour, may do it. *Dr. Withering's Cosmetic Lotion* for freckles was compounded as follows:

Take a teacupful of sour milk; scrape into it a quantity of horseradish; let it stand for several hours, then strain well, and apply with a camel's-hair brush two or three times a day.

The following recipes are also said to remove either freckles, tan or sunburn, and are certainly harmless:

Dip a bunch of green grapes in a basin of water; sprinkle it with powdered alum and salt mixed; wrap the grapes in paper and bake them under hot ashes; then express the juice, and wash the face with the liquid, which will usually remove either freckles, tan or sunburn.

Or, put two spoonfuls of sweet cream into half a pint of new milk; squeeze into it the juice of a lemon, add half a glass of genuine French brandy, a little alum and loaf sugar; boil the whole, skim it well, and when cool it is fit for use.

Birthmarks and *Moles* may be eradicated in infancy, but the advice of a skilful physician should be taken. Readers are admonished against the use of depilatories to remove hair from moles, as a fetid suppurating wound has frequently been a consequence of such attempts.

Wrinkles, being occasioned by the obstruction or obliteration of the finer blood-vessels, may be prevented by the use of lotions that stimulate the small threadlike blood-vessels and moisture pipes, which have been closed, and if the stimulating process be adopted previous to the closing of these vessels, they will not be obliterated.

Take two ounces of onion juice, two ounces of the white lily, two ounces of Narbonne honey, and one ounce of white wax; put the whole into a new earthen pipkin until the wax is melted, and then take the pipkin off the fire and continue stirring until it is cold. Apply on going to bed, and allow it to remain on until morning.

For Tetter or Ringworm in the face.—Take some aperient medicine daily, and when the eruption becomes painful, or itches violently, take the following sedative lotion:

R.—Liquor plumbi................1 drachm.
Distilled water.......... ....1 ounce.

This is an excellent lotion for allaying itching and inflammation generally.

The following is a novel cure for ringworm: Heat a shovel to a bright red, cover it with grains of Indian corn, press them with a cold flat-iron. They will burn to a coal and exude an oil on the surface of the flat-iron, with which rub the ringworm, and after one or two applications it will be cured.

How to Secure Beautiful Hair.

The hair has always been considered one of the most important appendages of the human form, and is the especial glory of women. In ancient times, red or auburn was the favorite color of poets and painters, but gradually this was supplanted in public favor by preference for black or dark-brown hair, though recently red has again been quoted as fashionable.

In order to secure a beautiful head of hair, whatever may be the color, it is necessary to begin in childhood, and to observe the following rules:

1. The hair of children should never be plaited, or braided, or twisted, or knotted.

2. Nothing should ever be put on it except simple, pure water, and not even this until the scalp is cleansed.

3. The hair should be kept short. It would be a valuable accomplishment if when a woman becomes a mother a few lessons were taken from a good barber, so that the child's hair, after the third year, might be trimmed by its mother once a week, only cutting off the longest hairs, by ever so little, so as to keep it of uniform length. This practice is proper for male and female.

4. The hair should be always combed leisurely, and for some considerable time, at least every morning, and neither brush nor comb ought to be allowed to pass against the direction of the hair's growth.

To Cure Baldness.—The growth of hair may be promoted on a fuzzy scalp, because in that case the root is not dead, but lacks vigor or needs nutriment, and new vigor can be imparted and additional nutriment bestowed, by whatever gives activity to the circulation of the blood about the roots of the hair, and what the following application fails to do in this direction all others will, simply because it is the most certain, the most powerful and safe stimulant known: Half an ounce of vinegar of cantharides, one ounce of cologne water, one ounce of rose water; to be rubbed in with a tooth-brush, gently and patiently, until the part is thoroughly moistened and smarts a little. To be repeated night and morning; if too powerful, dilute with water or use less.

Wash for Dandruff.—Take one pint of alcohol and a tablespoonful of castor oil, mix them together in a bottle by shaking them well a few minutes, then scent it with a few drops of oil of lavender. Alcohol dissolves castor oil, like gum-camphor, leaving the liquid or wash quite clear. It does not seem to dissolve any other unctuous oil so perfectly, hence no other is equally good for this purpose. Mr. John L. Davis, in the *American Journal of Pharmacy*, recommends a preparation of one ounce flowers of sulphur and one quart of water as an effectual remedy for dandruff. The clear liquid is to be poured off, after the mixture has been repeatedly agitated during intervals of a few hours, and the head saturated with the liquid every morning.

For Darkening the Hair.—Wash the head with spring water, and comb the hair in the sun, having dipped the comb in oil of tartar. Do this about three times a day, and in less than a fortnight the hair usually becomes quite black. The leaves of the wild vine, infused in water, are also said to render the hair black, and to prevent its falling off. Some persons use a metallic comb, which imparts a dark shade to the hair, and these are now generally kept by the perfumers.

To Remove Superfluous Hair.—The following is said to be an effectual depilatory: Orpiment, one part; finely powdered quick-lime and starch, of each, eleven parts; mix. It should be kept from the air. For use, make it into a paste with a little warm water, and apply it to the part, previously shaved close. As soon as it has become thoroughly dry, it may be washed off with a little warm water. This depilatory should be compounded by a druggist, and used with discretion, as orpiment is an arsenical preparation.

In Circassia and neighboring countries the eyelashes of children are clipped with scissors, at their extreme points, while asleep, every six weeks, giving them in time a beautiful gloss and curve, besides adding to their length and thickness.

How to Whiten the Hands and Beautify Nails.

A well-formed hand, white and soft, with tapering fingers and polished nails, is a rare gift; but where nature has denied these attractions, it is easy by proper attention to give at least softness and delicacy of appearance to the hand and improve the symmetry of the nails. It is well to wear kid or soft leather gloves at every opportunity, light being preferable, on account of the unctuous substances with which they are prepared, although not so healthy, and the application of warm bran poultice to the hands once a week. They should be washed in tepid water, as cold water hardens and predisposes them to roughness and chaps, while water beyond a certain heat makes them shrivelled and wrinkled. In drying them they ought to be rubbed with a moderately coarse towel, as friction always promotes a soft and polished ivory-appearing surface. The soaps to be preferred are such as are freest from alkaline impurities.

The growth and preservation of the *nails* depend in a great measure on the treatment they receive. They ought to be frequently cut in a circular form, and the whitened portion at the root, next the vessels which supply the nail with nutriment for its growth and preservation, should always be visible. When the nails are disposed to break, some simple pomade should be frequently applied, and salt freely partaken of in the daily diet.

For Chapped Hands.—A good recipe is: Almond oil, or sweet oil, three ounces; spermaceti, four ounces; pulverized camphor, one ounce; dissolve in an earthen vessel by the aid of heat, and stir while it is cooling. Apply night and morning.

Another good preparation for chapped hands, and which will preserve them smooth by constant use, is ALMOND PASTE.

Mix a quarter of a pound of unsalted hog's lard, which has been washed in common water and then in rose water, with the yelks of two new-laid eggs and a large spoonful of honey. Add as much paste from almonds well pounded in a mortar as will work it into a paste.

Perhaps no better ointment for beautifying the hands can be made than to take four parts, by weight, of the yelks of eggs and five parts of glycerine, rubbed together in a mortar. This compound may be preserved for years.

For Warts.—Common ink will remove them if applied night and morning on their first appearance. When they have been clearly developed, a certain means of extirpating them is the following:

Take a small piece of court-plaster made upon India rubber webbing, cut a hole in its centre, just sufficiently large to admit the head of the wart; rub the head with lunar caustic night and morning, and when it becomes hard pick off the top and again apply the caustic. The use of the court-plaster is to prevent the surrounding skin from being injured. Or,

Take oxymuriate of mercury, five grains; lime-water, one ounce. Mix, and apply with a camel's-hair brush two or three times a day. Be very careful in applying the solution, as it will injure clothes. Wash the camel's-hair pencil whenever used.

Care of the Eyes.

The eye is the most striking, delicate and beautiful feature of the human face, and no pains should be spared for its preservation. To this end spectacles or eye-glasses should not generally be used until they are imperatively required. Green spectacles are even worse than plain ones. If the eye is weak, nine times out of ten, cold water is the best lotion. Strengthening lotions, when composed of spirits or acids, are stimulants; such, of course, must occasionally be used, but judgment is required in using them, and an oculist's direction is generally required when these become necessary. Sometimes, when the eye is inflamed, it will be relieved by a lotion made of one teaspoonful of good brandy in a wineglassful of water; but as inflammation may arise from different causes, sometimes requiring anodynes, sometimes stimulants, no general directions of practical value can be given.

If the eyes are inclined to be inflamed after being up late, an unguent, composed of one drachm citrine ointment and three drachms fresh lard, rubbed on both lids when retiring to rest, will generally, almost magically, relieve them. Nine times out of ten, supposed affections of the eye are only inflammations of the eyelid: in such cases this unguent will effect a cure.

Raw-potato poultice for inflamed eyes is one of the very best applications in recent cases. *Slippery-elm* poultices are good. In nearly all the celebrated eye preparations sold in the stores sulphate of zinc is an ingredient.

Sometimes in travelling by rail, *cinders* from the locomotive get into the eye, causing great pain. These may be removed by introducing between the eyelid and the ball the bight of a horse or other strong hair, so as to include the spot where the particle appears to be, and gently draw out the hair; the relief is said to be instantaneous and permanent.

For squinting, science has discovered an operation that will effectually cure it. This is not either painful or dangerous; but we strongly advise none to submit to it until they have arrived at the age of from nineteen to twenty-one, as, if it be done before, it is more than probable that the eye will be drawn the contrary way by the time they reach that age. A more simple remedy is to cover the stronger eye, which will compel the weaker one to exertion, and thus increase its power. Perseverance in this plan is generally successful.

Women often injure the eye by wearing a white veil. The glitter which this causes, and the constant exercise to which its continual shifting exposes the eye in following its movements, is often the occasion of great injury to the sight. Spotted veils are equally injurious.

How to Preserve the Teeth Sound.

No remarks need be made at this day on the value of sound teeth, or the beauty of clear, regular, and white teeth. To prevent teeth from decay, it is necessary to keep them clean; to use the tooth-brush on the surface, and the tooth-pick to remove particles of food between the teeth. Dr. Lewis thinks no one need have decayed teeth, if he will observe the following rules:

First. On rising from the table, use a goose-quill tooth-pick thoroughly, and rinse the mouth so as to remove such particles as the tooth-pick may have left behind. [Avoid metallic tooth-picks.]

Second. On retiring at night, use a tooth-brush, broad and soft, with pulverized soap and prepared chalk, with a little camphor and orris-root to give a pleasant flavor. Do the same on rising in the morning.

Third. As often as you discover any tartar about the necks of your teeth, go to a dentist and have the tartar thoroughly removed—in fact, a dentist should be visited frequently, in order that the first appearance of decay in the teeth may be discovered and removed.

The following is an aromatic Tooth Powder that cannot possibly injure the teeth:

Take finely-powdered prepared chalk, two drachms; pure starch, two drachms; myrrh, two drachms; ginger, half a drachm; cuttle-fish bones, two drachms; flower of lavender and sugar at pleasure, and mix well together.

The following is said to be an infallible cure for all kinds of toothache, unless the disease is connected with rheumatism. It is known as—

Dr. Blake's Infallible Cure for Toothache. Take alum reduced to an impalpable powder, two drachms; nitrous spirits of ether, seven drachms. Mix and apply to the tooth.

The following is a *fomentation for the face, to assist in relieving Toothache:*

Take three poppy-heads and a handful of chamomile flowers, put them into a quart of soft water; boil until the quart is reduced to a pint, then apply repeatedly to the face by means of flannel, and as hot as can be borne. Take care no draught of air gets to the face while under its operation. In addition, lave the feet in hot water before going to bed.

Toothache frequently arises from indigestion or a disordered stomach; and when this is the case, it can be cured by the judicious use of aperient and tonic medicines.

Small pieces of cotton, soaked in a solution of half a teaspoonful of bicarbonate of soda (baking soda) in half a tumbler of water, and applied to an aching tooth, has frequently given instant relief.

Bad Breath.

One principal cause of an offensive breath is the accumulation of tartar on the teeth; the small particles of food not being removed, become decomposed and incorporated with the tartar and produce an abominable odor. A temporary remedy may be found in the use of some strong mouth-wash; but a cure can only be effected by having the tartar removed from the teeth, and those that are decayed filled or extracted. Dentists are the best mouth doctors.

To prevent the superabundance of phosphate of lime in the saliva, which produces tartar, and to sweeten the breath: Take five to ten drops of hydrochloric acid in half a tumbler of spring water, a little lemon juice and loaf sugar rubbed on lemon peel, to flavor it to suit the palate. Take three times a day for a month or six weeks, and then occasionally. It is a pleasant refrigerant and tonic draught.

As a toilet preparation for bad breath, probably the best is the concentrated solution of the chloride of soda from six to ten drops in a wineglassful of water, and rinsing the mouth with a teaspoonful of the solution in a tumbler of water.

For *breath tainted by onions*, parsley leaves, eaten with vinegar or burnt coffee, are recommended.

Care of the Feet.

The importance of attention to the feet is shown in the fact, that many of our most serious ailments come through neglecting them. It is an axiom among horsemen, "no foot, no horse." And a man with sore or tender feet is physically of little account.

To give the feet their just and proper attention, they should be soaked in warm water for at least twenty minutes, twice a week, and at the same time rubbed or scrubbed with a flesh-brush. Besides this they should be dipped in cold water once a day, summer and winter, rubbing them vigorously while immersed ankle-deep, then wiped dry and warmed. When the feet are tender, they should be bathed every other day in a strong solution of alum and water, in which might be added an infusion of galls or of oak-bark, and then well rubbed and dried; this will so strengthen them as to bid defiance to chilblains or sore feet from walking. It is also an excellent habit, during the season in which fires are kept burning, to hold the feet to the fire for a few minutes before retiring to bed, and rubbing them with the hands until thoroughly dry and warm. With attention of this kind, and care in the selection of shoes, corns and callosities would cease to exist, coldness of feet would, to a considerable extent, be removed, and "taking cold" would not occur once where it now occurs a dozen times.

Persons who are liable to *chilblains* should be very particular in thoroughly drying the hands and feet, and never go near a fire for some time after they come out of the external air. They should use the alum wash above mentioned, daily, and rub the feet and legs for ten or more minutes with a hair glove. If, in spite of these precautions, any symptoms of chilblains appear, anointing the feet night and morning with an ointment composed of two ounces of opodeldoc, and one ounce laudanum, will ordinarily prevent their appearance. If, however, chilblains have appeared, Sir Astley Cooper's *Chilblain Liniment* will generally remove them; viz.:

Take liquor of sub-acetate of lead, one ounce; camphorated spirits of wine, two ounces. Mix, and rub into the hands or feet two or three times a day; oftener if convenient.

To relieve feet *itching from frost-bites*, take hydrochloric acid, one ounce; rain water, seven ounces. Wash the feet with it two or three times daily, or wet the socks with the preparation, until relieved.

As a preventive against *frosting* the feet when they have become cold, warm them gradually; and, as remedies, apply cabbage leaves, wrapped round the feet at night; bathing with oak-bark tea, alum water, or glycerine and rosewater, and rubbing with white-lead ointment.

Those who suffer from COLD FEET, if the washing and rubbing recommended before do not prove effectual, are solicited to try the experiment of wearing cotton socks next the skin, and woollen stockings outside of them. Those who have tried this plan state that it was successful in keeping the feet warm and dry; and that they found the cotton socks next the skin to be quite dry at night, while the outside stockings were very damp.

Cure for Ingrowing Toe Nails.

A prompt and painless cure, it is said, may be effected by inserting the dry sesquichloride of iron between the nail and the protruding flesh, and powdering the latter with the same. Over all a large bandage should be applied. The exuberant flesh becomes hard as wood on the following day; suppuration ceases, and a cure follows two or three applications. In four or five days the original pain ceases, the swelling subsides, and the patient can walk. Dr. Gaillet, of France, first published an account of this cure as tested by Dr. Wahn and himself.

The Boston *Medical and Surgical Journal* publishes a communication from one who says he cured the worst case of *ingrowing nail* he ever saw—the patient being unable to put on a shoe for several months—by putting a very small piece of tallow in a spoon, heating it very hot and pouring it on the granulations. "The effect was almost magical. Pain and tenderness were all gone, the diseased parts dry and destitute of all feeling, and the edge of the nail exposed so as to admit of being pared away without any inconvenience. This application has been found effectual in many other cases, accomplishing *in one minute*, without pain, all that can be effected by the painful application of nitrate of silver for several weeks."

Ingrowing of the nail is often the result of improper cutting of the nail. Dr. Chavasse remarks: "There is, in this as in everything else, a right and a wrong way—the *right* way of cutting a toe-nail is to *cut it straight*, in a straight line. The *wrong* way is to cut the corners of the nail—to round the nail, as it is called. The latter may make work for the surgeon." Where there is a tendency towards ingrowing, the arch of the nail should be broken by curving the centre inwards and scraping the edge.

Fetid Feet

Are a sore trial to those who are afflicted with them. With some they are hereditary; an unpleasant peculiarity, if not disease, transmitted from one generation to another. With others, this peculiar and fetid odor is sometimes in the armpits, and again in the feet, flitting between the two. In most instances, however, the odor is the result of neglect in personal cleanliness. There are persons who wear socks or stockings without change from the time they are first put on until they are full of holes. Very many do not wash their feet oftener than once a month, only a few as often as once a week. The feet should be washed every night before going to bed, using the finger between each toe; and no stocking, boot or shoe should be put on the second time, until it has a whole day's sunning or drying—at least by those who have an ambition to be sweet and clean.

As a remedy for those whose skin and feet are disposed to be odorous, we would recommend that they put into the wash water two tablespoonfuls of the compound spirit of ammonia (hartshorn); or if this does not answer in connection with daily washings, a very efficient wash for the feet is found in *red oxide of lead, one part to twenty-nine parts of the liquor of the sub-acetate of lead; the former to be bruised in a porcelain mortar, gradually adding the latter;* apply a few drops, once a week, or oftener in summer.

Corns and Bunions

Are the most painful and troublesome excrescences that afflict the feet and torture humanity. They have their origin in either pressure from a tight shoe, or friction from a loose one; and though there are many remedies which will disperse them, they can never be so effectually cured that a misfitting boot or shoe will not cause them to return, because the structure of the skin about a corn is malformed for life, and would no more become natural than a finger would grow again if cut off. A man with consumption may get well; but he cannot be said to be perfectly cured, because he will always remain with a deficiency of lungs; yet, by making the remainder of the lungs work more fully, he may have even better health than he ever had before. So with corns; and as remedies are valuable for the multitude in proportion as they are safe, cheap and attainable, we shall only give a few of the simple remedies that it is claimed will cure corns.

Dr. Chase, of Michigan, says *corns may be cured in ten minutes*, by the following application:

Take a small piece of potash, and let it stand in the open air until it slacks; then thicken it to a paste with pulverized gum arabic, which prevents it from spreading where it is not wanted. Pare off the seeds of the wart or dead skin of the corn, and apply the paste, and let it remain on ten minutes; wash off and soak the place in sharp vinegar or sweet-oil, either of which will neutralize the alkali.

2. A man in Ohio offers to pay ten dollars apiece, for every corn not cured in three days, by binding a bit of cotton-batting upon it, and wetting this three times a day with spirits of turpentine.

3. The following is said to be an *infallible* Corn Plaster: Take two ounces of gum ammoniac; two ounces of yellow wax; six drachms of verdigris. Mix and spread the composition on a piece of linen or soft leather, first *filing* down the corn. Renew in a fortnight, if necessary.

4. Another positive cure for corns is: Take the strongest acetic acid, and apply night and morning with a camel's-hair brush. In one week, it is said, the corn, whether soft or hard, will disappear.

5. Another simple, available, and infallible cure is: First, to soak the feet in hot water for fifteen minutes, night and morning, for a week; and after the soaking, rub a little

sweet-oil on the corn, or any other mild form of grease, with the finger for about five minutes. Then, cut a hole in one, two or three thicknesses of soft buckskin, and bind it on the toe, so that the hole in the buckskin shall receive the corn. The object of the water and oil is to soften the corn and parts adjoining; and the use of the buckskin is to protect it from pressure. In a very short time the corn will be painless, and will subsequently fall out of itself, as it is a growth and is pushed upward and outward by the more natural growth beneath. It is thrown out of the body by the action of the parts, as a splinter or a crushed bone, as being no longer a part of the body. If anything else is done to the corn, it should be simply picked out with the finger nail; as cutting makes it take deeper root, and dangerous bleedings sometimes occur when the knife is used.

Bunions may be checked in their early development, by binding the joint with an adhesive plaster, and keeping it on as long as any uneasiness is felt. An inflamed bunion should be poulticed, and larger shoes be worn. Iodine, twelve grains; lard or spermaceti ointment, half an ounce, makes a capital ointment for bunions. It should be rubbed on gently, twice or thrice a day.

The *resolvent plaster*, usually known as the plaster of ammoniac and mercury, which can be obtained of any apothecary, is also of much benefit as an application to bunions.

To Remove Body Vermin.

Many persons, even the most cleanly, are liable at times to be placed in situations where they cannot escape the various kinds of vermin that infest the human body; and it is a very important item of practical information to know that an application of common sweet-oil will destroy body vermin. These insects breathe through their sides, and as the oil plugs up the air conduits, a speedy and certain death from suffocation is the consequence of its application.

Sulphur baths are an efficacious remedy for pediculi; one bath generally effecting an extinction of every one of them, even though they be all over the body. Dr. Culverwell says: Rubbing the parts affected well with a wash composed of half a drachm of calomel, and four ounces of lime-water, or even powdering with calomel, will also at once destroy these insects, and thereby remove the itching. The hair need not be removed, as the above remedies will be all-sufficient without its removal.

In this connection it may be of benefit to young housekeepers to tell them how to drive away or

Exterminate House Insects and Pests.

Roaches devour greedily flour paste, and die while eating it, if into half a pint of it, while hot, a dime's worth of *Phosphorus* is stirred with a stick. The *Persian Insect Powder* will also destroy roaches, and *borax* scattered about the places they frequent will drive them away.

House Flies may be banished from a room by hanging in it the common plantain, or "fleawort," dipped in milk, and may be destroyed by feeding them with ground black pepper and sugar, as much as will lie on a dime, moistened with two teaspoonfuls of cream or rich milk. They eat it, seek the air, and die out of doors. Farmers troubled with flies should plant before their doors the *Chinese Linden*, which seems to be an attractive poison for flies. Elder and walnut leaves, both in their natural state and as a decoction, will prevent attacks of flies, both on animals and meat, and drive them away. Horses may be protected from flies by washing the sensitive parts with a decoction of walnut leaves.

Bedbugs may be exterminated or kept away by many remedies, most of which we suppose are effectual in connection with cleanliness. It is said they are effectually destroyed by washing infected places with a decoction of common *smart weed*, or " water pepper," called by botanists *polygonum punctatum*. Pour a pint of boiling water on a pint of the weed, and let it cool. The liquor may be put on with a brush. The plant itself may be stuffed into cracks or corners.

Another remedy, said to be effectual, is to take two ounces of quicksilver and the whites of two eggs, or more or less for a larger or smaller quantity. Beat the quicksilver and the whites together until they unite and become a froth. With a feather then apply this compound to the crevices and holes in your bedsteads, and if done once or twice a year, this will keep away bugs.

Spirits of naphtha, also *oil of turpentine*, rubbed with a small painter's brush in every part of a bedstead, is said to be a certain way of getting rid of bugs. *Camphor* is also objectionable to them.

To destroy rats. Sir Humphrey Davy recommends the following as an infallible, tasteless and odorless rat poison:

"Mix carbonate of baryta two ounces, with grease one pound."

It produces great thirst; consequently water must be set by it, for death takes place immediately after drinking, not giving them time to go back to their holes. Should this be found as effectual as recommended, it will prove just the thing for rat killing, at they can be gathered up and carried away, thus avoiding the stench arising from their dead carcasses. Care must be taken that no other animal can get at it.

A few grains of strychnine on a little fresh broiled meat,

or an ounce of phosphorus mixed in butter and flour, will kill rats.

To drive them away alive, put Scotch snuff and pulverized Cayenne pepper or potash into their burrowing-holes. They will leave in disgust. Quick lime scattered over the bottom and sides of holes through which they pass, will also drive them away, as it eats off their skin and hair. To drive them away effectually, the lime must be renewed every week or two.

If some strong-scented cheese be mixed with an equal quantity of pulverized *squills*, and placed where rats and mice can have access to it, they will devour it ravenously and soon disappear from the premises.

Ants are averse to strong scents, and camphor, or a sponge saturated with creosote, will prevent them infesting a cupboard. It is also said that a chalk-mark half an inch in depth around the upper edge of sugar-buckets or barrels will exclude every ant from the interior. The same mark drawn on the edges of shelves will also prevent the approach of ants, as they are not able to crawl over the chalk. But if they are numerous among jam and jelly pots, take a large sponge, wet in cold water, squeeze it nearly dry, and then sprinkle fine white sugar over it. Place it on the infested shelf, and next morning dip it quickly and carefully into a bowl of boiling water. Red pepper dusted over their haunts will also destroy them, but the sponge is the surest method.

Fleas may be banished from houses by the use of *camphor*, and from animals by saturating strings with oil of pennyroyal and tying them around the neck, renewing the application every week; or, where the herb grows, by making a decoction of it and throwing the dogs or cats into it once a week. The herb should be mown and scattered in the beds of pigs once a month.

To get relief from *Musquitoes*, the most efficacious way is to put up a musquito-netting at the windows and around the beds; and the next best thing is to burn a small quantity of the *Persian Insect Powder*, which can be obtained of apothecaries generally. Take as much of the powder as can be heaped on an old-fashioned silver dollar, and place it on a plate at bedtime. Apply a lighted match to the top of the heap, and to aid the evolution of the fumes keep stirring it occasionally. The fumes will narcotize the musquitoes and keep them quiet several hours. The experiment may require repetition. The powder is said to be equally effectual with roaches, bedbugs, fleas, ants, etc.; not exterminating, but stupefying them. Its smell while burning is similar to that of a mild cigar.

A smart editor says that when musquitoes or other blood-suckers infest his sleeping-rooms at night, he uncorks a bottle of the oil of pennyroyal, and these insects leave in great haste, nor will they return so long as the air in the room is loaded with the fumes of the aromatic herb. If rats enter a cellar, a little powdered potash, thrown in the holes or mixed with meal and scattered in their runaways, never fails to drive them away. Cayenne pepper will keep the buttery and store-room free from ants and cockroaches. If a mouse makes an entrance into any part of your dwellings, saturate a rag with Cayenne in solution, and stuff it into the hole, which can then be repaired with wood or mortar. No rat or mouse will eat the rag for the purpose of opening communication with a depot of supplies.

For *Bites of Insects*, apply spirits of hartshorn to them as soon as possible, and almost instantaneous and permanent relief will be given. The reason is, the poison of

SECRETS OF THE TOILET.

insects, spiders, reptiles, etc., is an acid; the hartshorn is an alkali, and neutralizes the poison. Another remedy is, throw a handful of wood-ashes into a teacup of hot water, stir, and as soon as settled apply the liquid—which is common lye used for making soap—with a soft rag.

A medical writer observes: "Have we not, before now, looked with wonder on the old negro who ran out, when the wasp's sting made us 'holler,' caught up 'three kinds' of weed, rubbed the part well, and in five minutes we were happy in complete relief? But why 'three' kinds of weed? Why, in the first place, you know three, and all its multiples are mysterious numbers; and then again, you can scarcely gather up three kinds of plants anywhere, one of which will not have more or less of *alkali in it*."

[The two succeeding Chapters on Diseases have been read in proof and revised by six persons, including an eminent physician, and a first-class druggist.]

CHAPTER XIV.

THE FAMILY MEDICINE CHEST

"Physicians prescribe much, but use few medicines themselves. Let this hint suffice, by showing you that much is to be expected from simple remedies, discriminating judgment and the influence of the mind upon the corporeal body."—DR. RAYMOND.

SICKNESS is one of the great wastes and burdens of society, which deprives it of the useful services of nearly one out of every five of its members. How to preserve health and cure sickness is therefore a question of great economic importance, which comes within the scope of a work on Thrift in Housekeeping, especially so far as those diseases are concerned which can be cured as readily without as with the aid of a physician.

First, as to the management of a sick-room. Select for this apartment, says an anonymous but very sensible writer, the sunniest room in the house. There is life and healing in the solar ray, even if its light, which is only a part of the ray, is excluded. We all feel instantly, on entering a room on which the sunlight never directly falls, a chill and an absence of something essential to cheer and brightness. Observation shows that in hospitals more patients die in shady than in the sunny wards, and in cities disease is more fatal on the shady side of the street than on its opposite.

Next in importance to sunshine in the sick-room is ventilation. If well people need fresh air, much more do they that are sick. A free circulation of air must be provided without endangering at all the safety of the patient. In cool weather an open stove (if possible, a soapstone stove), with a wood fire, is perhaps as effective and pleasant a method as any other of securing this.

The aspect of the room should be inviting and pleasant. If the walls are bare, bring the pictures from that shut-up room, the parlor or the guest-chamber, and hang them where the patient can enjoy them. Set a rose or a geranium in the window. If plants were unhealthy, the air of greenhouses would be different from the outer air, which is not the case.

[*Well-aired bedding* is essential to the comfort of the patient. This can be secured with a little management. The patient may be removed to an easy-chair or a lounge, and the bedding be thoroughly shaken out of doors, if the weather is fair, or in a room with the windows opened, if the weather is foul; then warmed by the fire and put upon the bed. None but the sick are fully alive to the blessedness of clean sheets. How much of disease is only the choking in one form or another of the natural outlets of the body!

The comfort of the patient in many cases is greatly increased by *washing*. A cloth wrung from tepid saleratus or soda water may be passed over the body under the bedclothes, and, if followed by a dry towel, there is little danger that the patient will take cold.

If there must be light in the room all night, by all means use *tapers*. A box of these, costing ten cents, can be bought at the apothecary's, and will last many weeks. Each box contains a tiny socket or circle of tin with three sharp points, holding a bit of cork; into this socket sets a button-mould a quarter of an inch in diameter, with a hole in the middle, in which is inserted a bit of waxed wicking. The whole affair, not larger in circumference than a walnut, floats on the surface of a cup or tumbler full of lard oil. It gives a very soft and pleasant light, and is perfectly safe. Kerosene lamps cannot be turned down without filling the room with unconsumed products of combustion, which are very unwholesome; candles and oil lamps are apt to smoke. The taper is economical, pleasant and safe. We have been thus circumstantial in describing this little contrivance so that those at a distance from drug stores can make it for themselves. In the nursery it is invaluable. An outlay of 30 cents will keep a light in the sick-room for months.

To purify the air in a sick-room from noxious smells, especially of an animal character, put a few grains of coffee on a hot shovel, and roast them in the room. In a moment you will smell nothing but the coffee.]

Dr. Carmichael Smyth, of London, is said to have received $25,000 from the British Parliament, for making public the following recipe:

To Prevent Infection in Typhus Fever.—Take nitre (saltpetre) pulverized, three-fourths of an ounce; oil of vitriol, three-fourths of an ounce; put the nitre into a teacup and set it on a red-hot shovel, adding the vitriol, one-sixth at a time, stirring it with a pipe-stem, and taking care to avoid the fumes as they arise from the cup.

Colds and Cough.

The treatment of colds, as set forth in medical works, is radically different; but all agree that a cold must be broken up within the first forty-eight hours, or it will run its course. The regulars recommend, that as soon as a person discovers he has taken cold, he should shut himself up in a room of uniform temperature, drink warm drinks, bathe his feet in hot water, and take four compound cathartic pills at bed-time and a drachm of Epsom salts in the morning. He should also leave off animal food for a few days; and if the chest be painful, apply a common pitch or porous plaster.

Another school, of which *Drs.* Lewis and Hall are representative teachers, recommends, on the contrary, active exercise in the open air, sufficient to produce perspiration; abstinence from food, or not to eat anything except a piece of dry bread for breakfast and dinner, and nothing for supper; and liberal indulgence in cold water, drinking at least two tumblers on going to bed and on rising in the morning. They believe that the old saw, "stuff a cold and starve a fever," has been a source of infinite mischief. As food makes blood and blood makes phlegm, the more food the more phlegm, which is often the cause of most harassing coughs.

It is believed that a cold may be broken up almost infallibly, if the person, as soon as he discovers the premonitory symptoms, will abstain from food, for, say, thirty-six hours, go to bed in a warm room, wrap up well, and drink hot tea of any kind.

How to Avoid Taking Cold.

To *avoid catching cold*, a good preventive is, to sponge the body every morning with cold water, on getting out of bed. The distinguished physician, Sir Astley Cooper, said: "The methods by which I have preserved my own health are temperance, early rising, and sponging the body every morning with cold water—a practice I have adopted for thirty years, without ever catching cold."

Dr. Hill thinks that the great majority of colds are taken "by cooling off too quickly after exercise." Persons exercise until a perspiration is produced, and then seek a cool seat or a pleasant breeze. The wisest and safest plan after exercise is to go into the house, shut the windows and doors, keep hat and coat on, and wait until there is not the slightest perspiration seen on the forehead or felt on it with the hand.

If people who have been exposed to cold or wet through the day, would bathe their feet and hands in warm water at night, they would escape many colds and fatal diseases.

For the *cough* attending a common cold, the following is said to be the best, safest and cheapest cough syrup ever made:

Take one ounce of thoroughwort, one ounce of slippery elm, one ounce of stick licorice, and one ounce of flaxseed; simmer together in one quart of water, until the strength is entirely extracted. Strain carefully, add one pint of best molasses and half a pound of loaf sugar; simmer them all well together, and, when cold, bottle tight.

As a general rule, it is best not to stop a cough, especially in children. Dr. Chavasse remarks, "Any fool can stop a cough, but it requires a wise man to rectify the mischief. *A cough is an effort of nature to bring up the phlegm which would otherwise accumulate, and in the end cause death.* Again, therefore, let me urge upon you the immense importance of *not* stopping the cough of a child. Ipecacuanha wine will, by loosening the phlegm, loosen the cough, which is the only right way to get rid of a cough. Thousands of children are annually destroyed by having their coughs stopped."

Asthma

Is one of the diseases for which there are many remedies prescribed, though but few of them are effectual, except as palliatives. A quaint writer remarks, that for two dollars you can get in the drug-stores a box of stuff that you can burn up in three nights, and very certainly relieve asthmatic paroxysms; but an ounce of pulverized stramonium (Jamestown weed), with two drachms of powdered saltpetre, will do the same thing six times, and cost nine cents.

Dr. Finley, of Pittsburgh, is accredited with having cured many cases of asthma; and he has made public his prescription, which is as follows:

Oil of tar, one ounce; tincture of veratrum viride, two drachms; simple syrup, two drachms: mix. Dose—for adults, fifteen drops three or four times daily.

Iodide of potassium has cured asthma; and lobelia is considered by some a specific for this distressing complaint. Asthmatic persons should be very careful in their diet and regular in their habits.

Agues.

Dr. Chase, of Michigan, says he cured himself of ague, after having tried other remedies for three years ineffectually, by the following prescription:

Quinine, twenty grains; Dover's powder, ten grains; sub-carbonate of iron, ten grains. Mix with mucilage of gum-arabic, and form into twenty pills. *Dose*—two each hour, commencing five hours before the chill should set in. Then take one, night and morning, until all are taken.

In attacks of ague, it is best to take an active cathartic pill immediately after the first " fit," unless the bowels are lax, which is not generally the case.

An anonymous writer says, the following treatment has cured thousands of cases, and has never failed in a single instance, where directions have been strictly followed. "Take of calomel and jalap, each, ten grains, on going to bed. On rising in the morning, take one ounce of castor oil, previous to a light breakfast. If it is your 'shaking day,' do nothing further until the chill and subsequent fever have passed; or, if a day of respite from the chill, take one of these powders every three hours:

    R.—Tannin and Sulp. Quinine, aa gr. x.
    Piperine, gr. vj.
    Pulv. Root Licorice, gr. vij.

Mix, and divide into five powders. If your residence is *malarious*, you may get an attack the next season; but one course as above will cure again, as certain as the sun rises in the firmament."

Another anonymous writer says he cured himself of the ague, by putting into his boots a half gill of hot whiskey and putting the boots instantly on. The very first day he tried it, the fever came as usual, but *there was no chill;* the second day the symptoms were all modified; and after the third application, there was no return of the fever or the ague. He says: "I well remember, when a boy, there being a tavern in our neighborhood where teamsters stopped to rest and water their horses, of seeing the carters, instead of drinking their half gill of whiskey, pouring it into their boots cold, as a protection against the frost. They told me there was nothing equal to it to warm the feet; that it was better than fire, for the feet remained warm for a long time and prevented sickness. It is also excellent for a *cold*, or when from exposure the feet get wet or damp, and a cold or other disease may be apprehended. I have known it to act like a charm.

"I would advise your readers who may be attacked by chills and fever to use no other remedy, and particularly to reject all drugs, especially quinine. The foregoing is as simple as can be, and as cheap as can be. Try it and believe."

How to Prevent Fever and Ague.

Dr. Hall says miasmatic effects can always be prevented in two ways; hence, fever and ague and all classes of intermittents are preventable, and could be swept from the world. The first precaution is, to eat a hearty meal before going out of doors in the morning in warm weather, and take supper before sundown. He says, when he began the practice of medicine, he travelled day and night, through broiling suns and drenching rains, over one of the most malarious districts in the Southern States, and was never sick for a single second; but he never left the house, or went outside the door after daylight, until he had taken his breakfast. "While one class of persons died off like sheep, it was noticed that another class did not die at all. They lived and lived on indefinitely long and finally dried up. Some of them the author knew; they were old thirty years ago, are apparently no older now—the French Creole planters; they would have a cup of strong hot coffee brought to their bedsides every morning before they rose to dress." And the second precaution is, to have a lively fire kindled in the family room half an hour before sunrise and sunset in warm weather, to burn for an hour or longer. This is a most important suggestion to people in many sections of the United States.

Bleeding from the Nose

Often occurs in young persons from ten to fifteen years of age; and in cases where it is not excessive, is rather beneficial in relieving congestion and preventing headache.

It often stops of itself; but sometimes it is troublesome to arrest, which should always be done where weakness would result from loss of blood. It may be stopped in many cases by applying cold water or ice to the forehead and nose, the back of the neck, and the roof of the mouth, or wet a plug of dry cotton in strong alum water or tincture of the chloride of iron diluted, and introduce it into the nostril. Bleeding from the arm will often arrest it; or holding the hands above the head. When all these fail, the doctor should be called in.

Bleeding at the Lungs

Arises from different causes, and will usually require medical treatment. Take a tablespoonful of salt at intervals. If the spitting of blood lasts, take five grains of the sugar of lead and five of opium, every two hours as required. The diet should be light, and taken cool.

Blood Purifiers and Tonics.

Sarsaparilla root has long stood at the head of the list of articles used for spring medicines; but its value has been much overrated. Sassafras bark, which is much used as a blood-purifier in the rural districts, is now rarely prescribed by the medical faculty, many of whom think food is the best spring medicine; and to purify the blood, recommend people to abstain from the fat meats and gravies and coarse foods of winter; to use eggs, spinach, and vinegar. Keep Lent, at least partially; and wash the body daily.

If a bitter tonic is needed, half an ounce of ground quassia, an ounce of powdered gentian, with a drachm of golden-seal, steeped for several days in one pint of well-rectified whiskey, then strained and mixed with one gallon of clear water, will produce nine pints of "Tonic Stomachic" as good as the very best on sale. This preparation will cost but a few cents per quart, and is "warranted to keep in any climate."

Bruises and "Black Eyes."

The remedy for all bruises is a fomentation. This is best applied by wringing a piece of flannel out of hot water and keeping it to the injured part as long as it remains warm and moist. This should be persevered in while the pain and swelling continue.

The *tincture of arnica* is a favorite remedy for bruises; but it does not deserve the high popular estimation it has acquired. It may be applied, however, without fear of any bad result. A black eye generally must be patiently endured while it passes through the various discolorations, though it may be partially concealed by wearing a shade, or touching the skin artistically with chalk and paint. A "black eye" may generally be prevented, if the part receiving the blow or bruise be well buttered for an hour or two with fresh butter.

For the very severe kind of bruise caused by jamming the finger in a closing door or drawer, the quickest relief is obtained by plunging the finger into water as hot as it will bear. This will soften the nail, and cause it to yield and give room to the blood, the painful pressure of which will thus be relieved. After giving the finger a thorough soaking in hot water, you should wrap it up in a thick poultice of bread and water or milk. On the next day after, if the pain is troublesome, it is a good thing to scrape the nail, with a knife, so thin that it may readily yield to the pressure of blood or matter which frequently forms below. If this does not produce the desired relief, it will be well to make an opening into the scraped nail and let out the fluid beneath. The same remedy may be applied to a bruised toe as to a finger.

Chilblains and Frosted Feet.

Take a half pound of alum in a gallon of warm water; immerse the feet in this alum water, and let them remain ten or fifteen minutes; repeat until relief is obtained, and this will prove an effectual cure. Also, it is said that two white turnips, cut into thin slices without paring, mixed with three large tablespoonfuls of the best lard, simmered slowly for two hours, and mashed through a sieve, and applied to a chilblain at night on a soft linen cloth, will cure the most inveterate chilblain or frosted feet.

Diarrhœa—Hints for Travellers.

During the summer, persons travelling are liable to derangements of the bowels; and some one recommends as a safe remedy for diarrhœa, to stir a little wheat flour in a glass of water until it is of the consistency of thick cream; drink it down, and repeat it several times in the course of the day, if needed. Meanwhile, eat nothing, drink nothing, and lie down if practicable. The flour may act mechanically, not medicinally, by plugging up the relaxed mouths through which the watery particles are poured into the intestinal canal. Diarrhœas are often the result of the greater coolness of morning and evening over midday, and the injurious effects of bad air on an empty stomach; hence, one of the most important rules for travellers, in all seasons, climates, and countries, is, *Never fail to breakfast before you ride.*

Another authority on the subject claims that the following will always cure diarrhœa:

Procure "brandy coloring" from a rectifying liquor dealer, or make it by placing an ounce or two of good brown sugar in a pan or skillet; drop upon it just sufficient water to *dampen* the sugar; place the vessel over a quick fire; stir until the mass emits a thick, black smoke, but do not burn it crisp. Pour on half a pint of boiling water and stir till all is dissolved. Dose—a wineglassful every hour until relieved; after which eat an ounce or two of very tender beefsteak slightly broiled, dusted sparingly with pure black pepper. The regulars generally prescribe for diarrhœa, small doses of calomel.

How to Escape Cholera.

The premonitory symptom of an attack of cholera is looseness of the bowels; hence, when cholera is epidemic in a district, every one should watch carefully the action of his bowels; and whenever they are moved over once in twenty-four hours, recourse should be had to the proper remedies for checking diarrhœa. The body should be kept quiet; all drinks should be avoided, and the food should consist principally of common rice, parched brown and then boiled, and eaten with salt and butter. A tight compress should be bound around the abdomen; and the best material for a bandage for this purpose is a strip of stout flannel about a foot broad, and sufficiently long to double in front, but to be of but one thickness behind. Tape-strings should be attached to the outer end, and also to another part of the piece, a few inches beyond the lapping point, so as to make the flannel conveniently tight, and also aid in keeping it in place. When the cholera was prevailing in Europe, and broke out so suddenly among the Prussian soldiers that it was impossible to procure medical attendance for any considerable number, an order was issued that every soldier, sick or well, should instantly wear a flannel bandage around the stomach; and the disease disappeared in a few days.

Dysentery.

Sir Charles Locock, one of the Queen of England's physicians, says, "that in severe dysentery, especially where there is sickness, there is no remedy equal to pure calomel, in full dose," and recommends at the very outset of the disease to give from three to five grains (according to the age of the patient) of calomel, mixed with an equal quantity of powdered white sugar, and put dry on the tongue. In three hours after, let the following mixture be administered:

Take of compound ipecacuanha powder, five grains; ipecacuanha wine, half a drachm; simple syrup, three drachms; cinnamon water, nine drachms: to make a mixture. A teaspoonful every three or four hours, first *well* shaking the bottle.

Dr. Baily, who made this disease his particular study, recommends in cases where dysentery has continued for several days, a combination of castor-oil and opium—as for instance: Take of mixture of acacia, three drachms; simple syrup, three drachms; tincture of opium, ten drops (*not* minims); castor-oil, two drachms; cinnamon water, four drachms. Mix, and take a teaspoonful every four hours, first well shaking the bottle. A warm bath, at the *commencement* of the disease, is very efficacious; and a flannel bag, filled with hot table-salt, made hot in the oven, and applied to the bowels, will afford much comfort.

An American physician says *raw minced beef*, administered as the almost sole article of food, at the usual intervals of eating, and in quantities as great as the patient can comfortably swallow, seems to have an admirable effect in mastering this disease; and even in consumption some physicians are prescribing it, and with this agreeable circumstance, that although it is so repellent to our tastes at first thought, to be eating raw, bloody meat, yet the stomach soon becomes reconciled to it, and even to crave it. In the case of one of the members of the cabinet recently deceased, who had been using it in the hope of its benefiting a disease of the lungs, there seemed to be such a liking for it, that when the last meal was brought to his bedside, his eye brightened and he exclaimed, "Ah! that is a dish good enough for a king."

When raw beef is administered for dysentery, indicated by bloody discharges and a most distressing and ineffectual "bearing down," it should be minced very fine, and given *every four hours*, a tablespoonful at a time, eating nothing else in the meanwhile.

Dyspepsia or Indigestion

Is the great national disease of America. Bad cookery and eating too fast without proper mastication, and eating too much, have ruined thousands of stomachs.

We doubt whether there is any remedy in medicine, for confirmed dyspepsia. Medicine, says Dr. Hill, cannot make gastric juice, which is one of the essential requisites of a healthy digestion. "It is a liquid prepared as a consequence of the need of repair; this need of replenishment and repair is occasioned by a previous waste or wear; that waste or wear cannot be brought about without motion of the muscles, which is expressed by the word exercise; *it is muscular exercise which creates gastric juice.*" Hence, the first essential element in the cure of dyspepsia is *exercise*, more particularly out-of-door exercise.

Some years ago, a physician in New York attained so great a reputation for curing dyspepsia, that he was able to charge a fee of five hundred dollars for each case he undertook, payable in advance. His patients were bound by solemn oaths not to reveal the method of treatment; but after his death, some of them considered themselves absolved from their obligation, and revealed the secret, which consisted mainly in *slapping the stomach or bowels* with the palms of the hands for five or ten minutes on rising in the morning, a quarter of an hour or more about eleven o'clock, and in the evening before going to bed. Dr. Lewis calls this excellent treatment, and says he cannot conceive of a case of chronic indigestion which such manipulation would not relieve. Rubbing and kneading for chronic maladies is no new thing. For hundreds of years a class of women, known as "rubbers," have figured conspicuously in England and Mexico; and the authority just quoted says, "the most remarkable cures ever achieved among us have been the work of the rubbers."

In addition to slapping and kneading the stomach, and exercising freely out of doors, a dyspeptic should eat only when he is hungry, select digestible food, and chew it well. Voltaire claims that he cured himself of dyspepsia by living for nearly a year on the yelk of eggs, beaten up with flour of potatoes and water. The mode of preparation, as recommended by Sir John Sinclair, is as follows: Beat up an egg in a bowl; then add six tablespoonfuls of cold water; mix the whole together; then add two tablespoonfuls of the farina of potatoes, to be mixed thoroughly with the liquor in the bowl. Then pour in as much boiling water as will convert the whole into a jelly, and mix it well. It may be taken either alone or with a little milk and sugar not only for breakfast, but in cases of great stomach debility, or in consumptive disorders, at other meals. The dish is light, easily digested, extremely wholesome and nourishing. Bread or biscuit may be taken with it as the stomach gets stronger.

On the other hand, Mrs. Swisshelm announces that she was cured of a very bad case of dyspepsia, by the *hard bread and beer*, prescribed by a German physician. She says: "Some years after, when Pennsylvania doctors sent me back to Minnesota to die among my kindred, a German physician was called in; but heart and stomach were on a strike, and refused to assimilate food. In great perplexity he said: 'Can you take peer?' I could try, and he went on to prescribe: 'You get de Gheneral to get you some coot peer, fresh from the prewery. Dake von leetle half a glass, mit a pit of hart pread and leetle pit uv cheese. Chew de pread schlow, and sip de peer. Do not culp it like some beebles do; schust sip schlow, and eat de pread and cheese mit it. I dinks maype dat set de stoomach do vork vonce more!'

"His prescription worked like a charm, and in any fit of dyspepsia now, I go back to the hard bread and beer."

For *indigestion* produced by over-indulgence in an extra rich meal, immediate and generally perfect relief may be obtained by taking a cup of Thomson's Composition powders, which are made as follows:

Bayberry bark, two pounds; ginger root, one pound; cayenne pepper, two ounces; cloves, two ounces—all finely pulverized and well mixed. Take one-half of a teaspoonful of this, and a spoonful of sugar; put them into a teacup and pour it half full of boiling water; let it stand a few minutes, and fill the cup with milk or hot water, and drink.

This will stimulate the stomach to action, promote digestion, prevent the accumulation of gas which causes belching, and give tone to the whole system.

This dyspeptic tea or Composition powder may also be made a *cure for drunkenness.* Whenever the craving for liquor is felt, take a cup of this tea, which will give warmth and tone to the stomach; and, by avoiding places where intoxicating spirits are kept or sold, the desire for them will gradually pass away, and the whole system be restored to manly vigor.

Earache and Deafness.

Earache is often an extremely painful affection; and, when severe, a physician should be called in, as the inflammation may affect the brain. First, an examination should be made, to see whether an insect or any foreign body has been introduced into the ear; and if not, apply a neuralgia plaster behind the ear, and pour into the ear two or three drops of laudanum, with a little sweet-oil, or a few drops of glycerine. A teaspoonful of warm melted butter, dropped into the ear, is a favorite remedy for earache with a noted Philadelphia physician.

Glycerine is the best remedy for all cases of earache or deafness originating in concrete wax. It is perfectly safe, and as mild as milk and water; while it retains its moisture longer than any other substance yet discovered; hence, if hardened wax causes the deafness, it will certainly be softened and brought away. Auricles, or other aids to hearing, improve for a time, but only to bring ultimate deafness the sooner, and more certainly, as well as more completely. In ninety-nine cases out of a hundred of deafness, in the ordinary walks of life, all tampering with the ear is pernicious; and quite as often it will be found that whatever general good health, and the constant (once daily) moistening with pure glycerine does not accomplish in the way of an improved hearing, nothing else will.

Erysipelas

Is a blood poison, originating in causes not very well understood by physicians; though cold, mental anxiety and constipation are supposed to be the principal causes, while by some it is regarded as a contagious disease.

A poultice of cranberries, pounded when raw, affords a soothing and pleasant relief in erysipelas, and sometimes arrests its progress; while the repeated application of oxide of zinc ointment, which is preferable to the white-lead coating recommended by some physicians, relieves irritation by excluding the air from the parts affected.

Physicians in Philadelphia, however, mainly rely upon a remedy discovered by one of their number, Dr. Andrew Nebinger, which by some is regarded *as a specific in erysipelas*. It is used both internally and externally. The recipe, when anglicized, is as follows:

```
Bisulphite of sodium...................... 2 drachms.
Syrup..................................... 2 ounces.
Water..................................... 2 ounces.
```

Mix—Take a tablespoonful every two hours. For external application, use bisulphite of sodium, one ounce, in eight ounces of water.

In case the bisulphite of sodium does not agree with the stomach, take, as the next best remedy, twenty drops of *tincture of iron*, every hour, in water.

Fainting.

When a person faints, that is, becomes unconscious, with paleness, coldness, cessation of the pulse and breathing, he or she should be *laid down* at once, with the head lower than the body. The upright position might endanger life; as in fainting the heart fails to send fresh blood to the brain, and its flow must be favored by the recumbent posture.

In fainting there must be plenty of air, and avoidance of crowding; open the windows, unloose the patient's clothing and neck-tie, and apply hartshorn or sal volatile near to the nostrils at intervals.

When unconsciousness arises from *apoplexy*, or *liquor*, the head is warm or hot, the cheek flushed, the pulse full, and the breathing loud. In such cases the body should be laid down, having the head and shoulders elevated.

Felons.

Venice turpentine, one ounce; put into it half a teaspoonful of water, and stir with a rough stick until the mass looks like candied honey; then spread a good coat of the mixture on a cloth and wrap around the finger. If the case is only recent, this will remove the pain in six hours.

A poultice of fresh poke-root on a felon cures by absorption, unless matter is already formed; if it is, this soon brings it to a head, and saves much pain and suffering.

Lobelia is preferred, by many physicians, to either of the above; and by some is regarded as a "sure cure" of a felon.

Headache

Arises from such a variety of causes, that no one remedy will meet all its varying phases. In delicate females, it is often purely sympathetic; but the principal and general cause of headache is some derangement of the stomach or indigestion.

For *Sick Headache* arising from this cause, take a glass of warm water, into which has been rapidly stirred a heaping teaspoonful of salt and kitchen mustard; and this, by causing instantaneous vomiting, will empty the stomach of the bile or undigested sour food, and a grateful relief is often experienced on the spot; then rest, with a few hours of sound, refreshing sleep, completes the cure, especially if the principal part of the next day is spent in mental diversion and out-door activities, not eating an atom of food (but drinking freely of water or hot teas), until you feel as if a piece of plain, cold bread and butter would "taste really good."

Two teaspoonfuls of pulverized charcoal, stirred in half a glass of water, and drunk, generally give instant relief, especially when the headache arises from superabundance of acid in the stomach.

In nervous headaches, the elixir of valerianate of ammonia is generally prescribed; and a new remedy, called *Guarana*, is growing in favor.

For *Biliousness* or *Bilious Headache*, Dr. Lewis recommends the patient, on getting up and on going to bed, to drink plenty of cold water, to eat for breakfast a little stale bread and a piece half as large as your hand of boiled beef or mutton, for dinner about the same thing; to go without supper; and exercise freely, so as to produce perspiration. In a few days the biliousness will all be gone. A speedier remedy is a dose or two of anti-bilious or Mandrake Pills, when the first symptoms of bilious headache appear.

Heartburn or Waterbrash

May be relieved by taking twenty drops of *lemon juice* at the close of each meal, and by abstaining from drinks or fluids at meal-time. Any alkali, as bicarbonate of soda, will relieve; but Dr. Lewis says he has been in the habit of advising his patients who are temporarily afflicted with heartburn, to *chew spruce gum* and swallow all the saliva. This affords a grateful relief, and is not liable to the objections which may be urged against soda, saleratus, and other strong alkalies.

An agreeable effervescent drink for heartburn, which is highly recommended, is, to mix the juice of one orange, water and a lump of sugar in proportion to the acidity of the orange, together, and then add about half a teaspoonful of bicarbonate of soda; stir, and effervescing will ensue.

Hysterical Fits and Nervousness

Are very alarming to those who witness them for the first time. Women of all ages are liable to this complaint, as it generally arises from some irregularity in the functions of the parts peculiar to women; and it is very frequent with girls during the first few months of puberty, and with women when they have reached the "change of life."

A sensible writer recommends cold bathing, open-air exercise, strengthening diet, cheerful surroundings, with the removal of all care and perplexities; attention to a proper regularity of the bowels; frequent change of air and scene—are positively required. *All irksome family requirements should be suspended.* Iron pills may be taken two at a dose, night and morning; and a bitter tonic (quassia, gentian, etc.), in half wineglass doses, two hours before dinner and supper. At the proper season, sea-bathing will prove beneficial. Kindness from family and friends is imperatively required. Hysterical women should not *nurse* infants. Snuff, opium and camphor are not recommended. Strong tansy tea, taken cold and in small quantities, will be found serviceable. A long narrow strip of strengthening-plaster, worn the entire length of the spine during *cold* weather, will do good. This may be made by mixing by heat, dark resin with half its proportion of beeswax, adding a few drops of olive oil.

As a relief for *nervousness*, the following recipe has proved of great benefit to many:

Ammoniated tincture of valerian	1 drachm.
Compound tincture of bark	1 do.
Compound tincture of aloes	10 drops.
Camphor mixture	1½ ounces.

Mix, and take from twenty to thirty drops three or four times a day.

Neuralgia.

A remedy, which is sometimes successful in instantaneously allaying neuralgic pains, is found in mixing equal parts of sweet oil, spirits of hartshorn, and chloroform; shake well, and before time is allowed for the particles to separate, wet a bit of rag or lint, place it on the painful spot for about a minute, or less if relieved sooner; but hold a handkerchief on the lint, so as to confine the volatile ingredients; if kept on too long, the skin may be taken off.

The application of bruised horseradish to the wrist, on the side of the body suffering from pain, is a remedy, recently discovered, for the cure of "Nerve Ache," or neuralgia.

Pleurisy,

Which is an inflammation of the serous membrane enveloping the lungs, is a very painful affection, and usually requires the services of a physician. In nine cases out of ten, however, it is believed, the disease may be arrested, if the patient, at the beginning of the attack, take an alcohol or vapor bath until perspiration freely ensues, drinking freely of a strong tea made of pleurisy-root and catnip, and keeping well covered in bed. Turpentine may be applied over the seat of the pain and mustard upon the feet; and rubbing the arms and legs with dry flannel tends to moderate the severity of the attack. Call in a doctor, if relief is not obtained in a few hours.

Liver Complaint,

Or inflammation of the liver, also requires the services of a physician; but in its first or acute stage, the sweating process recommended in pleurisy will be beneficial, especially in combination with the use of Mandrake Pills.

Piles, or Hemorrhoids,

Are painful swellings at the lower extremity of the intestines, and are both internal and external. The internal are the most painful. The external vary in size and the pain often ceases when they break and discharge blood, but the swelling partially remains and they are soon as large as before. In cases of piles it is important to avoid strong and stimulating food, to take regular daily exercise, and to guard against costiveness.

The most successful treatment, judging from the certificates of cures which have been made, is the introduction into the rectum of an ointment composed of some astringent and oil or grease, as, for instance, two drachms of powdered gall nuts and an ounce of lard, or the extract of white oak bark and bacon oil, or powdered opium, rosin, and tallow, each one ounce, or equal weights of glycerine and tannin. All of these ointments, it is claimed, have cured piles.

Dr. Harriman, of Indiana, it is reported, has been very successful in curing piles with an ointment made of the extract of white oak bark, half a pint, and oil of old and strong bacon, half a pint, simmered together until an union takes place when cold. Apply every night until well.

For use internally, take a tablespoonful of sulphur in half a pint of milk every day. This of itself has been used with complete success by individuals who had spent scores of dollars in medical advice.

When the intestine falls down after evacuation, restore it by pressing gently with the finger, and use some astringent as a lotion to prevent its return.

Cold cream, or even fresh lard or tallow may often, if applied in time, be preventive of *erysipelas* and *piles*, the one a complaint dangerous to life, and the other painful and troublesome. For instance, if one feels a peculiar tenderness and soreness on the face about the eyebrow, which on examination shows a line of redness, the application of cold cream at once may ward off an attack of spreading erysipelas. Or, should the lower bowel feel ill at ease, and at the same time pain and soreness at its extremity, in going to stool, the free application of cold cream or lard three times a day may arrest the inflammation and prevent the formation of piles.

Quinsy, How to Prevent.

. Quinsy is an inflammation of the fauces or tonsils of the throat, attended by a painful and impeded deglutition, sometimes causing death by suffocation. When allowed to progress beyond a certain point very little can be done in this disease except to hasten suppuration. But if the patient applies in time to a physician possessing the requisite knowledge, there is seldom occasion for any one to have an attack of quinsy. Medical science has achieved one of its greatest triumphs in discovering a means of arresting the progress of this painful disorder. The editor of this work has been subject to occasional attacks of quinsy, but recently he had the good fortune to consult Dr. James Simpson, of Philadelphia, who dissipated a threatened attack by the following treatment:

Mix—Tincture of iron.................................. ½ ounce.
  Sulphate of quinine........................24 grains.
  Chlorate of potash........................... 2 drachms.
  Glycerine ....2½ ounces.
  Syrup... ½ ounce.

Take two teaspoonfuls every two hours in a wineglass of water. The peculiarity of this prescription is, that the chlorate of potash is not dissolved.

As a gargle, dissolve an ounce of chlorate of potash in a pint of water, and for external application use the following liniment:

Oil of amber (rectified).....................½ ounce.
Oil of turpentine..............................2 ounces.
Camphora......................................3 drachms.
Castor oil......................................2 drachms.

To be rubbed well and frequently over the throat.

This treatment, the doctor referred to, has found in an extensive practice to be almost a specific, not only for incipient attacks of quinsy, but for most inflammatory diseases of the throat, including even diphtheria.

Rheumatism.

Rheumatism is of two kinds, acute and chronic, and the former is divided into inflammatory and articular. All genuine rheumatism is a blood poison, originating, it is supposed, in excess of uric acid, and though not often fatal, is a serious disease requiring the services of a skilful physician to eliminate it from the system. The regulars generally prescribe alkalies, especially potash, in large doses to neutralize the acid, and do not believe much in liniments or external applications.

Chronic rheumatism, of two years' duration, has been cured, it is said, in twenty-four hours by mixing equal parts of alcohol, spirits of turpentine, sweet spirits of nitre, and oil of juniper, and rubbing this well into the parts affected; also taking internally ten drops in water at bedtime.

Many of the pains in the muscles and joints, which readily yield to liniments and rubbing, though called rheumatism, are not genuine rheumatism.

For *mercurial rheumatism* the following is recommended:

With four ounces of good oatmeal make three quarts of well-boiled gruel. In this dissolve four drachms of the *nitrate* of potassium. Stir well, and take of the mixture half a pint every two hours until all is consumed. Meantime bind a cloth steeped in turpentine one part, proof whiskey ten parts, to the region of the pain. Cover up quite warmly. If necessary, repeat the gruel remedy. In the interim take two "compound cathartic pills" every other night.

Sore Throat.

Bathe the throat externally with the liniment recommended in quinsy sore throat; gargle with *alum* water or alum in sage tea, and drink often and freely of flaxseed tea. A large draught of the latter may be made more agreeable by the addition of lemon juice and sugar, and may be taken at bed-time after a warm mustard foot bath.

Flaxseed tea should be made by pouring a pint of boiling water on one or two tablespoonfuls of whole flaxseed and stirring it up for a few minutes. The flaxseed should not be boiled, as that would bring out the oil, which is too heavy for the stomach. It is only the mucilage from the outside of the seeds that is useful.

Chlorate of potash, an ounce, in a pint of hot water, makes a very good gargle for a simple or ulcerated sore throat. It is nearly tasteless, and being not at all offensive to take, is well adapted for children. But for those who prefer something not so simple the following is recommended:

Take of very strong sage tea, half a pint; strained honey, common salt, and strong vinegar, of each two tablespoonfuls; one teaspoonful of pulverized cayenne pepper; steeping the cayenne with the sage, strain, mix, and bottle for use, gargling from four to a dozen times daily, according to the severity of the case. This is no doubt one of the very best gargles in use.

To smoke dried mullein leaves in an ordinary but new clay pipe has been found very beneficial where there is a tickling in the throat, or hacking cough, or other irritation. It is recommended by the *Eclectic Medical Journal*.

General Washington's remedy for sore throat and which others have found quite effectual in this disease, especially when accompanied by hoarseness, was—*onions boiled in molasses.*

Scrofula and Old Sores.

Nicholas Longworth, the Cincinnati millionnaire, used to say that he had done wonders in curing scrofula, and old sores, with the following recipe:

Put one ounce of aquafortis in a bowl, or saucer; drop into it two copper cents—it will effervesce—leave the cents in; when the effervescence ceases, add two ounces of strong vinegar. The fluid will be of a dark-green color. It should and will smart. If too severe, put in a little rain-water. Apply it to the sore, morning and evening, with a soft brush or a rag. Before applying it, wash the sore well with water.

Small-Pox, or Variola.

This is one of the terrible scourges of humanity, baffling often the best medical skill, and we would not allude to it except to show how pitting may be prevented, a matter that physicians overlook or regard as of secondary importance. We may state, however, that the mode of treatment prescribed for the English army in China, by general orders, is, just before the eruption appears the chest should be thoroughly rubbed with croton oil and tartar emetic ointment. This causes the whole of the eruption to appear on that part of the body to the relief of the rest, and prevents the disease from attacking the internal organs.*

---

*A Californian professes to have discovered, in sulphate of zinc and digitalis, a speedy remedy for small-pox. But as his announcement, though couched in the strongest language, has not attracted the attention of the medical faculty, there is probably nothing in it; and digitalis being a poison, non-professional readers should not experiment with it. He says: "It is as unfailing as fate, and conquers in every instance. It is harmless when taken by a well person. It will also cure scarlet fever. Here is the recipe as I have used it, and cured

But to guard against small-pox, the main reliance is upon vaccination in infancy and re-vaccination every seven years. Dr. Getchell, of the Jefferson Medical College, says, "Small-pox is a disgrace to any civilized land. My firm belief is, that if every person were, *every seven years*, duly and properly vaccinated, small-pox might be utterly exterminated." Even vaccination, however, is no certain preventive, unless the system is saturated with the vaccine virus, until it refuses, after repeated experiments, to absorb any more.

To Prevent Pitting in Small-Pox.

There seem to be so many remedies that will prevent pitting in this disease, that its frequency is disgraceful to the medical profession. Any doctor who brings a patient safely through the small-pox, yet has taken no measures to prevent pitting, deserves to lose his fee.

In all cases of small-pox, or variola, light should be excluded from the room as much as possible, as it aggravates the disease. One remedy to prevent pitting is to dissolve gum arabic in honey, and sufficient lamp-black to color the whole mixture. Then with a camel's-hair brush paint over every pustule or spot. Dr. Schonlien, of Hanover, has a still simpler process, which he says he has used most successfully to prevent pitting in small-pox and my children of the scarlet fever; here it is as I have used it to cure small-pox, when learned physicians said that the patient must die, it cured:—Sulphate of zinc, one grain; foxglove (digitalis), one grain; half a teaspoonful of sugar; mix with two tablespoonfuls of water; when thoroughly mixed, add four ounces of water. Take a spoonful every hour. *Either disease will disappear in twelve hours.* For a child smaller doses, according to age. If counties would compel their physicians to use this, there would be no need of pest-houses. If you value advice and experience, use this for that terrible disease."

also in measles, scarlatina, chicken-pox, to relieve the itching and irritation of these complaints. It consists in smearing the whole surface of the body, after the eruption is fairly out, with bacon fat, and the simplest way of employing it is to boil thoroughly a small piece of bacon with the skin on, and when cold cut off the skin with the fat adhering to it, which is to be scored crosswise with a knife, and then gently rubbed over the surface once, twice, or thrice a day, according to the extent of the eruption and the recurrence of itching and irritation.

Dr. Allshorn, of Edinburgh, uses three parts of oil and one of white wax, mixed by heat, and while warm to paint the face and neck with a camel's-hair brush dipped into the fluid. As this cools and hardens, it forms a mask which effectually excludes the air and prevents pitting.

A solution of India rubber in chloroform is used by some physicians, but others consider it injurious if not dangerous in suppressing the natural exudation of the skin.

How to Prevent Hydrophobia.

If hydrophobia be once developed in the human system we believe no cure for it has yet been found. But hydrophobia may be effectually prevented by the prompt use of proper remedies. As soon as a person has received a bite from an animal, whether dog or cat, that may possibly be mad, he should instantly run a stick of nitrate of silver (lunar caustic) into the wound for the space of five or ten seconds—not minutes. The stick of lunar caustic should be pointed, in order the more thoroughly to enter the wound, and may be obtained, ready for use, from any druggist. The nitrate of silver acts not only as a caustic, but neutralizes the poison. Mr. Youatt, the celebrated English veterinary surgeon, regarded this as an infallible preventive if properly and immediately applied. He himself had been bitten many times by rabid animals, but regarded that as a slight circumstance when he could apply lunar caustic.

Sea-Sickness.

An eminent French physician, Dr. Guardes, having heard that American physicians use syrup of chloral as a preventive of sea-sickness, experimented with it on two trips across the English Channel, and with successful results. He compounded a draught, composed of 45 grains of chloral, 50 grammes distilled water, 60 grammes gooseberry syrup, and two drops French essence of peppermint; and took half of the draught when the vessel left the harbor, and the other half on the return trip; and though as a rule affected by sea-sickness when crossing the Channel, he entirely avoided this disagreeable malady, and regards chloral as an efficacious preventive.—*Journal de Thérapeutique.*

Colonel Knox, an extensive traveller, says the following prescription has saved him, and many others to whom he has given it, from being sick at sea:

The night before you are to sail, take a blue pill—ten grains—just before going to bed; and when you get up in the morning, take, the first thing, a dose of citrate of magnesia. Then eat your breakfast and go on board, and I will wager four to one that you will not be sea-sick a moment.

How to Treat Sprains of the Wrist or Ankle.

As soon as possible after the accident, get a cotton bandage one or two yards long, and two to two and a half inches wide; wet it in cold water, and roll it smoothly and firmly around the injured part. Keep the limb at rest, exposed to the air, and continually damp with cold water. The sooner after the accident the bandage is applied, the less pain and swelling there will be; but if pain becomes excessive, care must be taken to slightly loosen the bandage.

What to do in Cases of Sunstroke and Fits.

Sunstroke, which is an instantaneous inflammation occasioned by the sun's rays affecting an enfeebled brain, requires prompt treatment or the patient will speedily die. The approved treatment for sunstroke is, to remove the sufferer into the shade, free the neck from all that binds it, and pour warm water on the head and dash it upon the body, or apply rags dipped in warm water, and renewed every minute. Sometimes it requires an hour or two, before relief is obtained. This, like all other inflammations, is more safely subdued by the use of warm than cold water.

Sunstroke may be prevented by wearing a silk handkerchief or a cabbage leaf, or a wet cloth of any kind, in the crown of the hat. Persons who indulge in stimulating drinks are more liable to sunstroke than others. Laborers exposed to the sun's rays should wash the head in cold water several times a day, and the body with a wet towel every night before going to bed, rubbing sufficiently to cause redness of the skin.

When a man falls in a *fit*, loosen the clothing but keep the head and shoulders raised. Give him plenty of air; the bystanders must not be permitted to crowd around him. He will soon come to himself if let alone, and should then be kept quiet till he is able to go or be removed to his home.

Tetter, Ringworm and Barber's Itch.

Dr. Chase, of Michigan, says he speaks from extensive experience in recommending cigar ashes, as a cure for these complaints. He says, that half of one cigar cured him of itch when a barber would not undertake to shave him. His remedy is as follows:

Take the best Cuba cigar, and smoke a sufficient length of time to accumulate a quarter or half inch of ashes upon the end of it; then wet the whole surface of the sore with saliva from the mouth, and rub the ashes thoroughly into and all over the sore or eruption; do this three times a day, and inside of a week all will be smooth and well. A more reliable remedy for itch and tetter is given in the succeeding chapter.

How to Avoid Curvature of the Spine.

In nineteen cases out of twenty, crook-back results from weakness of some of the ligaments and muscles which support and move the spine, or from irregularity of strength in their various parts. The age of curvature is from eight to eighteen; the subjects most liable to it are delicate children of the upper and middle classes, particularly schoolgirls. At this tender age, the bones, ligaments and muscles of the spine have not yet acquired that consolidation and firmness which is necessary to support the weight of the head, shoulders and chest. The prevention and remedy for this disease are as simple as is the mode of its production. The muscles must be strengthened by regular exercise; and that is the best exercise which calls all the muscles on each side of the spine into action. Nothing excels the old *skipping-rope* for the purpose, if used in moderation. The swing of the arms expands the chest and strengthens the respiratory muscles, thereby giving room for the admission of a larger amount of air to the lungs. The rapid bending of the body and the jump exercise every muscle of the back and hip equally. But the swing-rope and other calisthenic apparatus are also useful. Great fatigue must always be avoided, whether curvature has already taken place or is only impending.

When curvature has already occurred, the patient must not be taken to a quack or a specialist, to have all sorts of irons and cramping bandages applied. Gentle, but frequent and regular, exercise must be used, always short of fatigue; a little skipping, light dumb-bells, or the swing-rope, will answer the purpose better than long walks. The patient must maintain the erect position for a *very short period of time* at once, and then the horizontal position must be resorted to. Alternations of *short* periods of activity with *long* ones of repose, several times a day, succeed the best. For repose, a sofa with a hair mattrass, and with a cushion to rest the arms and forehead upon, is far preferable to the old-fashioned back board; or Verral's apparatus may be used. In any case, the patient should lie principally on her face, as the spine is thus placed in a better position for falling into its normal shape than when the supine position is adopted. In this position, the weight of the body is taken from off the spine and thrown upon the chest and abdomen, resting upon the couch.

In this connection, we submit two or three thoughts that seem to be of great practical importance; and the first is in relation to

Cold Water in Disease.

An anonymous writer remarks, forcibly: "It is very doubtful if there is a single possible disease in which the patient should not have cold water *ad libitum*. Oh, how the babes often suffer for cold water! A nursing babe is given, no matter how thirsty, nothing but milk. The little lips are dry and cracked, and the little tongue so parched it can scarcely nurse, and yet it has nothing but milk to assuage its craving thirst. Try it yourself, mother, when you have a fever, and we are sure that ever after, when your darling is dying with thirst, the teaspoon and a tumbler of cold water will be in constant use."

Uses of Alcohol as a Medicine.

Surgeon-General Hammond said in a recent lecture before the New York Neurological Society, "that alcohol, even in large quantities, is beneficial to some persons, is a point in regard to which I have no doubt, but those persons are not in a normal condition, and when they are restored to health their potations should cease. I have seen many weak, hysterical women drink a pint of whiskey or brandy a day, without experiencing the least intoxicating effects, or even feeling excited by it.

"The exhausted tissue has seemed to absorb it with an energy as though it were the one thing craved, and recovery has been rapid under its use when all other means have failed. I have seen strong men struck down with pneumonia and fever, and apparently saved from the grave by brandy or other alcoholic liquors. I have prevented epileptic seizures by its moderate use. Neuralgic attacks are often cut short by it, and sometimes entirely prevented. It has been efficacious in catalepsy, and in tetanus; it is one of the best antidotes to the bites of poisonous serpents, as I have repeatedly witnessed; in the convulsions of children from teething and other sources of reflex irritation it is invaluable; in the spinal irritation to which women, and especially American women, are so subject, nothing takes its place, and in certain forms of gastric dyspepsia it must be given if we wish to cure our patients."

Of Pyæmia, which is a dangerous disease and regarded as incurable by many physicians, Mrs. Swisshelm says she cured every case that came under her care in the army hospitals, by rubbing the body externally with alcohol and water, and giving internally milk punch, sherry wine, eggs, and broths.

Keep Ammonia in the House.

No housekeeper should be without a bottle of spirits of ammonia, for besides its medical value, it is invaluable for household purposes. It is nearly as useful as soap, and its cheapness brings it within reach of all. "Put a teaspoonful of ammonia in a quart of warm soap suds, dip in a flannel cloth, and wipe off dust and fly-specks, and see for yourself how much labor it will save. No scrubbing will be needful. It will cleanse and brighten silver wonderfully; in a pint of suds mix a teaspoonful of the spirits, dip in your silver spoons, forks, etc., rub with a brush, and polish with chamois skins.

"For washing mirrors and windows it is very desirable; put a few drops of ammonia on a piece of paper and it will readily take off every spot or finger-mark on the glass. It will take out grease spots from every fabric; put on the ammonia nearly clear, lay blotting paper over the place and press a hot flat-iron on it for a few moments. There is no better remedy for heartburn and dyspepsia, and the aromatic spirits of ammonia is especially prepared for these troubles. Ten drops of it in a wine-glass of water are often a great relief. The spirits of ammonia can be taken in the same way, but it is not as palatable.

"In addition to all these uses, the effect of ammonia on vegetation is beneficial. If you desire roses, geraniums, fuchsias, etc., to become more flourishing, you can try it upon them by adding five or six drops to every pint of warm water that you give them, but don't repeat the dose oftener than once in five or six days, lest you stimulate them too highly. So be sure and keep a large bottle of it in the house and have a glass stopper for it, as it is very evanescent and also injurious to corks."

Also keep a small quantity of

Chlorate of Potash in the House.

An anonymous writer says we have never found anything equal to it for a simple, ulcerated sore throat. Dissolve a small teaspoonful of it in a tumbler of water; then occasionally take a teaspoonful of the solution, and gargle the throat. It is nearly tasteless, and not at all offensive to take, and is hence well adapted for children. Nothing is better than this for chapped or cracked hands. Wash them in the weak solution, and they will soon be well. It is also good for a rough, pimply, or chapped face. It may be had of any druggist. Common salt has been recommended for the incipient stages of the dreaded disease, diphtheria; but we have no doubt this would be better. If some scheming medicine-man should, under a high-sounding Greek or Oriental name, introduce some ingredients to conceal its nature, and expend a hundred thousand dollars in advertising, he might make a fortune out of it, and possibly as honestly as some of the great patent-medicine vendors.

Medicinal Uses of Ice and Vinegar.

In all inflammations, whether internal or external, ice diminishes rapidly the size of the blood-vessels, and thus relieves the pain they give when thus swollen by their pressing against the nerves, which are always in the neighborhood of the arteries of the system. Swallowing ice freely in small lumps is the chief treatment in inflammation of the stomach, and the constant application of ice, pounded fine, and enveloping the head with it by means of a bladder or other contrivance, is said to be the best remedy for that dangerous malady, inflammation of the brain.

To "settle the stomach" when some discomfort is experienced after eating, some persons find relief by taking a pickle, or a little vinegar, which, in its action on food, is more nearly like the gastric juice than any other fluid known. A teaspoonful of vinegar in each glass of water will prevent any ill effects from using the water of limestone localities by those accustomed to other kinds of drinking water.

Hot Water Relieves Pain.

There is scarcely an ache or pain in the whole body which is not soothed or removed by hot water if applied as follows: Dip a piece of flannel or any cloth, of five or six folds or layers, in boiling water and lay it on the painful part, covering it instantly with a dry flannel of which the edges should extend over the wet one an inch or more: as soon as the wet flannel has dried a little, or in about five minutes, slip it out under one edge of the dry cloth and introduce another flannel as hot as can be handled; do this in so adroit a manner as to allow as little cold air as possible to get to the skin touched by the hot flannel;

persevere until the pain is removed. Physicians assert that by this hot-water poultice the most violent, dry, and distressing coughs have been relieved in a few minutes, and some forms of croup subdued in half an hour.

We cannot, perhaps, close this chapter with any observation more practically useful than the following from one of the most prolific writers on health topics America has produced:

The great practical lesson which I wish to inculcate, to be engraven as on a plate of steel, on the memory of children and youth, young men and women, the mature and the gray-headed: *Allow nothing short of fire or endangered life to induce you to resist, for one single moment, nature's alvine call.* So far from refusing a call for any reason short of life and death you should *go at the usual time and solicit*, and doing so you will have your reward in a degree of healthfulness, and in a length of life, which very few are ever permitted to enjoy.

If the love of health and life, or the fear of inducing painful disease cannot induce you to adopt the plan I have recommended, there is another argument which, to young gentlemen and young ladies, may appear more convincing —*personal cleanliness*. [If you suffer yourself to become and remain costive you will smell badly; the breath of a costive child even is scarcely to be endured.]

Cold feet, sick headache, piles, fistulas, these, with scores of other diseases, have their first foundations laid in constipation, which itself is infallibly induced by resisting nature's first calls. Reader, let it be your wisdom never to do it again.

CHAPTER XV.

CHILDREN AND THEIR DISEASES.

"Nothing can be too insignificant for the attention of the wisest which is not too insignificant to give pleasure or pain to the meanest."—
MACAULAY.

CHILDREN, in their health and appearance, are one of the tests of thrift and sources of comfort within a household. To rear up a family of children, strong in body and sound in mind, is about the only evidence that most persons can leave behind them that they have not lived in the world in vain; while puny, nervous, sickly and silly children betray their parents' secret weaknesses, and are living monuments that the laws of health have been somehow violated.*

---

* Travellers have frequently remarked, that females among the Indian and other uncivilized races bring forth children with far less pain, difficulty and danger than the women in Europe and the United States. The secret of this exemption from the pains of parturition appears to be, according to the views of modern physiologists, that their food consists less of those articles that form bone or osseous matter; and consequently the child, previous to birth, is an elastic, yielding and India-rubber-like substance, easily born. It is believed, therefore, by some, that if white women, during the last three or four months of gestation, were to confine their food principally to ripe fruits and green vegetables, roasted apples, oranges and fresh animal food, with very little bread and butter and no pastries, they would have no more difficulty in bringing forth children than their tawny or copper-colored sisters. Many instances are given in medical works

Proper Food for Infants.

In infancy, as all through life, food is an object that deserves especial attention. Dr. Combe remarks:

"Take particular care of the food of an infant. If it is nourished by the mother, her own diet should be simple, nourishing and temperate. If the child be brought up 'by hand,' the milk of a new milch cow, mixed with one-third water and sweetened a little with white sugar, should be the only food until the teeth come. This is more suitable than any preparations of flour or arrowroot, the nourishment of which is too highly concentrated. Never give a child bread, cake or meat before the teeth appear. If the food appear to distress the child after eating, first ascertain if the milk be really from a new milch cow, as it may otherwise be too old. Learn also whether the cow lives on proper food. Cows that are fed on *still-slops*, as is often the case in cities, furnish milk which is very unhealthful."

---

of women who, though they had suffered fearfully in child-bearing so long as they ate what people generally eat, by changing their food to fruits and articles not containing bone-making elements, brought forth their children with so little difficulty that, had they not been influenced by custom, they could have resumed their duties the next day.

It is greatly to be deplored that science has not discovered some certain method of regulating the number of offspring; so that parents need not have more children than they want or can care for; or rather, it is greatly to be deplored that this information is now possessed mainly by the wealthy and intelligent, who may or may not need it, while it is withheld from the poor, feeble and diseased who do need it. All theories for the improvement of society are mere vapor, so long as there are born into the world every day thousands of children who should never have been born, and who of necessity must become a curse to their fellows. "Fools die for want of wisdom," and thousands of feeble women are dying slow deaths daily; households are wrecked, and idiots are multiplied, for want of an item of scientific knowledge which every husband and wife ought to possess.

Dr. Clarke, physician in ordinary to the Queen of England, adds: "There is no greater error in the management of children, than of giving them animal food very early. Children so fed become very liable to attacks of fever and inflammation, affecting particularly the mucous membranes; and measles and other diseases incident to childhood are generally severe in their attacks."

Condensed Milk for Infants.

Many mothers are now using "Condensed Milk" for their infants, and when perfectly pure, it is well suited for the purpose. Dr. Cuibourt, of the French Academy, says, "Cow's milk with the addition of its weight of water and a little sugar is as nearly as possible equal to woman's milk." The "Condensed Milk" diluted with seven to nine parts of water exactly answers this description, and as it keeps sweet for a length of time without any tendency to sourness and without undergoing any chemical change, "it is superior as food for infants even to the present ordinary milk."

How to Treat Young Infants.

On the birth of an infant light should be excluded from its eyes for an hour, and when dressed it should be put to the breast, for though the secretion of milk may not have taken place, the effort will promote it and do the child good. The mother's milk is the only food the infant will require for months, and it should not be spoon-fed until it begins to cut its teeth.

Food from the first should be given at stated times, and with punctual regularity. A mother when healthy should suckle her own child, and if unable to do so, a wet nurse of good health and morals should be selected. She should be careful to have milk in good supply, and it should be of an age and quality suited to nourish the child. It should have a blue thin appearance, and sweet to the taste; it is not likely to be good when thick and yellow, and if the milk is not good the child will cease to thrive. Suckling infants at the breast exercises all their muscles, and the effort does them good, far more than taking food in any other way. The saliva promoted in suckling is carried into the stomach with the food and is a great aid to digestion.

Mental emotions have a direct influence on the secretions of the milk, and suckling mothers should be careful to avoid agitations as much as possible, or the heat of the milk may affect the bowels of the child and perhaps cause convulsions.

What is the proper period for *weaning a child* seems not to be definitely settled—some say six months, others twelve; but we think, when circumstances admit of it, and the mother is healthy and careful, it is better to continue the nursing until after the second summer, which is always a critical period in a child's existence. Infants should be weaned gradually, not suddenly, and rubbing the nipple with some innocent caustic solution, as a little powdered aloes made into a paste with a few drops of water, will soon give them a distaste for the breast. It is a good plan for a mother to send her infant away, or leave home herself for a week or two, in order to wean it.

The drink of young children at meal times should always be hot, but not hot enough to injure the teeth, and some very serious maladies result from eating cold food, in cold weather, for a long time. The very young and the very old are deficient in heat, and this should be supplied to the stomach by warm drinks. A good drink for young children is known as *Cambric tea*, which is made by pouring half a cup of hot milk into half a cup of boiling water, adding as much sugar as is agreeable. This resembles the *eau de Sucre*, or sweetened water, so popular on the Boulevards of Paris.

A very good *pap*, for infants not old enough to eat meat, is made as follows:

Put a tablespoonful of flour into a pap saucepan, to which add by degrees two gills of milk, mixing it into a very smooth batter with a wooden spoon; place the saucepan upon the fire, let it boil ten minutes, keeping it stirred the whole time or it is liable to burn or become brown; then add about half an ounce of sugar and a little salt; put it into a basin and it is ready for use. A little butter is also very good in it.

Soyer says that he has known a very robust man to make a hearty dinner of two plates of this pap by introducing bread into it.

Bread and milk is a good breakfast dish for infants of twelve months old. The bread should be cut into slices, the milk heated to the point of boiling and poured over the bread, the cup covered and allowed to stand for five minutes. This is better than to boil the bread and milk together, or to break bread into cold milk. When children are delicate, *porridge* is often preferable to bread and milk. Put two tablespoonfuls of Scotch grits or oatmeal in the milk saucepan, and pour over it half a pint of milk: let it boil ten minutes, keeping well stirred; add a small piece of butter and a little sugar, and the porridge is ready for use.

Dr. John Hunter, one of the most eminent of English physicians, summed up the proper treatment of infants by saying, "Give them a plenty of milk, a plenty of sleep, and a plenty of flannel."

What to do when a Baby Cries.

[Whenever an infant begins to cry, without any apparent cause, by day or night, says Mrs. Henry Ward Beecher, let your first act be to examine its clothing, loosen it, remove the pins, or untie the strings, and see if the lungs have full space to expand, and the body a chance to move every limb and muscle. Rub the body gently with your warm hand, particularly the back, lungs and bowels, to promote the circulation which the barbarous swaddling-bands have all day impeded. Try this remedy particularly at night, and unless you again "put on the screws," in most cases your baby will fall into a peaceful slumber and you may hope for unbroken rest.

But though the garments may be all properly adjusted it may be suffering from cold. Touch the little blue hands, and you will find them like ice; take the child in your lap, draw your chair to the fire, heat a blanket and wrap about it, lay it on the stomach, across your lap, shake out the foolishly long robes, and hold its toes to the fire till warm. Many a child who has cried for hours will, under this simple treatment, in a few minutes be fast asleep.

Endeavor to imagine yourself in an infant's place when it manifests symptoms you do not well understand. You wrap its hands and feet so closely, when you lay it down to sleep, that it cannot stir; could you remain two hours thus fettered without becoming cramped and full of pain? Loosen the wrappings; shake up the pillow, and turn it over occasionally (and by the way a good *hair pillow*, not too full, and well beaten every day, that it may not become lumpy, is far more healthful for any child than feathers). If awake, change its position; or if it has lain long, take it up, toss it gently and play with it a while to give it a pleasant variety, and cause the blood to circulate freely through the whole body.

If these simple methods do not pacify a crying child it is very probable that some of the above-mentioned causes have produced *colic,* but do not give the simplest medicine till you have tried what virtue there is in an injection of tepid water. Unless the crying indicates the beginning of some acute disease, we have invariably found the effects almost magical, and in no case will it be hurtful.]

We may add to these excellent suggestions, that infants often cry because they are tormented with thirst, which most nurses and mothers do not gratify. They suppose the crying proceeds from hunger, and the breast milk is given, but this does not satisfy. Dr. Dewees says, that he has often seen infants, when seeming to suffer exquisite agony, rendered perfectly quiet and easy by a draught of cool water.

What Crying sometimes Indicates.

The crying of a child will often indicate to an experienced medical man the nature of the trouble. The cry of teething, says Dr. Chavasse, is a fretful cry: the cry of earache is short, sharp, piercing, and decisive, the head being moved about from side to side, and the little hand being often put up to the affected side of the head; the cry of bowel-ache is also expressive—the cry is not so piercing as from earache, and is an interrupted straining cry, accompanied with a drawing up of the legs to the belly; the cry of bronchitis is a gruffy, phlegmatic cry; the cry of inflammation of the lungs is more a moan than a cry; the cry of croup is hoarse, and rough, and ringing, and is so characteristic that it may truly be called "the croupy cry," moreover he breathes as though he breathed through muslin; the cry of inflammation of the membrane of the brain is a piercing shriek—a danger signal—most painful to hear; the cry of a child recovering from a severe illness is a cross, and wayward, and tearful cry; he may truly be said to be in a quarrelsome mood; he bursts out without rhyme or reason into a passionate flood of tears; tears are always in a severe illness to be looked upon as a good omen, as a sign of amendment; tears, when a child is dangerously ill, are rarely if ever seen.

Proper Treatment in Childhood.

During infancy children should be encouraged to sleep, and to promote this object light should be excluded from the bed-room as much as possible, the bedding should be soft, the blankets fine and the counterpanes very light; the pillows should be small and not made of feathers, as they are too heating to the head. A good pillow for infants may be made of cotton-batting, enclosed in ticking, with threads run through it to keep the batting in place or from forming knots.

Towards evening the child should be kept active and wakeful, so that its rest during the night may be prolonged and undisturbed. Mothers will save themselves a world of trouble by not accustoming their babies to be rocked to sleep either in the cradle or in the arms. Young mothers are apt to err in this way, and bring upon themselves a vast deal of unnecessary trouble, and then resolve never to have any more children. A child, if placed in a crib or bed, without being rocked, will probably cry at first, but an hour's cry will not hurt it and it will soon get into the habit of going to sleep, especially if stated times are adhered to. During teething, children are always restless and fretful, but medicines should be administered with caution, and if the gums show indications of festering, or white spots, a physician should be called in, who will probably lance them.

Nothing tends so much to promote the comfort and the health of children as frequent bathing—in winter in warm or tepid water—but the operation should not be prolonged so as to weary or give pain, and the towels used in drying should be soft.

Teething children, says Dr. Hall, have often been cured of looseness of bowels by being allowed to chew the rind of bacon freely with some of the fat attached, and they chew it greedily; it seems to have a beneficial effect on the gums.

When a child has taken cold it is a good plan to spend five or ten minutes two or three times a day in rubbing into the whole breast, with a soft warm hand, about ten drops of common sweet-oil. The doctor just quoted thinks if such a course were promptly taken the moment a child is observed to be not as well as usual, *nine-tenths of the ailments of children would be averted.* It has a powerful influence in helping nature to cure the very worst forms of diseases to which childhood is liable.

When children have cut their teeth they should be allowed a variety of nutritious but easily digested food— no pork, veal, fried or greasy meats—and whatever meat is given should be cut fine or minced to facilitate mastication; *white crushed wheat*, boiled and sweetened, should form a staple article in their diet.

In the nursery or room where children play, fenders should be placed around the stove, the furniture should have rounded, not sharp corners, and the windows should be well guarded to prevent accidents; a panelling of blackboard is very suitable for a nursery. Parents are often ambitious to see their infants walk early, and this is the cause of the bow or curved legs and weak ankles so frequently seen. Children should be encouraged to crawl, but all are not prepared to walk at the same age, and this is a matter they can best regulate for themselves.

The clothing of infants should be warm, light, and free from compression. The practice of leaving children's limbs bare, especially in cold weather, which some parents adopt, is cruel as well as unsightly. The shoes should fit easily, and care should be taken that they do not become too short before they are worn out. Tight shoes are as torturing as tight-lacing.

It is very unsafe to change the winter clothing of children before the first of May, or to permit them to remain at any season out in the night-air. A well-known physician remarks, that if children were sent to bed within half an hour after sundown and not allowed to go out of doors in the morning until they have had a plain hearty breakfast, "half the diarrhœas, and summer complaints, and croups, which desolate our hearths and hearts so often in summer time," would be prevented.

Parents should compel each of their children, who are over five years of age, to go to a good dentist twice a year and have their teeth examined, and the first symptom of decay removed, and thus children will be spared much suffering and have reason for gratitude during life.

[The *London Sanitary Record* condemns the following as common faults in the treatment of young infants:

When they first wake up it is no uncommon thing to

have a candle flared before their eyes to amuse them with the "pretty red light;" then, perhaps, they are jumped, screamed or whistled at, tossed up in the air so violently that their nerves are thoroughly shaken. At other times the infants are "poked in the ribs," unclean fingers are thrust into their mouths, whether the poor things like it or not, or they may be tickled into spasms, or "bo-peeped" at so vigorously as to thoroughly scare them, if it does not induce St. Vitus' dance. Should the poor, helpless victim scream, which is the only protest it can make, it is libelled by being called fractious, and perhaps dosed with soothing syrup.

Other kind friends of the baby will, in the most thoughtless manner, kiss and hug the poor little victim, even when suffering themselves from sore throat or colds, and so entail an unknown amount of evil on the child, simply from want of common thoughtfulness. If some of these boisterous nurses and friends would remember that a very little violent excitement goes a long way with infants, they would save them much needless suffering, both in the present and in the future. Rest and quietness are the chief things they require, and yet seldom get, especially in a large family, or where there are many friends who take their turn to tickle and amuse the victim into a sort of hysterical spasm, and then think him or her happy. Again, in playing music to them, the most noisy and startling tunes are generally selected, to the acute torture of the sensitive tympanum, instead of those airs which are most soothing and gentle.

These are a few of the many needless sufferings to which children are thoughtlessly exposed. Another very common source of torture is carelessness in wheeling the perambulator. In street crossings these vehicles are more often than not allowed to bump down the full height of the curbstone, and then driven full tilt against the opposite curb. Such shocks try severely the spine and nerves of the tender infants who are unfortunately consigned to the mercies of a careless nurse. We once heard of a baby who was reported to have said, "How stupid parents are!" and if that infant prodigy should live to be a hundred it would never say a truer thing of the majority of fathers, mothers and relatives in general.]

Physical Defects.

In infancy or childhood is the proper time for removing all physical blemishes or imperfections, such as harelip, bad teeth, club-foot and the like. On these subjects, as Dr. Tichnor remarks, parents too often allow themselves to be governed by wrong motives; they start at the idea of causing pain to an infant, not thinking that their tenderheartedness will cause his feelings to be pained through a long life; and because a blemish or deformity does not seem particularly disagreeable to parents, they, therefore, conclude it is not so to others. Children, when they arrive at maturity, do not thank their parents for this misplaced tenderness, and would cheerfully endure almost any suffering to rid themselves of physical imperfections which could easily have been removed in childhood.

Infantile Diseases.

It often happens that within a few weeks after birth a child is affected with a common disease of the skin, called the red gum, or red spots on the breast, back, and loins. It will often disappear without treatment, or after taking a slight dose of aperient medicine. There is another skin affection with a red blush and slight excoriation, arising from want of cleanliness or the rubbing against each other of such parts as the thighs or arms. The best remedy is to wash gently with Castile soap, and use a little zinc ointment.

Vomiting is very common, and often arises from repletion, and in very young children ordinarily needs no treatment. The soured milk may be the cause, and in older children may be cured by two or three grains of powdered ipecacuanha in a little water. Should this not answer, send for the doctor.

Colic is a very common affection among children. Some infants are constantly tormented with colic for the first three or four months of their life, but probably a proper attention to clothing and food from the beginning will prevent these unpleasant visitations. Simple remedies will frequently remove the malady. Give the baby a teaspoonful of *soda mint* every hour or two, and it will be relieved. Place a warm flannel over the bowels and be sure that the feet and hands are warm. Sometimes a few teaspoonfuls of catnip tea will be effectual. A warm foot-bath or an injection of warm water with a little sweet-oil or soap in it are good remedies.

Worms may often be suspected to exist in the intestines, and are characterized by many and varied symptoms, of which the most certain are: irregular appetite, and craving for food after a meal, bowels one time relaxed and again costive; the child is feverish, often picks its nose or grinds its teeth, has fetid breath and often a livid circle under the eyes. Finding worms in the stool, however, is the only positive proof. There are several kinds of worms, of which the principal are the thread or common seat worm, and the long worm. Thread worms, which lodge in the lower part of the intestines, may be removed by injections of cold water, or a little aloes in water, or an infusion of quassia, or lime-water. Oil of chenopodium given, say, two drops in syrup, three times daily, will destroy seat worms.

Santonin is almost a specific for long worms; say, one or two grains every four hours. This is a favorite remedy in Germany, where it is known as the *German Worm-Seed*.

Children troubled with worms should have plenty of salt in their food, and be induced to partake freely of boiled onions.

Thrush is an inflammatory disease of the mouth and a name given to several diseases of a similar character, but distinct. It consists in small white vesicles inside of the mouth, or on the tongue, or inside the cheeks, and is usually accompanied with some derangement of the digestive organs, loss of appetite or diarrhœa. The child sucks with difficulty and pain, and the mouth is sore. It may be cured by the use of a little magnesia, and a lotion composed of borax, two drachms, in an ounce of glycerine, applied frequently by means of the finger on the parts affected.

Convulsions or *fits* frequently attend difficult teething, and are very alarming to inexperienced parents. As soon as a child has the symptoms of an attack it should be placed in a warm bath or tub of warm water, and cold water applied to the head if hot, and friction all over the body. When there is a succession of convulsions, with hours of interval between, there is danger, and a physician should be called in, who will probably lance the gums and order an enema composed of one tablespoonful of salt, one of olive-oil, and a teacupful of gruel to be administered until the bowels are well opened.

Irritant or Remittent Fever in infants, arising from disordered digestion, is very common between the ages of two and six. The symptoms are a dry burning skin, quick pulse and flushed face, redness of the eyes, headache, thirst, restlessness, and delirium. A child two years old should receive an emetic of five grains of ipecacuanha, and a dose of castor-oil. The warm bath will be useful, and the child will, it is likely, get better in a few hours, after a peaceful slumber. Abstinence is recommended, and a physician will probably not be needed. In this disease, after whooping-cough, scarlatina, or measles, more attention is required, and medical advice is necessary. If such is not at hand, use the warm bath, diet of barley-water, arrow-root, etc.

Croup.

This is a disease that frequently attacks children at night, and is distinguished by a peculiar resonant, barking sound from the throat, which any one who has once heard will never forget. Hoarseness is one of the earliest symptoms of croup. If treated properly in its first stage it is rarely dangerous; if allowed to pass to the second stage it is frequently fatal. Promptness in treatment is very essential. Every family with children should have a bottle of some kind of emetic in the house, as ipecacuanha syrup, or tinctures of lobelia and blood-root, equal parts; and as soon as a child shows symptoms of croup, apply hot water to the throat for fifteen or twenty minutes with a sponge or soft cloth, and give an emetic until vomiting takes place. Dr. Simpson, of Philadelphia, recommends powdered alum mixed in syrup, as the most efficient and least dangerous emetic; it can be given in half-teaspoonful doses, repeated every twenty minutes until vomiting takes place. He says no family containing young children should be without powdered alum and syrup of ipecac.

In *child-crowing*, or *spurious croup*, which sometimes occurs during teething, and which is very dangerous if not instantly relieved, the proper treatment is to imitate artificial respiration as soon as the paroxysm is upon the child, then put his feet and legs into *hot* water with salt and mustard in it; and, if necessary, place him up to his neck in a hot bath, still dashing water upon his face and head. If he does not quickly recover his breath, sharply smack his back and buttocks. The doctor when he arrives will probably lance the gums and prescribe some simple remedy. Regulate the diet, and watch the child, for the spasm is liable to recur, and may be instantly fatal.

Measles.

In the treatment of measles ordinarily very little medicine is required. Castor-oil may be given to keep the bowels open.

Children with the measles should not have their usual food, but plenty of warm milk and water, and as many roasted apples as they want. Warm teas of elderberry blossoms, sweet marjoram, or sage, may be used, until the rash is well defined. Keep the room moderately warm and of an equable temperature, not one hour hot and the next cold. Remember, children sick with the measles should be kept tolerably warm, while in small-pox the air which surrounds them should be cold rather than warm. To allay the itching which comes when the spots begin to disappear, powder with violet powder. When the breathing is short, and the wheezing is great, fifteen drops of ipecacuanha wine mixed with simple syrup and water should be given every two hours. Some physicians say that even in a mild case of measles and in favorable weather, a child should not be allowed to leave the house under a fortnight.

Mumps

Is a contagious disease, indicated by swelling and inflammation of the large salivary glands situated just in front of the ear, near the joint of the lower jaw. The peculiar appearance and irritable temper induced have given the name of mumps to this disease.

The treatment is simple, and friction with soap or camphor liniment will ordinarily cause mumps to disappear in four or five days, leaving not a trace behind. An oatmeal poultice, or a bag containing bran heated, may be applied at night. When the mumps show symptoms of migrating from the glands of the neck to the scrotum, call in a good physician.

Whooping-Cough.

Whooping-cough cannot be entirely cured until it has run its course, but it can be greatly mitigated by the use of proper remedies. Dr. Dailey says he has successfully treated more than one hundred cases by the following syrup:

> Take the strongest West India rum.......1 pint.
> Anise oil................................2 ounces.
> Honey..................................1 pint.
> Lemon juice...........................4 ounces.

Mix. Dose for children one teaspoonful with as much sugar and water, three or four times a day; for adults one tablespoonful.

The physicians in Philadelphia prescribe nitric acid, chloral and bromide of ammonium, one grain for each year of the child's age; and these remedies and judicious diet will greatly relieve the distressing spasms. If restless at night, give the child a warm bath.

To relieve soreness in the chest rub it with the following mixture:

Half an ounce of oil of amber; half an ounce of oil of cloves; one ounce of olive oil; and two teaspoonfuls of laudanum. The diet to consist principally of barley water and whey.

Dr. Delamere says whooping-cough may be simply and quickly cured, "if the child take, morning, noon, and night, a dose of *finely-ground alum* mixed in a small quantity of powdered sugar for three or four days. The dose varies from one to two grains, according to the age of the child, and goes on gradually increasing. If necessary, after the fourth day a child eight years old must take seven grains of ground alum three times a day. Milk diet must be abstained from, and all draughts of *cold air* carefully avoided."

When whooping-cough is not cured within a month, try a change of air, even from a pure country air to the air of a smoky, gas-laden town. Some persons assert that the *best* remedy for an *obstinate* case of whooping-cough is for a child to live the great part of every day in *gas-works.* Sea-breezes will often as by magic drive away the disease.

Dr. Valentine Mott strongly recommended the following prescription for whooping-cough:

>Hydrocyanic acid....................6 drops.
>Extract of belladonna................2 grs.
>Paregoric elixir...... ....3 drachms.
>Syrup of balsam of tolu..............1 ounce.
>Water................................3 ounces.

Mix. A teaspoonful three or four times daily.

Cholera Infantum.

This is commonly known to mothers as summer complaint, and at its commencement can, in most cases, be relieved by simple treatment. The patient should be put to bed, and a mustard plaster placed over the stomach and bowels. A small lump of ice should be given every few minutes, and take of this mixture:

Husband's magnesia, and aromatic spirit of ammonia, one teaspoonful of each, mixed and shaken in a bottle, with one-half tumblerful of peppermint water—a teaspoonful every twenty minutes. This is for common summer complaint or *Cholera Infantum*, and to be given at its commencement.

Diarrhœa.

Very many children as well as grown persons die annually of this disease, who might be saved by the use of the proper remedies. Rest in bed is the first requisite to effect a cure, in this and all other bowel disorders. If locomotion is compulsory, the misfortune of the necessity may be lessened by having a stout piece of woollen flannel bound tightly around the abdomen, so as to be doubled in front, and kept well in its place. Take a teaspoonful every three or four hours of the following

DIARRHŒA DROPS—Tincture of rhubarb, and compound spirits of lavender, of each four ounces; laudanum, two ounces; cinnamon oil, two drops; mix. In very bad cases it might be well to use after each passage an injection, composed of new milk, with thick mucilage of slippery elm, of each one pint; sweet oil, one gill; molasses, one-half pint; salt, one ounce; laudanum, one drachm; mix, and inject what the bowels will retain.

In all bowel complaints the only remedy, however, that is

worthy the name of specific, is a tea made of the bark of the sweet gum tree (liquid amber), that grows all over the United States, south of latitude 41°. It is said to be an invaluable medicine for children.

Diphtheria.

A physician of Jersey City, who claims that he has treated two hundred and ninety-three cases of diphtheria, within three months, without losing a single patient, though a majority of his cases were of the worst or malignant type of the disease, has published an outline of his treatment, which is as follows:

[Our first treatment is directed to destroying the fungoid virus which is deposited in the throat, bronchial tubes, or both: apply with camel's-hair pencil chromic acid, properly diluted, to every patch of diphtheritic membrane within your reach; give inhalations regularly by means of Codman & Shurtleff's steam atomizer of preparations containing lactic acid, aqua calcis, and chlorate potassa. If the patient is old enough, let him gargle his throat also with the above.

The effect of the atomizer is, that no matter how young the patients, every breath they draw will deposit the antiseptic spray directly upon the diphtheritic membrane, or the fungoid virus, where membrane is not deposited, thereby destroying and neutralizing its poisonous influence on the system, and controlling the spread of the disease, no matter how deep down in the bronchial tubes it may have reached. From the commencement give the most nourishing fluids, consisting of milk punch, Wommel's extract of malt ferrated, in milk and wine; ale, syrups lactate ferri; by this means we prepare the system to stand the debilitating influence of the disease which may follow.

To the throat apply cloths wet in cold water; if there is much inflammation use ice-water; if there is great swelling, endangering closure of the throat, use ice cracked fine and applied by means of a rubber ice-bag; this always relieves; also give small lumps of ice to hold in the mouth. When diphtheritic membrane is shedding off, there is at times great hemorrhage; the patient may bleed to death if it is not stopped shortly. A preparation of per chlor. ferri, used in a steam atomizer, will stop it immediately when nothing else can reach it. Never be without it.

Give directions, if patient in your absence suddenly turns cold and has a livid expression about the face, with very feeble pulse, evidencing danger of collapse, to give brandy freely and apply mustard and heat to extremities, with free rubbing of body with stimulating liniment or heated spirits. The third danger arises principally from weakness of the heart's action and albuminous deposits in kidneys, the latter inviting uramic poisoning, which causes coma, convulsions and death. Electricity in both cases will assist in removing the trouble.]

Diphtheria is decidedly contagious, and when one child in a family is taken down with it, the rest should be removed.

Earache.

Some children suffer exceedingly with pain in the ear, but generally instant relief may be had by dropping into the ear a little *ether combined with almond oil*, or applying a small flannel bag, filled with salt heated, or a hog's bladder partially filled with hot water. A bladder is the most effective instrument for applying moist heat, as it adapts itself to all the little inequalities of the external ear.

Among the domestic remedies for earache is this: put boiling water with a little soda or laudanum in it into a teapot, and hold the spout as near the ear as can be endured; keep a shawl or other covering around the head, and over the teapot, so as to confine the steam.

Another remedy is to take the heart from a roasted onion, cool it, and dip in sweet oil and laudanum, press the onion slightly into the ear, and tie a handkerchief around the head. Avoid all *cold* applications.

Burns, Scalds, etc.

Molasses, carbolic acid, flour, or the white of an egg well beaten' up in a tablespoonful of lard, are good to relieve the pain of a burn. For serious burns, the following salve has proved excellent, curing without blistering, or leaving a scar.

Take equal parts of turpentine, sweet-oil, beeswax; melt the oil and wax together, and when a little cool, add the turpentine, and stir until cold; apply by spreading on thin cloth—linen is the best. This is also good for chaps on hands or lips, or sore or cracked nipples.

To Cure Itching Feet from Frost Bites.

Take hydrochloric acid, one ounce; rain water, seven ounces; wash the feet with it two or three times daily, or wet the socks with the preparation, until relieved.

Itch.

A quaint writer says, "that about five dollars worth of advertised ointment will help the itch wonderfully, but a warm bath, a very coarse towel, and a few applications of *dry sulphur in powder*, which will cost five cents, will cure the trouble."

This may do for the common or dirty itch, which comes between the fingers, but for the regular Psora, or " seven years' itch," which is much more common, even among people of good circumstances, than most persons suppose, nothing will succeed so well as *red precipitate*, in lard or butter. Dr. Chase says the following ointment will cure all cases of "the Itch," and also pimples, blotches, etc.:

Unsalted butter, one pound; Burgundy pitch, two ounces; spirits of turpentine, two ounces; red precipitate pulverized, one and one-quarter ounce; melt the pitch, and add the butter, stirring well together; then remove from the fire, and when a little cool add the turpentine, and lastly the precipitate, and stir until cold.

Dr. J. F. Bird, of Philadelphia, who has been remarkably successful in curing cutaneous diseases, uses for the Itch the following ointment: Red precipitate, one ounce; Venice turpentine, half ounce; simple cerate or unsalted butter, one quarter pound.

Even tetterous affections are often readily cured, by the application of this ointment.

Hiccough

Is generally of such a trivial nature as not to require interference. But should it be severe, give four or five grains of calcined magnesia, with a little syrup, and anise-seed water. Hiccough may generally be traced to over-eating.

Scarlet Fever

Is one of those diseases that are very much dreaded when they make their appearance in the household, though it is by no means so fatal as is generally supposed. With proper treatment and careful nursing there is really very little danger to be apprehended from scarlet fever, unless it be of the malignant type. In order to distinguish a case of scarlatina from other eruptive diseases, as measles, erysipelas, etc., a French physician has discovered a very simple method; that is, by drawing the back of the nail or a penholder along the skin where the eruption is situated; and if a *white line* appears, or, in other words, if the skin is observed to grow pale, and to present a white trace which remains for one or two minutes or longer, then disappears, that is scarlatina.

It was the opinion of Dr. Sydenham that scarlet fever is oftentimes fatal "through the officiousness of the doctor;" and Dr. Chavasse says a truer remark was never made. The following plan of treatment has proved successful in so many cases, that, it is believed, if carefully observed, any ordinary case of scarlet fever may be cured by it and without leaving any ill consequences behind.

1. For the first five or six days, keep the room cool, thoroughly ventilated, and scant clothes on the bed.

2. Note carefully and warily when there is a change in the temperature of the skin, and the patient feels chilly, then instantly close the windows and put extra covering on the bed.

3. Apply to the throat a barm and oatmeal poultice, changed three times a day, and give every four hours a tablespoonful of the following mixture:

>   Diluted sulphuric acid................1 drachm.
>   Simple syrup........................1½ ounce.
>   Infusion of roses (rose leaves and boiling water)........................4½ ounces.

[The sulphuric acid in the mixture is regarded by some physicians as a *specific in scarlet fever* as much as quinine in ague.]

4. Administer no opening medicines for the first ten

days at least; and no leeches, blisters, emetics, spongings or painting the tonsils with caustic.

5. Keep the patient on a low diet for the first few days, but give cold water freely.

6. The patient must not leave the house in the summer under a month; in the winter under six weeks.

[This is the plan of treatment recommended by Dr. Chavasse, of Birmingham, England, who has written a paper on the *Treatment of Scarlet Fever*, which has been widely copied into medical journals, and as he claims to have been remarkably successful in his treatment, and the subject is a very important one, we will give his directions in full. He says:

Pray pay particular attention to my rules, and carry out my directions to the very letter—as I can promise you that if the scarlet fever be not malignant, the plan I am about to recommend will, with God's blessing, be generally successful.

What is the first thing to be done? Send the child to bed; throw open the windows, be it winter or summer, and have a thorough ventilation; for the *bed-room must be kept cool*—I may say cold. Do not be afraid of fresh air, for fresh air, for the first few days, is essential to recovery. *Fresh air and plenty of it, in scarlet fever, is the best doctor a child can have;* let these words be written legibly on your mind. Take down the curtains of the bed, remove the valance.

If it be summer time, let the child be only covered with a sheet: if it be winter time, in addition to the sheet, he should have one blanket over him.

Now for the THROAT.—The best *external* application is a barm and oatmeal poultice. How ought it to be applied and how made? Put a half teacupful of barm into a saucepan, put it on the fire to boil; as soon as it boils take it off the fire, and stir oatmeal into it, until it is of the consistence of a nice soft poultice; then place it on a rag and apply it to the throat; carefully fasten it on with bandage, two or three turns of the bandage going round the throat, and two or three over the crown of the head, so as nicely to apply the poultice where it is wanted—that is to say, to cover the tonsils. Tack the bandage; do not pin it. Let the poultice be changed three times a day. The best medicine is the acidulated infusion of roses, sweetened with syrup: diluted sulphuric acid, one drachm; simple syrup, one ounce and a half; infusion of roses, four ounces and a half; let the infusion of roses be made merely with the rose leaves and boiling water — a tablespoonful to be given every four hours. It is grateful and refreshing, it is pleasant to take, it abates fever and thirst, it cleans the throat and tongue of mucus and is peculiarly efficacious in scarlet fever; as soon as the fever is abated it gives an appetite. My belief is *that the sulphuric acid in the mixture is a specific in scarlet fever*, as much as quinine is in ague, and sulphur in itch. I have reason to say so, for, in numerous cases, I have seen its immense value. Now with regard to food.—If the child be at the breast, keep him entirely to it. If he be weaned, and under two years old, give him milk and water and cold water to drink. If he be older, give him toast and water, and plain water from the pump, as much as he chooses; let it be quite cold—the colder the better. Weak black tea, or thin gruel, may be given, but not caring, unless he be an infant at the breast, if he take nothing but *cold* water. If the child be two years old and upwards, roasted apples with sugar, and grapes will be very refreshing, and will tend to cleanse both the mouth and the throat. Avoid broths and stimulants of every kind. When the appetite returns you may consider the patient to be safe. The diet ought now to be gradually improved. Bread and butter, milk and water, and arrow-root made with equal parts of new milk and water, should for the first two or three days be given. Then a light batter or rice pudding may be added, and in a few days afterward, either a little chicken or a mutton-chop.

The essential remedies, then, in scarlet fever, are, for the first few days: (1) plenty of fresh air and ventilation; (2) plenty of cold water to drink; (3) barm poultices to the throat; and (4) the acidulated infusion of roses' mixture as a medicine.

Now, then, comes very important advice. After the first five days, probably five or six, sometimes as early as the fourth day, *watch carefully and warily, and note the time the skin will suddenly become cool*, the child will say that he feels chilly; now is the time you must change your tactics —*instantly close the windows*, and *put extra clothing*, a blanket or two, on his bed. A flannel night-gown should be now worn next to the skin, until the dead skin has peeled off, when it should be discontinued. The patient ought, however, to wear in the daytime a flannel waistcoat. His drinks must now be given with the chill off; he ought to have a warm cup of tea, and gradually his diet should, as I have previously recommended, be improved. There is one important caution I wish to impress upon you: do not give opening medicine during the time the eruption is out. In all probability the bowels will be opened; if so, all well and good; but do not, on any account, for the first ten days, use artificial means to open them. It is my firm conviction, that the administration of purgatives in scarlet fever is a fruitful source of dropsy, of disease, and death. When we take into consideration the sympathy there is between the skin and the mucous membrane, I think that we should pause before giving irritating medicines, such as purgatives.

The irritation of aperients on the mucous membrane may cause the poison of the skin disease (for scarlet fever is a blood poison) to be driven internally to the kidneys, to the throat, to the pericardium (bag of the heart), or to the brain. You may say, Do you not purge if the bowels be not open for a week? I say emphatically, No! I consider my great success in the treatment of scarlet fever to be partly owing to my avoidance of aperients during the first ten days of the child's illness. If the bowels, after the ten days, are not properly opened, a dose or two of the following mixture should be given: take of simple syrup, three drachms; essence of senna, nine drachms: to make a mixture. Two teaspoonfuls to be given early in the morning occasionally, and to be repeated in four hours, if the first dose should not operate.]

These directions are plain, practical and based upon extensive experience in the treatment of scarlet fever; but there is one thing omitted, which physicians in Philadelphia regard as very important—and that is, to anoint the body all over, two or three times daily, with some fatty substance, as bacon or ham fat. This allays irritability, and is found to be very beneficial to the patient.

The late Simon Gartland, of Philadelphia, was in the habit, for many years, of distributing the following directions for use in cases of scarlet fever and typhus fever, and said he never knew a death to occur when they were followed:

Put one peck of charcoal in a furnace and burn the gas off in the open air; take it to the sick-room, and sprinkle over it gradually about five pounds of common brown sugar; then sprinkle over this one gallon of cider vinegar. It should be tried every day for three days to make it effectual. Of course medical advice is required besides.

CHAPTER XVI.

SLEEP AND ITS APPLIANCES.

"The real cause of sleep has been a matter of much guessing and speculation with medical men, and even very learned philosophers have disagreed in opinion on the subject. Napoleon, whose genius seemed capable of seizing every subject of contemplation with giant grasp, remarked, while distinguishing between *sleep* and *death*, that sleep was the suspension of the *voluntary* powers of man, and death was the suspension of those that were *involuntary*."—DR. GUNN.

OF all medicines for the cure of most of life's ailments, the best is sleep. It is what Shakspeare called it,

"The death of each day's life, sore labor's bath,
Balm of hurt minds, great nature's second course,
Chief nourisher in life's feast."

One-third of nearly every man's life is spent in sleep; and to many of the busy dwellers in cities, home has no other meaning than a place in which to sleep.

Proper Time to Sleep.

In former times, it was supposed that six hours passed in sleep were sufficient to recruit the wasted powers of man; but modern physiologists think eight hours little enough for the majority of grown-up persons, especially those whose nervous waste is great, whether occasioned by anxieties in business or study. Children should be allowed a larger quantity of sleep than adults, in proportion to their youth. Up to six or seven years of age, they require, in winter, twelve hours; in summer, an hour less. From this age to fourteen or sixteen, nine or ten hours may be allowed; and so, gradually diminishing to the eight hours, as above stated. Women are supposed to require more sleep than men. This is only partly true. Those who have the cares of a family, perhaps the duties of child-bearing and nursing in addition to the routine of the household to undergo, may take an hour extra with advantage; but ladies in society, and young females employed in indoor labor, frequently require less sleep than men.

As so much of our short lives is passed in bed, it becomes an important question for thrifty housekeepers to know what kind of bed is best. There are writers on hygiene who argue that to be healthy, a man should live on "hard tack," and sleep on the soft side of a plank; but the weight of authority is altogether in favor of

Luxurious Beds.

In former times it was considered a great luxury to possess a feather bed, and a straw tick laid upon a network of cords; but of late years, feathers have fallen into disfavor; though Dr. Strange, of London, still thinks that the best bed that can be devised is a moderately-soft feather bed, placed over a hair mattress in winter, and under it in summer. But in cities, feathers are now nearly discarded, and mattresses filled with wool, hair or other materials are substituted in their stead.

A good *wool mattress* is at once the most costly and the most desirable for all seasons. *Curled hair* ranks next to wool or down, and is the substance of which most first-class beds are made. *Husks, palm-leaf,* and *oak-splits,* make beds which are about alike in softness, and all equally wholesome and durable. *Spanish moss*, which grows in long festoons upon most of the trees in extensive forests in the Southern States, makes a better mattress, if well prepared, than poor hair. For lower mattresses, *corn husks, German grass*, and *beech leaves*, are a very clean and durable material. Probably there is no material which makes so economical and at the same time so comfortable a bed as husks, or "shucks," as they are sometimes called. They have also the advantage of being very easily obtained; so that almost every housekeeper in the country can prepare and make her own beds at a very small expense. Lyman says, "the labor of children may be successfully employed in sorting and splitting the shucks, and removing all ends and fragments of the stalk that are found adhering. A mattress needle may be purchased for twenty-five cents. The cost of ten yards of ticking is from three to five dollars, according to quality; so that by labor that would otherwise be unproductive, or nearly so, and an expenditure of about five dollars, almost any housekeeper can readily produce a mattress comfortable, durable, new, fresh and wholesome."

It must be admitted, however, that only wool and hair mattresses make an entirely comfortable bed without either springs beneath them or a softer substance above. The ordinary spiral coils, which make the best springs, may be obtained at any upholstery establishment, for about seventy-five cents a dozen, and five dozen are sufficient for the longest bed. A person moderately skilled in the use of tools can bore the holes, and fasten them to the slats of an ordinary bedstead. With proper usage, these springs will last a lifetime.

Best Covering for Beds.

The value of bed-clothing depends more on the quality than the quantity of the articles used. The most satisfactory covering for a bed in cold weather is a double rose-blanket, thick and warm. No other substance will compare with fine wool, or comforter of down, in the property of retaining warmth, and of feeling light and agreeable. Blankets, however, to be comfortable and wholesome, must be frequently exposed to fresh air. Even those made of the finest wool, if constantly used, without careful airing, will cease to be the luxurious covering that they are when new. When washed, they should be dried as rapidly as possible, *and the nap raised by going over them with a fine and short toothed wool card.* By this means the newness of feeling may be retained in blankets and other woollens, as long as they are worn, and their warmth greatly increased.

With regard to sheets, the preference that so many housekeepers show for linen sheets rather than cotton is not, in the opinion of philosophical writers, supported by sound rules of health. Sheets of fine bleached cotton, costing not half as much as fine linen, are more comfortable in cool weather, nearly as much so in warm; are washed and ironed with greater facility, and are wholly unobjectionable on sanitary considerations. Linen retains its whiteness longer than cotton, is somewhat more durable, and in the hottest weather is cool and soothing to the touch. But for pillow-slips, linen is decidedly, and at all times, preferable to muslin, being whiter, pleasanter to the touch, smoother and more lasting.

When sheets are perfectly dried and laid away for the ironing table, if sprigs of lavender or some other pleasant perfume, as little perfume-bags of powdered orris-root, are laid between the folds, the luxury of the bed will be very much increased.

Some writers on hygiene think horse-hair pillows much more conducive to health than feathers, especially for children, as they keep the head cooler.

How to Ventilate Sleeping Apartments.

So soon as the occupants have left the room, the bed-clothes should be entirely removed from the bed, and hung upon a clothes-horse or the backs of chairs, the bed shaken up, and all curtains, if used, drawn closely to the bedposts. The windows should then be opened both at top and at bottom. Dr. Strange, in his treatise on health, says: "I find in warm weather, healthy people wish to dress with the windows open, to enjoy the invigorating breeze: this should not be done until the proper amount of friction shall have braced the relaxed skin."

The windows should remain open in summer, or in very fine weather, until a little before sunset; in very sultry weather some outside air may be admitted all night. In winter and early spring, windows should remain open until *a little after midday*, when the warmth of the air is greatest, and then closed. In this way the air of the best portion of the day is shut in and reserved for respiration during the night, when the external air is at the worst. When it is essential, from the construction of the room or the number of persons sleeping in it, a fire should be lighted for a few hours during the afternoon, in very cold and damp weather, so as to dry the air which has been shut in. This is the only way in which the exhalations from the bed-clothing can be got rid of in such a state of the atmosphere, and the sweetness and purity of the clothing and other materials, which are kept in drawers and wardrobes, secured.

It sometimes happens that sleep is partial and fickle, visiting "the ship-boy on the high and giddy mast," yet denied to a king "with all appliances and means to boot;" and it therefore is important to consult physiologists, to learn

What can be Done to Induce Sleep.

The first rule they recommend is, to exclude the light from acting on the tired retina of the eye, and, as much as possible, noises or sounds from the ear, except such as are of a low, monotonous character. Cold air must not blow upon the face, or rush into the lungs to excite the circulation; and the warmth of the skin should be preserved by an immovable layer of warm air in contact with it. Second, with regard to the amount of warmth required to be furnished by the bedding and bed-clothes, there is great difference in the feelings of individuals. Whilst weight of clothing is oppressive to some and prevents sleep, others are cold and uncomfortable without it. Invalids and aged people should have fires in their bed-rooms; and in severe weather, fires should be kindled in bed-rooms generally, both to heat and to dry them. For this purpose, it is best to light them some hours before retiring to rest and after the windows have been closed. They may then with advantage be allowed to go out at, or soon after, bed-time, except in very severe weather or in the case of very delicate or invalid persons. Used in this way, there is no weather when sleeping apartments may not be sufficiently ventilated; and in low or damp situations and the closer part of towns, this is the only way in which pure air can be secured during a considerable portion of the winter and early spring.

Thirdly. It is better to go to sleep on the right side than the left; for "then the stomach is very much in the position of a bottle turned upside-down, and the contents are aided in passing out by gravitation. If one goes to sleep on the left side, the operation of emptying the stomach of its contents is more like drawing water from a well. After going to sleep, let the body take its own position. If you sleep on your back, especially soon after a hearty meal, the weight of the digestive organs and that of the food, resting on the great vein of the body near the back-bone, compresses it and arrests the flow of the blood more or less. If the arrest is partial, the sleep is disturbed, and there are unpleasant dreams. If the meal is more recent or hearty, the arrest is more decided, and the various sensations, such as falling over a precipice or the pursuit of a wild beast, or what is commonly called 'nightmare,' attacks us; and the desperate effort to get rid of it arouses the sleeper."

Fourthly. The condition of the body exercises a great influence, either good or evil, upon the chances of obtaining sleep. When the feet are cold or damp on going to bed, a refreshing sleep is impossible; therefore it is a good plan to spend a few minutes, before going to bed, in drying and heating the feet before the fire, with the stockings off. Indians and hunters, it has been observed, always sleep with their feet towards the camp fire.

The condition of the stomach, also, has a great effect upon the quality of the sleep. When the food is not being properly digested, the sleep will be disturbed; and some physiologists recommend that persons should not try to sleep until digestion has been completed. But too long a time since the last food was taken should not be allowed to elapse before bed-time, or the want of sustenance in the system will cause, especially in weakly persons, a feeling of exhaustion and sinking, which is antagonistic to sleep. Many persons rest better after taking a little supper a short time before going to bed. Dr. Strange recommends a cup of cocoa, with bread and butter, or a cupful of arrowroot with a tablespoonful of brandy in it, to divert the blood from the brain to the stomach.

Mr. Buckland, the son of the author of the "Bridgeport Treatise," has given this subject considerable attention, and is in favor of sleeping after eating. He says "I have no hesitation in saying that the proper thing to do is to go to sleep immediately (or at least very soon) after the meal of the day. All animals always go to sleep, if they are not disturbed, after eating. This is especially noticeable in dogs; and the great John Hunter showed by an experiment that digestion went on during sleep more than when the animal was awake and going about. This is his experiment: He took two dogs and gave them both the same quantity of food. One of them was then allowed to go to sleep; the other was taken out hunting. At the end of three or four hours, he killed both these dogs. The food in the stomach of the dog which had been asleep was quite digested; in that of the one which had been hunting the food was not digested at all. This fact, I think, shows the advisability of going to sleep immediately after eating." He condemns both tea and coffee as evening drinks; for they stimulate the brain, and are therefore unfavorable to rest, though he admits they "actually send some people into sound slumber."

If the brain be overexcited by amusement, or important business transacted in heated apartments, a stroll for a half hour or more in the cool air will often calm the nerves and promote sleep.

Professor Terrier, of King's College, London, who has made the phenomena of sleep a special study, recently said in a lecture thereon, that anything which has a tendency to abstract blood from the brain favors sleep. Exercise does this, because the moment the weary muscles are at rest the blood rushes to them to repair their loss, and is absorbed by them. Digestion and hot drinks produce the same result by drawing the blood supply from the brain to the stomach. Conversely, anything that stimulates the brain, such as sights, sounds, thought or anxiety, will keep a man awake. If we, therefore, wish for a refreshing slumber, we must begin by avoiding care and anxiety and take sufficient bodily exercise to induce the necessary muscular exhaustion.

Fifthly, with regard to the use of narcotics, it may be said, generally, that they should be used sparingly, or only with the concurrence of a physician. One of the best medicines for this purpose is the *syrup of lactucarium;* though sometimes the effect is produced by *Hoffman's anodyne.* Hop tea is unobjectionable, and sleep may be procured by laying the head on a hop-pillow, made from hops heated and sprinkled with alcohol. Onions are also soporific in their nature. Mr. Buckland, already quoted, remarks: "I now venture to suggest a new but simple remedy for want of sleep. Opiates in any form, even the *liquor opii sedat.*, and chloroform, will leave traces of their influence the next morning. I therefore prescribe for myself—and have frequently done so for others—onions; simply common onions raw, but Spanish onions stewed will do. Everybody knows the taste of onions: this is due to a peculiar essential oil contained in this most valuable and healthy root. This oil has, I am sure, highly soporific powers. In my own case they never fail. If I am much pressed with work, and feel I shall not sleep, I eat two or three small onions, and the effect is magical. Onions are also excellent things to eat when much exposed to intense cold."

Franklin's Art of Procuring Sleep.

When you are awakened by uneasiness, and find you cannot easily sleep again, get out of bed, beat up and turn your pillow, shake the bedclothes well with at least twenty shakes; then throw the bed open and leave it to cool, in the mean while continuing undressed; walk about your chamber, till your skin has had time to discharge its load, which it will do sooner as the air may be drier and colder. When you begin to feel the cold air unpleasant, then return to your bed and you will soon fall asleep, and your sleep will be sweet and pleasant. All the scenes presented by your fancy will be of a pleasing kind. I am often as agreeably entertained with them as by the scenery of an opera. If you happen to be too indolent to get out of bed, you may, instead of it, lift up your bedclothes so as to draw in a good deal of fresh air, and, by letting them fall, *force it out* again. This, repeated twenty times, will so clear them of the perspirable matter they have imbibed as to permit your sleeping well afterward. But the latter method is not equal to the former.

Those who do not love trouble, and can afford to have two beds, will find great luxury in rising when they wake in a hot bed and going into a cool one. Such shifting of beds would be of great service to persons ill in fever, as it refreshes and frequently procures sleep. A very large bed that will admit a removal so distant from the first situation as to be cool and sweet, may, in a degree, answer the same end.

These are the rules of the art; and observing them, and

maintaining a conscience void of offence, one may realize "that to be able to lie down at nights and fall to sleep within ten minutes, and to know no dream or waking until morning comes; and then to bound out of bed, full of health, freshness and good humor, is a blessing well worthy the warmest outgushings of a thankful heart towards Him who giveth us all things richly to enjoy."

CHAPTER XVII.

THE ART OF PROLONGING LIFE.

"Acute theologists have shown that the chronology of the early ages was not the same as that used at present. Some, particularly Hensler, have proved, with the highest probability, that the year till the time of Abraham consisted only of three months; that it was afterwards extended to eight; and that it was not till the time of Joseph that it was made to consist of twelve. These assertions are, in a certain degree, confirmed by some of the eastern nations, who still reckon only three months to the year; and besides, it would be altogether inexplicable why the life of man should have been shortened one-half immediately after the flood. It would be equally inexplicable why the patriarchs did not marry till their sixtieth, seventieth, and even hundredth year; but this difficulty vanishes when we reckon these ages according to the before-mentioned standard, which will give the twentieth or thirtieth year; and consequently, the same periods at which people marry at present. The whole, therefore, according to this explanation, assumes a different appearance. The sixteen hundred years before the flood will become four hundred and fourteen; and the nine hundred years (the highest record) which Methuselah lived, will be reduced to two hundred,—an age which is not impossible, and to which some men in modern times have nearly approached."—DR. HUFELAND.

FROM the earliest ages, men have sought to discover some means by which death may be averted and life may be prolonged. The favorite prescription of the old Egyptian physicians to remove disorders from the human system was a frequent emetic and to keep up perspiration. "So general was this idea, that it became a custom among the people to address each other with ' How do you sweat?' instead of 'How do you do?' The degree of perspiration was supposed to indicate the state or degree of health." In Greece and Rome, the physicians prescribed pills and balsams, and the philosophers wrote in favor of gymnastics, bathing, bodily friction, and temperance in eating and drinking, as the best means of preserving health and prolonging life.

Among the empirical ideas that have from time to time had their advocates, was the belief that there are fountains in some parts of the world that will renew the youth of those who bathe in their waters. One of these was located in the island of Negropont, in the Grecian Archipelago; another at Lefucaya, in Peru; and Ponce de Leon reported that he had discovered one of these priceless fountains in Florida. In order to relieve persons from the necessity of travelling to foreign countries to enjoy these waters, physicians at different times have announced that they had compounded some wonderful preparation from mineral, vegetable and animal substances, as the Stone of Fire, the Quintessence of Ambergris and the Essence of Vipers— which, if taken as they direct, would re-establish broken constitutions, purify the blood, substitute new spirits, re-animate those which were exhausted; in short, restore youth and give immortality. Paracelsus boasted that by his "Mercury of Life" it was as easy for him to metamorphose an old man into a young one, as to change iron into gold; and yet the very man who promised to prolong the life of others died at the early age of thirty-seven.

The average period of human life has considerably declined since the days of Noah, when, and for several centuries after, it was reckoned at 120 years; but there are well-authenticated instances of individuals in modern times, who lived more than six-score years. In Great Britain there are records containing the names of over fifty persons who lived to be centenarians, some of them by no means models of sobriety and abstemiousness, quite the contrary; and at least three of them lived for one hundred and fifty and more years.

FRANCIS CONFIT, a native of Yorkshire, England, lived to be one hundred and fifty years old, and retained his senses to the last. No extended notice of his life has been written, but it appears that he was temperate in his living, that he used a great deal of exercise, and ate largely of raw new-laid eggs.

Old THOMAS PARR was one of the most notable instances of longevity in English history. He was born in 1483, and died in 1635, in the one hundred and fifty-second year of his age. He was first married when he was eighty-eight, and again at the age of one hundred and twenty; and when he was one hundred and forty-five, he was able to run races, thrash out grain, and accomplish almost any kind of laborious work. He was accustomed to eat at night as well as in the daytime, but always of the plainest food. His body was covered with hair; and of him it was written:

> "From head to heel, his body had all over,
> A quick set, thick set, nat'ral hairy cover."

HENRY JENKINS, though less known than Parr, it appears was the longest-lived Englishman of whom there is any reliable record. He was born in Yorkshire, on the 17th of May, 1500, and died in 1670, in his one hundred and seventieth year. He was the son of a market gardener, and in his early years assisted his father as a fruit-grower. He rose early, drank a half pint of water every morning before breakfast, and lived simply; his food consisting principally of cold meats and salads. Following the directions of his mother, he always continued the use of flannel and warm clothing which had been commenced in infancy. When hops were introduced into England from Flanders, he became interested in the manufacture of beer, and drank a moderate portion of that beverage every day.

In his youth he was crossed or disappointed in a love-affair, which gave him a distaste for marriage, but not for the fair sex; for it is recorded, that in his hundredth year he became involved in a "woman scrape," for which he was severely lectured by the minister of the parish, "and nothing but his age excused him from doing penance."

When Jenkins was in his hundred and sixtieth year, Charles II. heard of him, and sent a carriage to convey him to London. He, however, declined the carriage, though he accepted the invitation, and actually walked to the metropolis in easy stages—a distance of two hundred miles. On his arrival in London, he was introduced to the King, and by him to the Queen, who, among other questions, asked him, "Well, my good man, may I ask of you, what you have done in the long period of life granted you, more than any other man of shorter longevity?" The old man, looking the Queen in the face, with a low bow, naively replied, "Indeed, madam, I know of nothing greater than becoming a father when I was over a hundred years old." He was allowed a pension, which he enjoyed the remainder of his life.

It is a remarkable circumstance that very little addition has been made to our knowledge of the best means of preserving health and prolonging life, by modern discoveries;

and that some of the best books on the subject are more than a century old. One of the early writers on health and regimen was COMIERS, a learned Italian, who obliged the world by publishing rules for a long life; some of which, like the following, cannot even at this day be improved upon:

One should eat to live, and never eat to Satiety.

One should act in every thing with Moderation to Keep the Body in a reasonable Activity.

One should live chastely, if one would live long.

One must abstain from eating different Meats, and drinking several sorts of Drink at the same Repast, lest the heterogeneous Juices hurt the stomach by their contrary Qualities.

One must chew perfectly what one eats. Mastication is the first Digestion; it is performed by the acid Humor which issues out of the Salival Glands near the eye-teeth.

At Meals one should eat alternately moist things after dry, fat after lean, sweet after sour, and cold after hot, to the end that one may be corrective of the other.

In an extraordinary Sweat one should not be uncovered in the least; and one should walk moderately when one is heated, for fear of catching cold, drinking then a little wine, but no water, unless first warmed, and that too drop by drop, to avoid Pleurisy or Rheumatism.

After coming out of bed, one should never go to look out of the window, no more than to run to the Fire immediately coming out of the Cold; because every sudden change is dangerous.

One should eat very little of new Fruits at one time, that the Stomach may be accustomed thereto by degrees, and may also be freed from Fermentations whence proceed most dangerous Fevers.

One should sleep not only with the eyelids, but even lay our thoughts asleep likewise; which will never be the happy lot of those who use Wine immoderately, and Liquors composed of Brandy and (what is much worse) Spirit of Wine.

One should Sweat three times in the year, in Autumn, Winter, and the Spring, and be rubbed twice a week, at least, with hot cloths to excite Transpiration, so necessary for Life.

If one has a bad stomach, one must keep Diet for 24 hours, and walk in the open Air, to reanimate the natural Heat, loaded with too much nutritive Juice.

Diet and Sweating are a Species of universal Medicine, capable of preserving our bodies, and to acquire a long Life. Diet restores appetite; the Appetite moderately contented, augments Strength; Strength contributes to Health; and Health bestows Life. Sweating disperses ill Humours, and eases Obstructions, whence proceed all our Distempers.

Near the close of the last century, a book was written by a German physician, a professor in the University of Jena, on the *Art of Prolonging Life*, which is remarkable from the fact that it contains about all that more modern writers have said pertinent to the subject. Its English editor, Erasmus Wilson, remarks: "The reader will be struck with the little real progress which has been made in the science of living, during more than half a century since the original work was first written." A brief digest of this important treatise will appropriately close this volume.

What Shortens Life.

In the first place, in order to prolong life, it is necessary to avoid all those things that tend to shorten life. Of these the principal are, *Delicate nursing and treatment in infancy*, as keeping the infant from every breath of air, burying it in pillows and blankets, and at the same time stuffing it with food; *physical excess in youth*, especially indulgence in physical love at an immature age; *overstrained exertion of the mental faculties*, as thinking hard, and neglecting bodily exercise, or curtailing sleep; using artificial means to stimulate the mind, as wine, coffee, and snuff; studying in a confined air and in a bent posture (students should accustom themselves to study lying down, standing, walking, not always in the closet, but sometimes in the open air); *diseases, and the injudicious manner of treating them*, as taking food when there is no appetite, and stimulating drinks in feverish disorders; excluding the air in scarlet fever and small-pox; neglecting colds; and especially neglecting to regulate the bowels, which is the cause of three-fourths of all the ailments that afflict humanity; *impure air; eating too much*, and *improperly*, as eating until one experiences a heaviness or fullness of the stomach, yawning, and confusion of the head; and eating highly-spiced or highly-concentrated food, and drinking spirituous liquors; *fear*, as fear of thunder, fear of ghosts, and fear of death; *idleness, inactivity and languor;* no idler ever attained to a great age, and regular employment is favorable to health; *overstrained power of the imagination*, as constant fear and dread of diseases, by reading of their symptoms or indulgence in imaginary sorrows from reading sentimental novels; *exposure to poisons and infectious diseases;* and, lastly, *engrafting old age on youth*, by wasting the vital power profusely, by exposure to great fatigue early in life, as taking long journeys, continual dancing, sitting up all night, or by indulging in care, fear and sorrow, and especially by attempting to harden the organs by means of *cold bathing*, indulged in frequently and for a long time in cold water. "Nothing," says Dr. Hufeland, "can be more proper to produce every symptom of age."

What Prolongs Life.

Secondly, in order to prolong life, it is necessary to adopt those means and observe those precautions which promote health and physical vigor. Of these, the principal are proper *care, nursing* and *feeding in infancy;* an *active and laborious youth* free from indulgences that weaken the system; a *happy marriage;* not less than six nor more than eight hours *sleep* in well-ventilated apartments, free from poisonous exhalations, whether of plants or of animals; *exercise in the free air;* occasional *journeys and excursions,* avoiding travelling in the night-time; *cleanliness and care of the skin,* washing in cold water frequently, taking tepid baths occasionally, and sea-baths when practicable; and wearing flannel next the skin the greater part of the year; using *proper food in moderation,* and preserving the teeth to chew it well; cultivating a contented, hopeful, even joyful, disposition; guarding against diseases, especially those to which one is constitutionally disposed; and a knowledge of the proper remedies to employ in case of danger of sudden death, as from drowning, suffocation, poisoning or being struck by lightning.

What to do in Cases of Suffocation.

In all cases of danger of death from suffocation, as drowning or hanging, be as expeditious as possible to draw the body from the water or to cut the rope; in a word, to remove the cause of death. This alone is sufficient to save the unfortunate person, if it be done speedily; but attention to that point is too much neglected.

2d. The body should be immediately stripped, and every endeavor should be made as speedily as possible to excite in it a general warmth. Heat is the first and most general stimulus of life. The same means which Nature employs to quicken life in the beginning are also the most powerful to restore animation. The best thing for that purpose is the tepid bath; but if this cannot be had, the patient may be covered with warm sand, ashes, or thick blankets in a bed; and hot stones should be applied to various parts of the body. Without these means, all others will be of little avail; and it is much better to warm thoroughly persons apparently dead, than to use cupping, friction or the like, and at the same time to suffer them to become stiff with cold.

3d. To convey air into the lungs is the next process in point of importance, and may be connected with the excitation of heat. It is, indeed, most beneficial when it is done with oxygen gas by means of a pipe and a pair of bellows. But in urgent cases, and to save precious time, it will be sufficient if one presses on the chest so as to expel the air which it contains, and then by its withdrawing the pressure, allows it to expand by its own elasticity, and thus fill the lungs with air. This should be done with regularity, so as to imitate ordinary breathing.

4th. Let fall now and then, from a certain height, drops of frigid water or wine on the pit of the stomach. This sometimes has given the first stimulus to restore the motion of the heart.

5th. Rub with a cloth or a flesh-brush the hands, soles of the feet, the belly and the back; irritate the sensible parts of the body, such as the soles of the feet and hollow of the hands, by friction with stimulating oils; the nose and throat by means of a feather, or by holding to the nostrils and dropping on the tongue volatile spirit of ammonia, etc.

6th. As soon as signs of life begin to appear, pour a spoonful of good wine into the mouth; and when the patient swallows it, repeat the same thing often. In cases of necessity brandy may be used, but mixed with two-thirds of water.

To Restore those Struck by Lightning.

For those who have been *struck by lightning*, the *earth bath* is to be recommended. The body may be either laid with the mouth open, against a spot of earth newly dug up, or fresh earth may be scraped around it up to the neck. If these simple means, which every one can and ought to use in behalf of his fellow-man, when exposed to the danger of sudden death, be speedily employed, they will be of more service than anything science can suggest, if applied half an hour later; and at any rate the intermediate time will not be entirely lost, and the feeble vital spark may be prevented from being totally extinguished.

To Restore those who have been Frozen.

These require a mode of treatment entirely different; for by warmth they would be destroyed altogether. Nothing further is to be done than to immerse them in snow up to the head; or to place them in a bath of the coldest water that can be procured without being frozen. Then life will return of itself; and as soon as any signs of it appear, give the patients a little warm tea or wine, and put them to bed.

Antidotes for Poisoning.

The third class includes those who have been *poisoned*. It is here to be observed, that we are in possession of two invaluable remedies, says the doctor, which may be everywhere found, and which require no previous acquaintance with medicine—I mean *milk* and *oil*. By the help of these only, the most dreadful of all the kinds of poisoning, that by arsenic, has been cured. Both of them answer the principal object, which is to expel the poison or to destroy its power. Let persons, therefore, who have been poisoned, drink as much milk as they can (if it in part comes up again, so much the better); and let them, every quarter of an hour, take a cupful of oil of any sort; for it is all the same whether it be oil of linseed, almonds, poppies, or common oil. If it be known with certainty that the poison is arsenic, corrosive sublimate, or any other metallic salt, dissolve soap in water, and let the patient swallow it. This will be sufficient till a physician arrive, and will often render his assistance unnecessary.

Among the modern theories for the prolongation of human life, which have been advanced by modern writers, that seem worthy of attention, are those of Drs. Bostwick and Hall, and George Catlin.

Homer Bostwick, of New York, has written a book to demonstrate that the cause of "Natural Death," or death from old age, is an obstructed circulation of the blood; and the direct cause of this obstruction is the presence of earthy inorganic matter, derived originally from food and drink. His grand secret for preserving health, activity and life, therefore, is to diminish the necessity, so far as possible, for eating and drinking, and to select from different kinds of food those which contain the least solid earthy matter. According to his analysis of articles of diet, common table salt, Indian corn, spices, wheat flour, and beans, contain the largest proportion of the matter which ossifies and chokes up the system, while eggs, cheese, cabbage, and greens in general, turnips, carrots and onions contain very little; and grapes, oranges, apples and fruits generally, scarcely any at all.* He thinks he has brought

---

* Grapes are very conducive to health, not only in consequence of being free from earthy matter, "but they possess the power of thinning the blood and gently stimulating it and causing it to be sent through all the countless capillary vessels. And those who have never observed the fact will be surprised to be told, the aged whose hands and other parts of the body are much dried up will rapidly become soft, and the little vessels that have for years been closed will reappear, as also will the fine vessels of the cheeks again put on the hue of youth; the appetite

forward facts that will prove incontestably that in proportion as individuals, classes, or even nations, subsist upon aliment containing the smallest proportion of earthy elements, so do they prevent or retard the process of consolidation, maintain a state of health and activity, and prolong existence. "As long," he says, "as we can supply fuel to the fire and keep it free from the ashes, it will continue to burn. If this can be done for one hundred or a thousand ages, the fire will continue to warm and enliven for that period; so, in the same manner, if we can supply the body with proper food, and keep it free from earthy matter—the ashes which choke it up—will it continue to live. Time, or the number of years, has nothing whatever to do with old age or death."

The late Dr. Hall, of New York, laid great stress on the posture of the human body in walking, as affecting the health and longevity of mankind. He says, walking with the head downward, or with a staff or cane, promotes a stooping position and brings on an appearance of old age prematurely, not only by the effects upon the structure of the spinal column, but by throwing the weight of the body on the chest, thus compressing the lungs, and diminishing their capability of receiving an adequate quantity of pure air, thus gradually purifying the blood less and less perfectly, until the whole mass of it becomes imperfect, impure and diseased; *then slight causes carry a man to the grave.* An absolute preventive of all this is an habitual, persistent attention to the following rules:

Walk with the toes thrown outward.

---

will improve, the bowels will become regular, elasticity of limb and a more buoyant spirit are sure to follow those who eat plentifully of good grapes. The old man will again become young i

Walk with the chin slightly above the horizontal line, as if looking at the top of a man's hat in front of you, or at the eaves or roof of a house.

Walk a good deal with your hands behind you.

Sit with the lower portion of your spine pressed against the chair-back.

George Catlin, who for many years resided among the Indian tribes, in North and South America, became so much impressed with the conviction that he had made an important discovery in the art of prolonging life, that he issued a pamphlet in script, entitled "The Breath of Life, a manugraph." He observed that Indian mothers, before transferring their infants from the arms to the crib or plank, pressed the lips tightly together and placed under the head a small curved cushion or pillow just high enough to elevate or bow the head a little forward, so that the mouth would not fall open during sleep; thus establishing in infancy the habit of breathing through the nostrils. He ascertained that the Indian men, when they wished to express contempt for another, said he was a man who kept his mouth open.* He noticed that the Indians of all ages were exempt from most of the diseases that afflict civilized humanity, especially asthma, bronchitis, quinsy, croup, and other throat and lung diseases, and had good teeth and well-shaped mouths; and these considerations led him to reflect that the nostrils were made to convey air to the

---

* A Sioux brave, who had gone out to fight a duel with knives, and no quarter, with a Hudson Bay trader, who was physically his superior, was asked, after a reconciliation had been effected, whether he had not felt afraid of a white man who was so much stronger and larger than himself—replied: "I never fear harm from a man who don't keep his mouth shut, no matter how large or how strong he may be."

lungs which is their food, while the mouth was made to select and masticate food for the stomach. The more he reflected upon his discovery, the more he became convinced of its importance, until he believed that if mankind would walk and sleep with their mouths shut, not only would snoring in a great measure be abolished, but consumption would become a comparatively rare disease, and men could walk unharmed through epidemics of cholera and yellow-fever. Finally, he says, "If I were to endeavor to bequeath to posterity the most important motto which human language can convey, it should be in three words—

'SHUT—YOUR—MOUTH.'"

There are, undoubtedly, the elements of important truths in these suggestions; and thousands of men would greatly prolong their lives by keeping their bowels open, their heads up, and their mouths shut, even if they did not observe that other rule, which is, in sleeping the head should always be towards the north.

How the Old may become Older.

Passing on to those means by which people, already old, may prolong their life, Dr. Hufeland prescribes the following rules:

1st. As the natural heat of the body decreases in old age, one must endeavor to support and increase it externally as much as possible. Warm clothing, warm apartments and beds, heating nourishment, and, when it can be done, removal to a warmer climate, are all means, therefore, that contribute greatly to the prolongation of life.

2d. The food must be easy of digestion, rather fluid than solid; abundant in concentrated nourishment; and at the same time much more stimulating than would be advisable at an earlier period. Warm, strong, and well-seasoned soups are therefore beneficial to old age; and also tender roast meat, nutritive vegetables, good nourishing beer, and, above all, oily generous wine, free from acid, earthy and watery particles, etc., such as Tokay, Spanish, Cyprus and Cape wines. Wine of this kind is one of the most excellent stimulants of life, and that best suited to old age. It does not inflame, but nourishes and strengthens: it is milk for old people.

3d. The tepid bath is exceedingly well calculated to increase the natural heat, to promote excretion, particularly of the skin, and to lessen the aridity and stiffness of the whole frame.

4th. Guard against all violent evacuations, such as letting blood, unless when required by particular circumstances; strong purging, exciting perspiration by too much heat, indulging in excesses of any kind. These exhaust the few powers still remaining, and increase aridity.

5th. People, with increasing years, should accustom themselves more and more to a certain order in all the vital operations. Eating, drinking, motion and rest, the evacuations and employment, must have their determined periods and successions. Such mechanical order and regularity at this season of life may contribute greatly to the prolongation of it.

6th. The body, however, must have exercise, but not violent or exhausting. That which is rather passive will be the best, such as riding in a carriage, and frequent friction of the whole skin, for which sweet-scented and strong ointments may be employed with great advantage, in order to lessen the rigidity of the skin and to preserve it in a state of softness. Violent bodily shocks must in particular be avoided.

7th. A pleasant frame of mind, and agreeable employment for it, are also of uncommon utility; but violent passions, which disturb equanimity and which in old age may occasion instant death, ought to be avoided. That serenity and contentment which are excited by domestic felicity, by the pleasant review of a life spent not in vain, and by a consoling prospect of the future even on this side the grave, are the most salutary. The frame of mind best fitted and most beneficial to old age is that produced by intercourse with children and young people. Their innocent pastimes and youthful frolics have something which tend, as it were, to renovate and revive. Hope, and extending our views of life, are especially valuable assistants for this purpose. New proposals, new plans and undertakings, which, however, must be attended with nothing dangerous, or that can create uneasiness, in a word, the means of continuing life longer in idea, may even contribute something towards the physical prolongation of it. We find, therefore, that old people are impelled to this as if by internal instinct. They begin to build houses, to lay out gardens, etc., and seem in this little self-deception, by which they imagine they secure life, to find an uncommon degree of pleasure.

Such is, in brief, an abstract or digest of the rules prescribed by doctors, for the prolongation of human existence.

But there comes a time for all men, when the wisdom of the wisest philosophers and the skill of the most skilful physicians will avail nothing to prolong life. We may bar the doors for many years against the arch-enemy who rides on the passing breeze and "lurks in every flower," but sooner or later he effects an entrance into every habitation and robs every human being of what most persons would give all else that they possess to retain. What

Death is, except it be the permanent cessation of all the vital functions, the disintegration of the minute cells composing the human body, no one certainly knows; and whether natural death be painless or the extremest agony, no one who has undergone the ordeal has ever returned to tell us (though the few who have been resuscitated, when almost dead, have described their last sensations of consciousness as delightful); but we do know, from the records of many death-beds, that a child-like faith in the promises of the gospel, a belief that the tomb is but a tunnel through which it is necessary to pass in order to reach the mansion in the skies prepared for us by our heavenly Father, will deprive death of its terrors and the grave of a victory. When the blood courses through the veins in riotous, vigorous health, we may indulge in the luxury of skepticism, we may propound questions that the most learned theologians cannot answer, and then mock at their perplexity; but when we see the ghostly finger beckoning to us from the farther shore of the mysterious river, we instinctively grasp at the hand of religion as the only pilot that can carry us safely over. So, dear reader, when the dread summons comes, as it will come sooner or later, may you have the consciousness not only that you have used this world wisely and contributed something for the comfort of others, but that you have also secured a well-founded hope of happiness in the eternal world, and thus,

> "—— Sustained and soothed
> By an unfaltering trust, approach thy grave
> Like one that wraps the drapery of his couch
> About him, and lies down to pleasant dreams."

INDEX.

ACID, hydrochloric, 225; hydrocyanic, 321; sulphuric, 330.
Ague, proper treatment for, 271; whiskey a novel remedy for, 272; how to prevent fever and, 273.
Alcohol, uses of, as a medicine, 300.
Ammonia, a remedy for bites of insects 264; should be kept in every house, 301.
Ants, how to expel and destroy, 263.
Apples, machines for paring, 75; how to preserve, 95; how to thaw, when frozen, 95; an excellent dish of, 197.
Apple sauce, the garnish for roast pork, 175; an improved, 197.
ART OF PROLONGING LIFE, chapter on, 344.
Asthma, remedies for, 271; preventive of, 356.

BACON, points in good, 83; fried rashers of, 144; how to boil, 171; how to extract salt from, 171; bacon-fat prevents pitting in small-pox, 295.
Bain marié, a useful utensil, 172.
Baldness, remedies for, 247.
Bathing, cold, injurious to health, 350; in the sea, 351; tepid, beneficial to old persons, 358.
Bass, how to cook, 97.
Beans, new method of shelling, 69; nutriment in, 137; how to cook, 138.
Beds, luxurious, recommended, 334; best coverings for, 336.
Bedding, airing of, in sickness, 267; shaking up, induces sleep, 337.
Bed-bugs, how to exterminate, 262.
Bedrooms, proper size of, 47.
Bedsteads, different kinds of, 59.

INDEX.

Beef, how to choose, 81; how divided, 81–83; most economical pieces to buy, 83; for roasting, 83; analysis of, 124; best parts of corned, 143; beef-stew an economical dish, 144; what may be done with cold, 146; how to roast, English style, 180–182.

Beef's liver, how to distinguish good, 84.

Beef's heart, an economical food, 84; how to roast, 145.

Beefsteaks, how to broil, 152; fungi equal to, 149; Macbeth's recipe for broiling, 152; should look well on the table, 156; how to broil, Wakefield style, 184.

Beef's tongue a great delicacy, 84.

Benzine will extract grease from marble, 61.

Bills of fare, for the sick, 176; for young children, 177; for sedentary persons, 177; of food containing brain-making elements, 178; costly, 207; of a dinner for twelve persons, 208.

Birthmarks, how to eradicate, 246.

Black eyes from bruises, remedies for, 275.

Bleeding from the nose, a cure for, 274; from the lungs, 274.

Blood, food best purifier of the, 274.

Boiling meats, points in, 151.

Boots and shoes, suggestions on buying, 222; how to preserve, 223; to cure squeaking, 223; whiskey in, a preventive of ague, 272.

Borax, value of, in washing clothes, 237; will drive away roaches, 261.

Brains, developed by certain kinds of food, 178.

Breath, causes of bad, 254; how to sweeten, 254; best toilet preparation for, 254.

Bread, how to make good family, 158–163; how to make stale, fresh, 164; how to keep, 164; various uses of, dough, 164; an elegant, pudding, 196.

Bread and milk, best method of preparing, 309.

Breakfast, importance of a substantial, 39; standard dishes for, 177; a nice dish for, 197.

Breasts, how to reduce, 242; how to enlarge, 243.

Broiling, secret of, 152.

Brooms, how to preserve, 67.

Broth, the foundation of cookery, 72; Blot's recipe for making French beef, 166.

Bunions, cures for, 260.

Bureaus, depth of drawers in, 59.

Burns, admirable remedies for, 120, 326.

Butter, how to make drawn, 176.

INDEX. 363

CABBAGE, how to keep, 94; how to boil, 151; with milk, to render digestible, 171.

Cake, recipe for making the national French, 200; imperial southern, 201; Baltimore tea, 201; southern waffles, 201.

Candles, improved by age, 102.

Cambric tea, how to make, 309.

Carpets, points in buying, 64; large patterns in, objectionable, 65; how to make cheap, 64; Brussels, the best, 65; economical way of laying, 65; in bedrooms, 65; how to sweep, 66; how to destroy moths in, 67; to clean and brighten Brussels, 67.

Calves' heads, how to buy, 85.

Calves' feet, how to judge, 85.

Calves' sweetbreads a delicacy, 85.

Cauliflowers, points in good, 93.

Ceilings should be only moderately high, 47.

Celery, how to choose, 93; how to preserve, 94; the garnish for boiled turkey, 75.

Chairs, faults in construction of, 57; for drawing and dining rooms, 58; for bedrooms, 59; how to clean and tighten cane-seat, 62.

Charles II., interview of, with Jenkins, 347.

Charcoal, value of, 105.

Cheerfulness promotes digestion, 42.

Cheese, how to judge, 102; how to make macaroni, 169.

Chilblains, remedies for, 276.

CHILDREN AND THEIR DISEASES, 305.

Chimneys, best form of, 47.

China, how to cement broken, 63.

Chocolate, points about, 174.

Cholera, how to escape, 277, 357.

Cinders, how to remove from grates, 110; value of, 112.

Cinder-sifters, economy of, 77.

Clams, how to judge fresh, 97; best recipe for making, chowder, 193; best method of baking clams, 193.

Closets should be numerous, 49.

Cloth, to extract grease from, 63; points in buying, 217; how to cleanse broadcloth, 221; to render, waterproof, 222.

CLOTHING, chapter on, 216; for children, suggestions on, 218; on men's, 219–221; how to treat wet, 221; suggestions on women's, 223; of infants, 314.

Clothes lines, protection for, 78.

Coal, how to judge good, 108; how to kindle a, fire, 109; economical use of, 110; waste in burning, 111; how to measure, 112.

Coffee, how to buy advantageously, 101; how to keep, 101; substitutes for, 148; novel mode of making, 172; Turkish method of making, 172.
Coffee-pots, best kinds of, 74.
Coke, utility of, 106.
Cold-cream, useful in piles, 289.
Colds, proper treatment of, 268; how to avoid catching, 269.
Colic, in infants, remedy for, 317.
Comfort, definition of, 33; elements of, 33–43.
Complexion, how to beautify, 43.
Convulsions in children, remedy for, 318.
Cookery, extravagance of American, 131; in France, 132; of cold meats, 146; best books on, 155; HIGH CLASS, 206.
Cook-books, practical value of, 41.
Coughs, best syrups for, 270; stopping, in children dangerous, 271; whooping-cough, how relieved, 322.
Corn-bread, how to make, 139; best recipe for, 202; Virginia corn pone, 202.
Corn-fritters, recipe for, 198.
Cornmeal, quantity to buy at a time, 99; healthfulness of, 99, 123; errors in preparing, 139.
Corns, cured in ten minutes, 259; remedies for, 258, 260.
Cranberries, how to keep, 95.
Cream, good substitute for, 172; recipe for fried, 215.
Croup, treatment of, 319; spurious or child-crowing, 320.
Crying, of babies, how to prevent, 310; what it sometimes indicates, 312.

DAINTY DISHES, chapters on, viz., domestic cookery, 179; high-class cookery, 206.
Dandruff, an effectual remedy for, 248.
Deafness, a relief for, 282.
Death, reflections on, 357, 358.
Diarrhœa, hints to travellers for curing, 276; simple remedy for, 277; treatment of, in children, 323.
Digestion, process of, illustrated, 129; food easy of, suitable for old people, 357.
Dinners, bills of fare for, 177, 179, 208.
Diphtheria, remarkable success in the cure of, 324.
Domestic economy, an interesting study, 33.
Doors, faults in construction of, 46.
Dress, suggestions on, 224–228; combinations of colors in, 228.
Drowning, what to do in cases of, 351.

INDEX. 365

Drunkenness, a cure for, 280.
Ducks, how to roast canvas-back, 182; to extract fishy flavor from, 182.
Dysentery, recipes of eminent physicians, 278.
Dyspepsia, the national disease, 279; slapping the stomach a remedy for, 280; other novel remedies, 281.

EARACHE, the best remedy for, in adults, 282; in children, 325.
Earth-closets, advantages of, 49.
Eastlake, his directions for hanging wall-paper, 53.
EATING, chapter on, 121; philosophy of, 126; how and when to eat, 130; before going to sleep, 340.
ECONOMICAL FOOD, chapter on, 131.
Edge tools, new way of sharpening, 78; how to remove rust from, 79.
Eggs, different ways to keep fresh, 103; how to fry, 165; how to boil, 167; and cheese an excellent dish, 189.
Egg-beaters, different kinds of, 74.
Egg-boiler, peculiarity of a novel, 73.
Egg-steamer, a recent invention, 73.
Egg-plants, characteristics of best, 93.
Erysipelas, a specific for cure of, 283.
Exercise, physical, neglected by ladies, 38; kind best suited for old people, 358.
Eyes, care of, 251; how to remove cinders from the, 252; how to cure squinting in, 252; veils injurious to the, 252.
Eyelashes, how to secure beautiful, 249.

Fainting, proper remedy for, 284.
Fairies, anecdote of, 43.
Feet, proper care of the, 255; remedies for fetid, 256; for frosted, 276; for itching, 326; when cold, prevent sleep, 339.
Felons, cure for, 284.
Fever, remittent, in infants, treatment of, 319.
Filter, how to make a cheap, 77.
Fire, protection against, 47; how to kindle a coal, 109; how to extinguish clothing on fire, 118; how to regulate in cooking, 157.
Fires, how to extinguish, 116; home brigade for extinguishing, 117; suggestions for preventing, 117.
Fish, how to judge fresh, 97; how to cook, 97; Chinese method of catching, 98; chemical analysis of, 125.
Fits, hysterical, how to treat, 236; what to do when a man falls in a fit, 297; in children, 318.

Flannel, not suitable for infants, 218; healthfulness of, 235; when to change, 236; how to wash, 236; wearing of, promotes long life, 347, 351.

Fleas, how to destroy, 261.

Flies, how to banish from houses and animals, 261.

Flour, how to test quality of, 99; how to keep sweet, 99; how to buy rye, 100; a remedy for burns, 120; to select, for bread, 158.

Food, quantity consumed by epicures in a lifetime, 35; may be divided into four classes, 120; most economical kinds of, 129; quantity of, necessary to sustain life, 132; for the sick, 176; for young children, 177; for sedentary persons, 177.

France, cookery in, 36.

Franklin, his rules for inducing sleep, 342.

Freckles, remedy for, 245.

Frost-bites, cures for, 276; how to restore those who have been frozen, 353.

Fruits, to neutralize the acid in, 157; pleasant dessert of, 196; eating of promotes long life, 347, 351.

Frying, process of, 152; defects in pans for, 72; how to clean pans for, 157.

FUEL AND FIRES, chapter on, 105; best woods for, 107.

Furnace and refrigerator, a combined, 50.

Furniture, what to avoid in buying, 56; points in buying, 58; novelties in, 59; marble tops on, 61; to take bruises out of, 62.

Furs, how to protect from moths, 238; how to judge, 239.

GAME, how to judge, 91; currant jelly the garnish for, 175; how to add to flavor of, 182.

Garnishes, different kinds of, 175.

Gas, how to save, 113; as a fuel, 113; burners, importance of, 114; different kinds of, 114; regulators, economy in the use of, 115; carbonizing, 116; best way to regulate flow of, 116.

Gas-stoves desirable in summer, 77.

Geese, points of young, 90.

Gloves, kid, 231; hints to wearers of, 231.

Grapes, conducive to health, 354.

Gridirons, revolving, a novelty, 73.

Grits, a cheap and palatable food, 137.

Groceries, hints on buying, 99.

Guinea fowls roasted, a dainty dish, 184.

INDEX. 367

HAIR, how to secure beautiful, 247; rules for improving children's, 247; wash for dandruff in, 248; how to darken, 248; to remove superfluous, 248; Circassian method of clipping, 249.
Hams, how to select, 87; best method of frying ham and eggs, 165.
Hands, how to whiten, 249; good recipe for chapped, 250; to remove warts from, 250.
Headache, different kinds of, 284; remedies for, 285.
Health, how to preserve, 38, 349, 350.
Heartburn, how to relieve, 286.
Herbs, when to gather, 95.
Hominy, how to buy, 100; valuable for laborers, 123; how to cook, 140.
Horses, to keep flies from, 261.
Horseradish, a remedy for neuralgia, 287.
HOUSEHOLD CONVENIENCES, chapter on, 69.
Housekeeping, few improvements in, 69.
HOUSE FURNISHING, chapter on, 55.
HOUSE PLANNING, chapter on, 44.
House-thrift, meaning of, 33.
Hydrophobia, how to prevent, 295.

ICE, medicinal uses of, 303.
Ice-cream, best methods of making, 205; freezers, a household convenience, 76.
Indigo, how to buy, 101.
Indians, a valuable secret known to the, 356.
Indigestion, remedies to relieve, 281.
Infants, clothing of, 218; proper food for, 306; condensed milk for, 307; how to care for, 307; cold water refreshing to, 300.
Ink, a cure for warts, 250.
Itch, cures for, 326; a specific for the seven years, 326; how Dr. Chase cured the barber's, 293.

JEALOUSY, danger of exciting, 42.
Jenkins, Henry, oldest man in English history, 346.
Johnson, Samuel, his opinion of women as cooks, 36; his remark on dinners, 40.

KITCHEN, best location of, 45; advantage of towels in, 69; compact in steamships, 70; sinks in, 70; what a, should contain, 70; a laboratory, 155; cleanliness in utensils in, 156.
Kitchiner, Dr., his rules for marketing, 80.
Knife-cleaners save labor, 77.

LAMB, how to choose, 86; analysis of, 124; mint, the best garnish for roast, 175.
Lamps, how to keep from smoking, 79; how to prevent explosions of, 119.
Lard, adulterations of, 89.
Larding-needles, common in French kitchens, 72.
Leanness, how to cure, 242.
Lent, the keeping of, recommended, 128.
Lentils, an excellent vegetable, 142.
LIFE, ART OF PROLONGING, 344; Comier's rules for prolonging, 348.
Lightning, to restore those struck by, 352.
Linen, how to detect cotton in, 234.
Liver complaint, remedy for, 288.
Lobsters, how to select, 98.
Longevity, before the flood, 344; illustrations of, in modern times, 346, 347; rules for promoting, 357–359.

MARBLE, uses of by cabinet-makers, 61; how to choose, tops for furniture, 61; recipe for extracting stains from, 61.
Marble cement, valuable recipe for, 62.
Mackerel, Lyman's method of cooking salt, 170.
MARKETING, chapter on, 80.
Markets, excellence of American, 37.
Marmalade, an exquisite, 203.
Mattresses, best kinds of, 335.
Measles, proper treatment for, 320.
Meats, recipes for keeping sweet in warm weather, 89; economy in buying, 143; how to use cold, 146; how to boil, 151; how to broil, 152; how to fry, 152; French method of sautéing, 153; how to roast, 154, 180; how to stew, 154.
MEDICINES, FAMILY, chapter on, 266.
Milk, a substitute for, 172; uses of condensed, 307; an antidote for poison, 353.
Mirrors, how to clean, 62.
Molasses, where to be kept, 102.
Moles and birthmarks, how to eradicate, 246.
Moths, how to destroy, in carpets, 67; in furniture, 68; protection against, 68; in woollens and furs, 238; in sofas, 239.
Mumps, best remedy for, 321.
Mushrooms, how to distinguish edible from poisonous, 93; good test of, 93; recipes for cooking, 191.

INDEX.

Musquitoes, best protection against, 264.
Mutton, how to select, 86; analysis of, 124; what can be done with cold, 146; equal to venison, 187.

NAILS, how to beautify, 249; a cure for ingrowing, 256.
Narcotics, the best, 341.
Nervousness, a recipe that will relieve, 287.
Neuralgia, remedies for, 287.
Noah, longevity in days of, 345.
Nutmegs, how to test, 102.

OAK, best wood for dining-room furniture, 56.
Oatmeal, value of, as food, 123; best way to make porridge of, 143.
Oil, how to test good kerosene, 104; an antidote to poisons, 353.
Oilcloth, points in buying, 67; how to clean, 68.
Omelettes, French recipe for making, 190; how to make a sweet, 190; recipe for a cheap, 190; soufflè, 215.
Onions, how to preserve, 95; how to cook without smell, 169; boiled, a remedy for worms, 318; an excellent narcotic, 341.
Oysters, how to judge fresh, 97; best for frying, 97; the remedy when too many have been eaten, 98; suitable for the sedentary, 126; broiled on the shell, 187; finest way of stewing, 188.

PAPER-HANGINGS suggestions on, 51; how to clean, 53.
Parr, Thomas, biographical sketch of, 346.
Parsley, the garnish for cold poultry, 175.
Pasty-pans, utility of, 73.
Peas, when best, 93; how to eat, 124; how to boil, 152; a novel machine for shelling, 76.
Peat, peculiarities of, and objections to, 106.
Pepperpot, how to make a genuine, 145.
Photograph, how to dress for, 232.
Pictures, proper arrangement of, 52; proper height for hanging, 60; wire cords for, 60.
Pickles, what kind to avoid in buying, 102.
Pie, the nicest ever eaten, 199; delicious mince, 204.
Pig, Lamb's eulogy of roast, 186.
Pigeons, how to broil, 183.
Piles, remedies for, 288.
Pillows, of cotton batting for infants, 312; horsehair better than feathers, 337.

Pleurisy, how to treat first attacks of, 288; how to avoid, 348.
Poisons, antidotes for, 353.
Pork, how to judge, 87; best piece for roasting, 87; how to cook, 87; Soyer's plan for testing freshness of, 87; analysis of, 124; and beans, when wholesome, 125; how to cook pork and beans, 138.
Porridge, recipe for making oatmeal, 143.
Potatoes, how to select, 92; for meats, 91; how to keep, 94; how to thaw when frozen, 94; value of, as food, 124; how to boil, 152; Irish method of boiling, 167; cold, utilized, 168; how to cook sweet, 168; Saratoga and Philadelphia fried, 203.
Potato-slicer, an ingenious invention, 75.
Potash, chlorate of, the gargle for quinsy, 290; in sore throat, 292; many uses of, 302.
POULTRY, how to judge, 90; how to make tender, 90; contains muscle-making elements, 125; how to roast, 154; the garnish for cold, 175.
Puddings, queen of, 196; an excellent bread, 196; green-corn pudding, 199.
Pyæmia, a remedy for, 301.

QUAKER, anecdote of a, 42.
Quinsy, how to prevent an attack of, 290.

RABBITS, how to barbecue, 183.
Raisins, a novel invention for seeding, 75.
Rarebit, recipe for making a Swiss, 191; the genuine Welsh, 191.
Rats, how to destroy, 262; to drive away, 263, 264.
Reedbirds, broiled, a dainty dish, 186.
Refrigerators, utility of, 76; the remedy for impure gases in, 76.
Rheumatism, different kinds of, 291; remedies for, 291; how to avoid, 348.
Rice, a popular food, 123; how to cook, 141; to make a pudding of, without eggs, 141; how to make farmer's, 142; croquettes, 214.
Ringworm, novel cure for, 246.
Roaches, how to destroy, 261.
Roasting, secrets in, 154; beef, English style, 180.
Rooms, novel method of cooling, 50.
Rust, how to prevent, 79; to remove, from cutlery, 79.

SAGO, most desirable kind of, 102.
Salads, novel method of preparing, 174; best method of dressing, 194; Valadon's recipe for dressing, 213.
Salt, best for table use, 101.
Santanin, a specific for worms, 318.

INDEX.

Sauces, suitable for every kind of fish, 192; recipes for, 214.
Sausages, how buyers may be protected against deception in, 88; meat for, 88; fried, a garnish for poultry, 175; machines for making, 76.
Savarin, remark of, on food, 80; experiments of, in coffee, 172.
Scales and weights, useful in kitchen, 173.
Scarlet fever, specifics for the cure of, 327–332.
Scrofula, Longworth's remedy for, 293.
Sea-sickness, how to prevent, 296.
Seasoning, rules for, 155.
SECRETS IN COOKING, chapter on, 150.
SECRETS OF THE TOILET, chapter on, 240.
Seeds, how to test quality of, 96.
Shawls, when becoming to ladies, 226.
Short-cake, an excellent buckwheat, 199; how to make strawberry, 200.
Sickness, a burden on society, 266.
Silks, what kinds to buy, 225: how to test, 225.
SLEEP, AND ITS APPLIANCES, 333; importance of, to health, 39; proper time for, 333; how to induce, 338; best narcotics, 341.
Small-pox, novel remedy for, 293; to prevent pitting in, 294.
Snoring, how to abolish, 357.
Soap, economy in buying, 102.
Sofas, defects in, 57.
Sore throat, remedies for, 292; Washington's treatment of, 292; in scarlet fever, 329.
Soups, Soyer's recipes for cheap, 134; for French beef broth, 166; à la Julienne, 167.
Soyer, Alexis, a remarkable calculation by, 34; his cheap soups, 134; his plan of broiling steaks, 152; novel mode of making coffee, 172; his method of making tea, 173; his recipe for melted butter, 176; for cooking mushrooms, 192.
Spine, how to avoid curvature of, 298.
Spices, how to preserve, 102.
Sprains, proper treatment of, 296.
Squinting, cure for, 252.
Starch, most economical, to buy, 101.
Stewing, best fire for, 154.
Stock-pot, a fixture in French kitchens, 171.
Strawberries with orange juice, 194.
Students, suggestions for, 349.
Sturgeon, how to cook equal to veal-cutlet, 148.
Suffocation, what to do in cases of, 351.

Sugars, how to buy, 100; different kinds of, 100.
Sulphuric acid, a specific in scarlet fever, 330.
Sulphur baths, efficacy of, in destroying vermin, 261.
Sunstroke, the approved treatment for, 297.
Sweating, recommended by old physicians, 348.
Sweden, ladies of, good cooks, 40.
Sweetbreads, how to cook, 185.

TABLES, how to remove stains in, 63.
Tapers, best light for the sick, 267.
Taste, a thing of culture, 44.
Tea, how to keep, 101; best methods of making, 173.
Tea-kettles, faults in, 79.
Teeth, how to preserve sound, 252; a good powder for the, 253; cures for aches in the, 253; frequent examination of, recommended, 314.
Teething, a relief for pain of, 313; convulsions resulting from, 318.
Terrapin, how to select, 98; chicken dressed as, 188.
Tetter, remedies for, 246, 298, 327.
Thrush, in infants, cure for, 318.
Tinware, which is the cheapest, 71.
Toast, to make good, 165.
Toilet, preparations for the, 240-260.
Tomatoes, best kinds of, 92; accompaniment for roast-beef, 92.
Toothache, cures for, 253.
Trout, salmon and brook, baked and broiled, 185, 186.
Turkeys, how to tell young, 90.
Turnips, how to select, 92; how to boil, 168.
Typhus, to prevent infection in, 268.

Veal, points of good, 84; choice part of, 84; most economical piece to buy, 85; how to roast, 86; analysis of, 124; what can be done with cold, 147, 170; veal-cutlets, 148; how to cook cutlets, 156; cutlets with tomatoes or oysters, 184.
Vegetables, how to select and preserve, 92-95; as food, 123, 124; injurious when not sufficiently cooked, 155; how to cook greens, 155; washing greens, 175.
Venison, how to buy, 91.
Ventilation, of bedrooms, 39, 337; of sick-rooms, 267.
Vermin, how to destroy, on the body, 260.
Vinegar, a corrective of stomach disorders, 303; which is the best, 101.
Voltaire, his recipe for curing dyspepsia, 281.

INDEX.

WALKING, a healthful exercise, 38; proper carriage of body in, 355, 356.
Wall-paper, selecting, 44; suggestions on, 51.
Warts, remedies for, 250.
Warren's cooker, advantages of, 75.
Washing, of body neglected by women, 39; comfort of, in sickness, 267; preferable to cold bathing, 351; of clothes, viz., chintz and summer dresses, 234; of flannels, 236; an easy way to wash clothes, 237.
Water, how to soften hard, 237; drinking of, a relief to the sick, 299; beneficial to infants, 300, 311; hot water, a remedy for pain, 303.
Water-closets, defects in the construction of, 49.
Water-pipes, danger of metallic, 48.
Weaning infants, proper time for, 308.
Wheat, value of, as food, 122; crushed, an excellent food, 137.
Whitewash, a recipe for a permanent, 54.
Whooping-cough, remedies for, 321.
Wife, qualifications of a good, 37–43; should be a physician, 42.
Wine, quantity consumed by ladies, 40; how to decant and cool in bottles, 96; good wine is milk for old people, 358.
Woods, best kind for buildings, 47; for furniture, 55; for fuel, 106.
Working-classes, extravagance of, 34.
Worms, in children, 317; remedies for thread, 317; a specific for long, 318.
Wrinkles, how to prevent, 246.

YEAST, how to make hop and potato, 159.
Yellow-fever, observation of Dr. Rush on, 47; a protection against, 357.
Youth, fountains that were said to restore, 345.

www.ingramcontent.com/pod-product-compliance
Lightning Source LLC
Chambersburg PA
CBHW020232240426
43672CB00006B/497